# A GIFT OF FREEDOM

# A GIFT OF FREEDOM

### HOW THE
### JOHN M. OLIN FOUNDATION
### CHANGED AMERICA

## JOHN J. MILLER

ENCOUNTER BOOKS
SAN FRANCISCO

First edition published in 2006 by Encounter Books, an activity of Encounter for Culture and Education, Inc., a nonprofit, tax exempt corporation.

Encounter Books website address: www.encounterbooks.com

Manufactured in the United States and printed on acid-free paper.

The paper used in this publication meets the minimum requirements of ANSI/NISO Z39.48-1992 (R 1997) (*Permanence of Paper*).

FIRST EDITION

Library of Congress Cataloging-in-Publication Data

Miller, John J.
  A Gift of Freedom/ John J. Miller.
    p.   cm.
    Includes index.
    ISBN 1-59403-117-7 (alk. paper)
    1. Olin, John M., 1892–1982.   2. John M. Olin Foundation—History.
    3. Conservatism—United States.   I. Title.
  JC573.2.U6 M55 2005
  320.520973—dc 22

                              2005025102

10  9  8  7  6  5  4  3  2  1

*For Linda Chavez,*
*mentor and friend*

# CONTENTS

# "RECOVER THE FUNDAMENTALS"

SECURITY WAS UNUSUALLY TIGHT AT THE St. Louis Club on the evening of April 16, 1981. More than 160 academic and business leaders from around the country were gathering to celebrate the life and work of John M. Olin, and much of the small talk before dinner focused on a mystery guest who had not yet arrived. Although many people figured out his identity—several men at the club looked suspiciously like Secret Service agents—only a few of them knew for certain and they were keeping it to themselves. The eighty-eight-year-old Olin seemed happily unaware that there would be a mystery guest at all.

Curiosity heightened as people took their seats and noticed an empty chair at the head table. Was that where the mystery guest would be sitting? Finally the master of ceremonies directed everyone's attention to the back of the room. In bounded Richard M. Nixon. Everyone stood and applauded the former president. Olin beamed as the two men embraced. "You boys pulled one this time!" he declared. They certainly had. Some weeks earlier Nixon had told William E. Simon, his former Treasury secretary and a close associate of Olin's, that he would like to attend the dinner. They decided to keep their plans under wraps until the moment Nixon entered the room. Tricky Dick had even written a letter to Olin apologizing for his absence from the dinner: "I only wish that my schedule had been such that I could attend in person."

Olin was thrilled to see a man he had known, admired, and supported for decades. After sitting down, he and Nixon discussed families and fishing. But Olin had larger questions on his mind. It was a time of economic and political turmoil. A new president had come into office only a few months earlier—and had been shot by a deranged gunman less than three weeks before the dinner. Inflation seemed out of control and Cold War relations were tense. In the seven years since Nixon's resignation, Olin's hair had turned white. The aging industrialist must have known he did not have much time in front of him. And yet he peppered his longtime friend with earnest questions about the future. "Tell me honestly," he asked Nixon, "how do you think everything is going to turn out?"

Nixon shared his thoughts with Olin and later, when it was his turn to speak to the audience, announced them for all to hear. He provided a short analysis of U.S.-Soviet relations and offered a cautious prediction for the 1980s: "We may see a major breakthrough in dealing with those who may oppose us." Yet Nixon had not flown to St. Louis to talk foreign policy. Like everybody in the room, the former president wanted to honor a remarkable man. "It all really comes back to what John Olin stood for, what he's contributed to, and what his foundation still stands for: the strength of the American economy, the strength of the American spirit," said Nixon. "We have been fortunate to know this man," he continued. "The country has been fortunate to have him."

Then Nixon raised a wine glass in his right hand and offered a toast noteworthy as much for its obvious sincerity as for its high praise:

> Due to the offices I have held and only because of that, I have toasted virtually everybody you can imagine: presidents, kings, prime ministers, dukes, queens, you name it. But I can assure you that as I look back over the years—thirty-five years that I have done it in Washington and virtually every major capital of the free world and the Communist world—there is none that gives me more pleasure than this toast tonight. He isn't a king. He isn't an emperor. He sure isn't a queen. [Laughter.] He has been a president, of course, of his company, and a chairman. But I toast him tonight as one of the best and most loyal friends and one of

the finest human beings that any of us could know. Gentlemen, ladies: To John Olin.

Olin had received letters from Gerald Ford, Ronald Reagan, and many others—enough to fill the small volume presented to him that evening. Yet Nixon's words were the high mark of a special night.

"Dick, I thank you from the bottom of my heart," he said. Then Olin addressed the men and women who had come to honor him, speaking briefly about his career, his foundation and his hope for America. In his final words of the night, he issued a challenge: "We have to recover the fundamentals of our country without delay."

This was the ambitious project to which John M. Olin devoted the final years of his life—as well as the bulk of the fortune he had spent a lifetime amassing. Before he became one of America's great philanthropists, he was one of its great businessmen. With his father and brother, Olin built a corporate empire that was the envy of many would-be captains of industry. He found himself counted on lists of the country's wealthiest people. He traveled in its most elite circles. He was a friend of presidents. And as with Carnegie, Rockefeller, and Ford before him, he eventually turned his sights away from accumulating and maintaining his riches and concentrated on the matter of giving them away. Yet there was almost nothing conventional about the way he chose to do it.

In *The Devil's Dictionary,* that biting lexicon of satire and cynicism, Ambrose Bierce defined a "Philanthropist" as "A rich (and usually bald) old gentleman who has trained himself to grin while his conscience is picking his pocket." Olin was wealthy, thin on top, and able to flash a nice smile. Yet he had none of the guilt that Bierce believed was behind the robber barons' making hasty amends for their crimes of success. By opposing this view, Olin was out of step not only with Bierce's definition but also with the prevailing liberalism of his own times.

Olin gave away his money for a reason. The political and social tumult of the late 1960s and early 1970s had convinced him that the American system of free enterprise was in danger of collapse—not because of any intrinsic weaknesses, but because too many people either did not understand or refused to appreciate the country's most basic principles. Many of them occupied positions of influence and prestige at colleges and universities, in the government and the media, and, increasingly, among philanthropic foundations and nonprofit organizations. Irving Kristol referred to this group collectively as "the new class" and observed that its members dedicated their professional lives to expanding the size and scope of the welfare state.

Olin aimed to frustrate them—and to recover the fundamentals. He wanted to promote free enterprise, limited government, and individual freedom by funding a "counterintelligentsia" of scholars, think tanks, and publications. This was no easy task in the 1960s and 1970s, when the conservative movement was still young. Its scholars were few, its think tanks rare, and its publications essentially limited to William F. Buckley Jr.'s *National Review*. Conservatism may have started to emerge from its intellectual ghetto, where it had been stuck for much of the postwar era, but Lionel Trilling's legendary condemnation remained fresh in many minds: "There are no conservative or reactionary ideas in general circulation," he had written in 1950, only "irritable mental gestures."

Conservatives like to cite an old Richard Weaver aphorism: "Ideas have consequences." Olin probably never read anything Weaver wrote, but he certainly would have agreed with this observation. He also realized that ideas alone, however powerful, are not enough. They must come from somewhere. Once they are hatched, they require testing and refinement. Only then may they begin percolating down into policy. The process takes more than sheer brainpower; it requires financial support, which is why Olin turned the John M. Olin Foundation into a venture capital fund for the conservative movement.

How successful was he? If Trilling were to come back and assess the political and social scene in the first years of the twenty-first century, he certainly would reverse his earlier judgment. Conservative ideas are ascendant; indeed, America may be in the middle of a "conservative moment." The success of conservatism owes much to the inherent power of its ideas, as well as to the talents of individual men and women who promote them.

Yet it is impossible not to see the steady influence of the John M. Olin Foundation in this triumph. If the conservative intellectual movement were a NASCAR race, and if the scholars and organizations who compose it were drivers zipping around a race track, virtually all of their vehicles at least would sport an Olin bumper sticker. And many of the champion drivers would have O-L-I-N splashed across their hoods in big letters.

Some of the foundation's major accomplishments were already in the works on that evening in 1981 and would become even more dramatic in the years to come:

• **Law and Economics**: The John M. Olin Foundation has devoted more of its resources to studying how laws influence economic behavior than any other project. The law schools at Chicago, Harvard, Stanford, Virginia, and Yale all have law and economics programs named in honor of Olin. "You should not forget that without all the work in Law and Economics, a great part of which has been supported by the John M. Olin Foundation, it is doubtful whether the importance of my work would have been recognized," said Ronald Coase, the 1991 Nobel Prize winner in economics.

• **The Federalist Society**: It is impossible to say which grant in the history of the John M. Olin Foundation has mattered more than any other, but a strong candidate would be the foundation's support for a 1982 conference of law students and professors that served as a springboard for the creation of the Federalist Society. "There are many members of the Federalist Society in our administration," said Vice President Dick Cheney in a 2001 speech. "We know that because they were quizzed about it under oath."

• **The Collegiate Network**: The consortium of conservative college newspapers got its start in 1980 with a small grant to a student publication at the University of Chicago by the Institute for Educational Affairs, a group chaired by William E. Simon and supported by the foundation. Today, most of the country's top colleges and universities are home to an established student newspaper or magazine that presents an alternative voice on campus and provides a training ground for future conservative leaders.

- **Welfare policy**: A small grant to Charles Murray helped make possible the publication in 1984 of *Losing Ground,* a landmark book whose full impact became apparent when President Bill Clinton signed a welfare-reform bill into law in 1996.

- **School choice**: Another small grant was made for another pioneering book, in this case *Politics, Markets, and America's Schools,* by John E. Chubb and Terry M. Moe. It became an intellectual cornerstone of the school-choice movement and was arguably the most important book of its time on K-12 education.

- **"The End of History" vs. "The Clash of Civilizations"**: The most fascinating foreign-policy debate in the aftermath of the Cold War was born when Francis Fukuyama delivered his famous "End of History" lecture at the University of Chicago's John M. Olin Center—and then had it published in *The National Interest,* a journal created and sustained by the foundation's dollars. Fukuyama's most prominent critic was Samuel P. Huntington, the national security expert who led the John M. Olin Institute for Strategic Studies at Harvard.

- **Intellectual opinion makers**: No two men have done more to discredit the left-wing dominance of America's campuses than Allan Bloom and Dinesh D'Souza, both of them bestselling authors. The foundation supplied Bloom with a grant that helped him write an article for *National Review* that became the basis of *The Closing of the American Mind,* and also backed Bloom's John M. Olin Center for Inquiry into the Theory and Practice of Democracy at the University of Chicago. D'Souza wrote his own groundbreaking book, *Illiberal Education,* as a John M. Olin Fellow at the American Enterprise Institute—and sparked the debate that helped turn the term "politically correct" into a pejorative. Other prominent beneficiaries of the John M. Olin Foundation's grants included Linda Chavez, Milton Friedman, Henry Manne, Harvey Mansfield, Richard John Neuhaus, Michael Novak, and George Stigler, as well as the American Enterprise Institute, the Center for Individual Rights, the Heritage Foundation, the Hoover Institution, the Manhattan Institute, the National Association of Scholars, *The New Criterion,* and the Philanthropy Roundtable.

In addition to these accomplishments, the John M. Olin Foundation achieved an influence far greater than the sum of its parts. It was by no means the only source of philanthropic dollars for conservatives. Yet it became a leader among more than a dozen other foundations of varying sizes, and it helped turn a collection of outposts and tendencies into a full-fledged movement. Its partners in this effort included the Lynde and Harry Bradley Foundation, the Sarah Scaife Foundation, and the Smith Richardson Foundation, as well as the W. H. Brady Foundation, the Carthage Foundation, the Earhart Foundation, the Charles G. Koch, David H. Koch and Claude R. Lambe charitable foundations, the Philip M. McKenna Foundation, the JM Foundation, the Samuel Roberts Noble Foundation, the Randolph Foundation, and the Henry Salvatori Foundation. Together, these foundations made sure that conservative ideas really did have consequences, even though their combined assets did not begin to approach the massive endowments of their liberal counterparts. Liberal foundations outspent conservative ones on an annual basis by a factor of at least 10 to 1 and, depending on how the political biases of foundations are defined, perhaps by as much as 20 to 1.

The fact that the John M. Olin Foundation was able to do so much with so little is a testimony to the people who ran it. Apart from Olin himself, the foundation's most significant figure was William E. Simon, whom Olin had recruited to become chairman of the board and president in 1977. Simon was Olin's junior by thirty-five years, and he provided the foundation with dynamic leadership during its most active period. He professionalized its operations, put it on firm footing to become a major philanthropic force, and oversaw its programs until his death in 2000. All the while, he abided by Olin's philosophical and organizational principles. His lieutenants were three smart and energetic executive directors who managed the foundation's day-to-day operations: Frank O'Connell, who shaped much of the foundation's grantmaking in the 1970s and was preparing to retire as Simon joined; Michael Joyce, who guided the foundation during its most creative phase and helped it become a major

supporter of neoconservatism; and James Piereson, who administered the foundation's activities as they matured over the course
of more than two decades.

The story of the John M. Olin Foundation is essentially the
story of these men—Olin, Simon, O'Connell, Joyce, and Piereson. They are the central characters, but hardly the only ones.
Their story is, in turn, the tale of the conservative intellectual
movement during the final years of the twentieth century, told
from the perspective of venture capitalists. They searched for
promising talent and new opportunities. They experienced many
successes and endured several failures. Over time, their priorities shifted and their strategies evolved. And they stayed true to
Olin's unusual request that his foundation not outlive him by
more than a generation. Most important, however, was their devotion to the foundation's mission "to recover the fundamentals,"
as John M. Olin put it in 1981. At that memorable dinner in St.
Louis, when Nixon and all the others had finished their tributes,
Olin reflected upon his extraordinary life as a businessman and
philanthropist. "That all started with one black powder mill," he
said. "And I point out that is the fundamental of free enterprise
in this country, that principle: You grew out of hard work and
out of accumulating profits. . . . That's America."

# CHAPTER ONE

# A MAN AND HIS FORTUNE

THE *St. Louis Post-Dispatch* DID NOT COMMENT on the birth of John Merrill Olin on Thursday, November 10, 1892, in Alton, Illinois. Nor did it say much about the fresh blanket of snow covering the countryside and causing trains throughout the Midwest to lose time on their routes. The big news in St. Louis—and everywhere else in the United States—concerned the presidential election held two days earlier. "The feature of today's election returns," reported the *Post-Dispatch,* "is the strong probability that Ohio has cast her vote for Cleveland." The newspaper was not referring to a city, but to a man: Grover Cleveland had just driven Benjamin Harrison from the White House. He was about to become the only president to serve nonconsecutive terms in office.

Nobody in America yet drove cars, flew airplanes, or even zipped zippers as they would in a few years, though Whitcomb L. Judson was about to patent a hook-and-eye shoe fastener he called a "clasp locker," which would be a commercial flop. Yet the country was fast assuming many recognizably modern features. Ellis Island had just opened as a processing center for millions of immigrants from Europe. In politics, partisans debated the extravagant spending of the "Billion-Dollar Congress." The presidential election had turned on free trade, and in particular a high tariff that inflated consumer prices. The result reversed the decision of four years earlier, when Cleveland carried the popular vote but Harrison won the Electoral College. Plenty of Americans welcomed sensational distractions: Many readers who paid a nickel for a copy of the *Post-Dispatch* were probably more interested in the latest developments in the Lizzie Borden murder case than they were in the comparatively dull Cleveland/Harrison contest. In the world of Gilded Age commerce, names like Carnegie, Morgan, and Vanderbilt held sway.

The rise of the name Olin may be traced not to the arrival of a baby boy, but to a business venture his father had started some weeks earlier, when Franklin W. Olin founded a black powder mill in East Alton. As his wife was giving birth to a son, he was giving birth to one of the great American success stories of the twentieth century—a story in which his son would play a decisive role.

John M. Olin was a seventh-generation member of a family that had arrived in the New World in the seventeenth century. His namesake, John Olin, was reportedly born in France in 1664, arrested in Wales in 1678, and pressed into the British navy. When his man-of-war docked in Boston Harbor, he escaped and settled in Rhode Island. Another story has it that he deserted in Providence and changed his name from Llewellyn to Olin. Whatever the truth, in 1708 he married Susanna Spencer, a Welsh immigrant sixteen years his junior. His descendants included Stephen Olin, who served as president of Randolph-Macon College in Virginia and Wesleyan University in Connecticut in the nineteenth century. This Olin also fathered a son, Stephen Henry Olin, who served as acting president of Wesleyan, which named the campus library after these two men in 1928.

Franklin Walter Olin sprouted from a different branch of the same tree. Born in a logging camp in Vermont in 1860, he received little formal education in his youth, but his intelligence was obvious. When an older friend gave him a batch of *Scientific American* magazines, he read every line. At the age of twenty-one, in 1881, he entered Cornell University as an engineering student. He excelled at sports, especially baseball. A left-handed power hitter, he captained the school team for three years. In 1884, he played professionally in Washington and Toledo before returning to his studies. He graduated from Cornell the next year and went on to hire out his service in building five powder mills in New Jersey, Pennsylvania, and West Virginia. Then he headed west to Illinois, where the growing coal industry in the southern part of the state needed more blasting powder. On a train ride to St. Louis, he spotted an attractive piece of land and took title to it on July 4, 1892. He always considered it signifi-cant that he became an independent businessman on Indepen-dence Day. At the age of thirty-two, he settled in Alton, Illinois, with his wife and a one-year-old son, Franklin Jr. He founded the Equitable Powder Company shortly before the birth of his sec-ond son, John.

The powder mill did well, paying its first dividend in 1895. Franklin fought off a takeover attempt orchestrated by Du Pont, which was looking to purchase its competitors in the powder and explosives industry. He managed to stay in control, however, and in 1898 he expanded his operation into the manufacture of small-arms ammunition by starting the Western Cartridge Com-pany. In 1900, a devastating fire ripped through a loading facil-ity, destroying equipment and supplies. Western Cartridge lost money for several years, but the company eventually found its footing. During the first half of the twentieth century, it would sit at the center of the Olin family's growing enterprise.

As his father's business began to flourish, John spent his summers with Uncle Amos and Aunt Mary on a farm in New Hampshire, where he milked cows and tended crops. Their last name was Merrill, and John chose to take it as his own middle name, even though he had been baptized as John Moulton Olin. "During my boyhood," he later explained, "my mother's brother betrayed my father with respect to stock ownership in the origi-nal Olin Company and I changed my middle name from Moul-ton to Merrill, a token of my admiration and association with Uncle Amos."

The time on the farm in New Hampshire was crucial to John's formation. "I learned to work there, and to save my earn-ings. My uncle paid me 15 cents an hour to dig kale out of corn, and if I didn't work I didn't get paid," he said. When he was seven years old, John gathered his hard-earned savings of $15 and bought his first fly rod. "By the end of that summer I knew where every trout in every pool was, and I could jump from rock to rock like a cat." This work ethic and love of the outdoors would last his whole life.

He went on to attend Cascadilla, a boarding school in Ithaca, New York, that prepared boys for college in general and Cornell in particular. When he was vacationing back home in Illinois, he participated in the family business, testing as many as two thousand shot shells in a single day. After eight hours of trigger pulling, he would go home with a sore finger—and years later he would revel in telling his friends about the experience. This was a real job and he was paid for it. Although the Olins were prospering, Franklin Sr. was determined not to spoil his boys. Rather than bring home all the shot they wanted for their own hunting and target practice, he made his sons purchase ammunition with money they had earned. "He was a tough taskmaster," John would say of his father in 1973.

John entered Cornell in the fall of 1909. He was not an eager athlete as his father had been. He was less outgoing, mostly keeping to himself and his studies, though he did join the Kappa Sigma fraternity. As a freshman, he struggled with calculus and repeated two courses in the summer session following his first year. His grades improved steadily over his four years at Cornell, as he shifted away from the degree in mechanical engineering that his father wanted him to pursue and instead majored in chemistry. The department allowed Olin to conduct research in areas touching on the family company's interests. He worked closely with Emile Chamot, a professor who became another important influence. In one project, he and Chamot studied why paper shot shells sometimes misfired. "We had difficulty in making much progress in solving this problem," Olin recalled. Then, late one night, Chamot leaned back in his chair and offered a piece of wisdom that his student never forgot. "Olin," he said, "we are being defeated in this study because we have not ascertained 'why' a defect occurs. It has been my experience in such cases if the reason 'why' the defect occurs is found, often the remedy suggests itself." Although seemingly banal, these words inspired Olin in his approach to problem solving. He repeated them many times. "This professor made a tremendous contribution to my future and I shall forever be in his debt because I have

used his philosophy thousands of times in my analysis of problems in my career which followed college," he recalled many
years later.

One of Olin's classmates remembered him for owning a
car—a genuine novelty in those days—in the spring term of his
senior year. It was a sure sign that his father's company was doing
well. In 1913, Olin graduated with a degree in chemistry and
joined the family business. He had received his first share of
stock a year earlier, and now he quickly assimilated into company life. He oversaw the construction of a smokeless powder
mill in Springfield, Illinois, and later ran operations at a brass
mill. Just before the First World War broke out in Europe, Western Cartridge revenues approached $3 million. Over the next
few years, this figure more than quintupled as Franklin Olin and
his sons secured some two dozen arms contracts with the United
States and its allies. Western ammunition was noted for its high
quality. When the war was over, General John J. Pershing sent a
letter of thanks and praise. Franklin Sr. was so proud that he had
the letter framed and displayed it in his office.

During the war years, John usually worked eighteen-hour
days, taking after his father's habits and demonstrating the near-
complete devotion to the family company that would last until
his retirement. Yet he found the time to marry Adele Levis in
1917. Together, they had three daughters. (One of them, Joan,
died at the age of five; Georgene and Louise both predeceased
him, too, dying in the 1970s.) Two years after the marriage, Olin
became a vice president and increasingly demonstrated executive skills. Like his father, he had a good head for finances. Yet
he was more of a natural risk-taker, a quality that caused the two
men to clash from time to time but one that also served the interests of the company. By the start of the 1920s, business could
hardly have been better. Whereas Remington and Winchester
were suffering from excess capacity, Western was benefiting from
Franklin's decision to sign only short-term contracts with
customers.

Tragedy struck when John's brother Franklin Jr. developed
a painful abdominal condition that required hospitalization in
New York City. His parents traveled with him and nervously

awaited the outcome. The surgeons who conducted the operation considered it a success, but the young man apparently fell
into a fit of depression during his convalescence. On the night
of February 4, 1921, he threw himself from the third-story window of St. Bartholomew's Hospital on East 42nd Street.

The sudden death of his older brother made John even
more important to Western Cartridge, though his burden was
lightened somewhat when his younger brother, Spencer, joined
the business. John was at heart a scientist who loved to tinker
with products; twenty-four patents bear his name, all for arms
and ammunition manufacture and design. His most important
innovation was a shotgun shell that extended firing range by
twenty yards. The inspiration for it came on a duck-hunting excur-
sion along the Illinois River, in which his partner killed his quarry
on the water rather than in flight. Olin protested this unsports-
manlike conduct. "We had a hell of a fight that evening," said
Olin, who vowed to get even. The next year, he returned to the
scene with his new shell. When some ducks flew into sight, the
other man waited for them to put down on the water. Olin, however, started firing before they came into his partner's range. He
called his new shell "super excellent." A colleague with a mind
for marketing dubbed it the Super-X. The shell's enormous popularity with wildfowl hunters thrust Western Cartridge into the
front ranks of ammunition companies.

By 1931, as the country stumbled into an extended economic depression, one of the Olin family's main competitors,
Winchester Repeating Arms, fell on hard times. It had flourished
during the war but afterward had to absorb excess capacity and
pay down debts—a set of thorny problems that the Olins had
managed to avoid. Poor management decisions complicated matters further. One of America's best-known gun makers was sell-
ing everything from refrigerators to roller skates. The Olins saw
their chance to take over a company that would allow them to
achieve a goal they had always talked about: manufacturing guns
in addition to producing the ammunition for them. With heavy
borrowing, they bought Winchester three days before Christmas. "The Olin family went into their safety deposit boxes and
brought out all the securities we owned, and every member of

the family put what he had down on ninety-day loans, and we bought Winchester," John remembered later on. "Believe me, I didn't think we had any Christmas present."

John understood that the acquisition by itself would not solve Winchester's problems, so he moved his family to the company's base in New Haven, Connecticutt. There, he could return Winchester to its core business of gun making and revive it as a division of Western Cartridge. He produced astonishing results, including a profit of $168,000 in his first year there—which did not sound like much until it was compared against the $8 million that Winchester had lost in the year before Olin's intervention. John called it "the most important, the most satisfying profit that I ever made in my entire life." Despite the joy of success, John's time in New Haven was excruciatingly difficult. To breathe new life into Winchester, he had to make difficult cost-cutting decisions. He took no pleasure in releasing hundreds of workers who had done nothing wrong except join a company that had suffered from poor leadership. Yet the greatest trials took place at home. His marriage appears to have collapsed during these hard years in New Haven, probably from the stress of working and living far away from St. Louis. In 1935, it ended in divorce. Olin fell into a year-long depression, neglecting some of his work obligations for the only time in his life. He went on a few long hunting trips and stayed away from New Haven for almost a year. Despite this personal turmoil, Winchester rebounded under his guidance.

In the midst of the Depression, Winchester began to prosper once more. By 1934, revenues topped $17 million. By 1940, they had nearly tripled to $45 million. Franklin Olin remained the titular president of the company during these years, though he was in his seventies and slipping into retirement. John and Spencer increasingly made most of the important business decisions. Of the two sons, John took after his father in his intense focus on the company. Spencer was far more easygoing. During disputes between his brother and his father—often with John urging an aggressive course of action and Franklin urging caution—Spencer usually sided with the father, in part because it was the easiest course. He was an important contributor to the company, but was more passionate about leisure than business; he was a champion trapshooter and enjoyed an excellent reputation for his golf game. (In 1954, in fact, Spencer participated in Sam Snead's pro-am tournament with a struggling professional named Arnold Palmer; their performance earned Palmer a much-needed check for $1,500, and Palmer was even more thrilled when Spencer gave him the entire proceeds of his wager on the team, almost $10,000.)

In 1938, with war looming in Europe again, government officials anxious to plan for possible U.S. involvement sought Olin's help in selecting, designing, and constructing the St. Louis Ordnance Ammunition Plant, a massive facility for the production of small-arms ammunition. Olin was also asked to set up the U.S. Cartridge Company and oversee all aspects of production. He threw himself into the project, choosing a site for the plant and suggesting an innovative design concept. He recommended a multistory structure with cups for cartridge casings and bullet jackets stationed on the top floors and successive stages of manufacture below them, with the bottom floor devoted to shipping finished rounds. Olin believed his plan would boost efficiency.

The government rejected his idea, on the grounds that such a building would suffer too much damage if enemy bombers targeted it. Olin considered this critique bizarre: If enemy bombers were flying over St. Louis, then the United States would have a lot more to worry about than the blueprints of a small-arms ammunition plant. But he acquiesced, and the factory was built to the government's inefficient standards. Work began in December of 1940. Ten months later, the plant was producing ammunition. At the height of its activity, the plant employed more than 34,000 people. Over the course of the war, the various Olin operations churned out more than 15 billion rounds of ammunition as well as nearly 1.5 million rifles and shotguns. By one reckoning, all of these Olin-produced cartridges, laid end to end, would have circled the equator more than eighteen times. Revenues boomed, with total sales worth $650 million between 1941 and 1945, including $40 million in profit.

Olin was pleased to do well and do good at the same time, though the experience of contributing to the war effort also made him think that government activity simply could not match private enterprise. He was one of the country's leading experts on the manufacture of ammunition—and yet he was forced to take orders from federal officials who were placed in positions of authority despite their lack of practical knowledge. The result, he believed, was a level of wastefulness that would sink a company if it were tried in the marketplace. Olin was especially upset by one directive from Washington demanding that he lower the copper content in his brass cartridge casings from 67 to 62 percent. The motive apparently was to conserve copper, but Olin insisted that the quality of his ammunition suffered for it. Decrees on staffing and other matters only aggravated the problem. Olin complained that he was being forced to manufacture inferior products, but his protests were ignored.

Olin's frustration in dealing with the government at least was countered by the personal satisfaction of succeeding his father as president of the family business, which consolidated itself as Olin Industries in 1944. Yet an enormous disappointment loomed, affecting both his personal and his business life. Franklin owned most of the company stock, which he donated to the F. W. Olin Foundation, an organization that would spend most of its resources on educational projects. (This entity, founded in 1938, is not to be confused with the John M. Olin Foundation.) By giving away his shares, Franklin made it impossible for John and Spencer to inherit them. This decision astonished the boys, who thought they had contributed mightily to the stock's value. Yet their father was a frugal man who had lived continuously in the same house he had bought for $6,000 in 1892. He believed they were wealthy enough already. "I've done enough for you boys and I'm putting my stock in a foundation," he said. If they wanted more money, they would have to go out and make it themselves. Franklin was not moved by their bitter complaints that upon his death (which came in 1951) they might lose control of the company their family had built. To complicate matters further, neither of the sons was placed on the board of the new foundation. Their only recourse was to buy back their father's stock—something they did at great personal cost over the next few years.

The postwar boom saw Olin Industries expand into many new areas. In 1949, it entered the cellophane business, drawing on its experience making cellulose-based products such as explosives. It acquired paper companies that owned large tracts of land in Louisiana and North Carolina, which led the company into forest products. Soon the company was producing most of America's cigarette paper. In 1952, Olin bought Ramset Fasteners, a maker of nail guns and other powder-actuated building tools. In 1953, it went into the production of hydrazine, a rocket fuel. This enterprise particularly interested John because hydrazine was the subject of his senior research project at Cornell, and he watched with interest as the company developed derivative uses for this increasingly affordable chemical.

One of Olin's most important acquisitions at the start of this period involved a person rather than a company. John Hanes, formerly an undersecretary at the Department of the Treasury and a commissioner at the Securities and Exchange Commission, was a charismatic financial wizard who had saved William Randolph Hearst's publishing empire from financial ruin. His job at Olin Industries was not to avert disaster, but to exploit opportunity. Hanes made much of Olin's rapid expansion possible, and he would remain one of John's most trusted associates.

In 1953, *Fortune* magazine called Olin Industries "one of the few great family-owned corporations." It went public and then took an even bigger step. John was entering his sixties and looking for a successor. Without any obvious candidates in his family or at the company, he had to search beyond his immediate circle. His thoughts turned to Thomas S. Nichols, the forty-four-year-old president of the Mathieson Chemical Corporation, based in Baltimore. Attempts to recruit him failed, but they led to a series of intense talks between Hanes and Nichols. The result was a merger. The new company was called the Olin Mathieson Chemical Corporation. (In 1969, the company changed its name to Olin Corporation and launched a public-relations campaign asking everyone "to call us by our first name.")

John M. Olin suddenly found himself chairman of the board of a company that had doubled in size instantly. Annual revenues totaled half a billion dollars. Although Mathieson's core technologies of chemicals, metals, and ammunition were familiar to him, the merger put Olin in charge of a huge enterprise that made everything from brown paper bags to pharmaceuticals. (One of Mathieson's divisions was Squibb, the drug maker.) The company grew at first, but sales slumped during the recession of 1957. By this point, John was thinking more seriously about his retirement. He may also have recognized that his skills were better suited to the construction of a business empire than to the maintenance of one. In May, he resigned as chairman of the board but remained active as chairman of Olin Mathieson's executive committee. That same year, *Fortune* included the Olin brothers on its list of people whose personal wealth was estimated at $75 million or higher; John and Spencer were ranked no. 31. They must have bristled at the writer's claim that their wealth was "inherited," given that they had created so much of it themselves and then been forced to buy back the stock their father had given to his foundation.

Like so many captains of industry, John Olin was highly intelligent and fiercely competitive. "Show me a good loser and I'll show you a loser," he liked to say. He was determined to win at everything he did, and most of all at leading his company. His gruff exterior made him more respected than loved. Like his father, he had a difficult time congratulating or rewarding his employees. Many of them felt intimidated in his presence, though colleagues who knew him well also found him deeply loyal.

Olin had strong opinions on a variety of subjects and was not reluctant to share his views on everything from labor unions (which he did not admire) to dog breeding (a hobby he enjoyed). Although he never questioned certain principles, such as the value of a free-enterprise system, he was not stubborn or inflexible. At bottom, he had the mind of a scientist who was willing to test assumptions and try new ideas—just as Professor Chamot had advised many years earlier. Olin also loved gadgets and would give away batches of them each Christmas. "I remember when those dodecahedron calendars came out," said Connie Josse, Olin's longtime secretary in St. Louis. "Suddenly we all had to have a dodecahedron calendar on our desks."

Olin was a workaholic who did not understand why people wanted time off on Good Friday or Labor Day. "I've been getting up before daybreak since I was a boy, and it's just become the natural way to start a day," he once said. Josse remembered a moment shortly after his daughter Louise died. "I went into his office and saw him just staring out the window," she said. The sight startled her because she had never seen Olin do that before; he was always busy, refusing to squander a moment of his time when he could be confronting his company's latest challenge or thinking about its next opportunity. He was well known for never leaving a piece of mail unanswered. He was nominally Episcopalian but not an especially religious man. Toward the end of his life, however, he said that the world's problems would be solved "if all mankind adopted belief in a Supreme Power."

Corporate affairs consumed most of his substantial energies, but not all of them. In 1940, Olin married Evelyn Brown Niedringhaus. It was her second marriage as well—and a remarkable match for both of them. There were no children, though Olin took an immediate liking to his new stepdaughter, also named Evelyn. Just as Uncle Amos in New Hampshire had treated Olin as the son he never had, Olin became close to Evelyn, taught her how to use a gun, and took her hunting.

Hunting, in fact, was one of Olin's great passions. He was known to stop a business meeting to watch a group of ducks fly by. He traced his love of the outdoors to those summers in New Hampshire. As the head of a company that manufactured small arms, he was delighted to see more hunters take to the fields and forests following the Second World War, but he also recognized that the growing popularity of the sport would require improved conservation efforts. He believed that well-trained dogs would reduce game losses and that effective habitat management would minimize hunting's impact on wildlife. On business trips, he would often go out of his way to speak on these subjects to sporting clubs; yet his devotion went well beyond stump speeches and bird watching. In 1951, he founded Nilo Kennels in Illinois to breed and train retrievers; the next year, he founded Nilo Farms to promote the idea of hunting preserves. Both ventures were successful. The black Labradors of Nilo (Olin spelled backwards) became famous as contest animals, especially King Buck, who won championships in 1952 and 1953 and later served as the model for a U.S. postage stamp. *Sports Illustrated* was so impressed with these achievements that it featured a picture of Mr. and Mrs. Olin on the cover of its November 17, 1958 issue.

Olin was an avid fisherman as well. Each June, he visited Quebec's Moisie River and shipped boxes of salmon to friends around the United States. Richard Nixon was among the regular recipients. Olin was active in Atlantic salmon conservation efforts and served as a director of the World Wildlife Fund.

In 1963, Olin retired as chairman of the Olin Corporation's executive committee. He was made honorary chairman of the board and continued to participate in board meetings, but his obligations were reduced and he found time for many other activities. "I will continue to work until I become either senile or too weak to carry on," he once said. One of his main interests was education. He had joined the board of Washington University in St. Louis in 1942 (becoming a life trustee in 1972) and also served on the board of Johns Hopkins University (1953–65). At Cornell, he served a single term on an alumni leadership panel known as the Cornell University Council (1950–54), followed by a dozen years on the board of trustees (1954–66), after which he became a trustee emeritus, a lifetime position. Olin gave generously to each of these institutions, especially his alma mater. He donated millions of dollars to Cornell, including $3 million for a major library that now bears his name.

Washington University conferred an honorary degree upon him in 1963, as did Blackburn University in 1956, Springfield College in 1957, and the St. Louis School of Pharmacy in 1962. In 1968, Olin won the Charles F. Kettering Award from George Washington University's Patent, Trademark, and Copyright Research Institute. Six years later, he was inducted into the Hunting Hall of Fame. He also received the Chevalier de la Légion d'Honneur of France and the Grande Ufficiale dell'Ordine al Merito della Repubblica Italiana.

As these honors poured in, however, age began to slow him down. He underwent surgery several times to improve a bad hip; at some point in the 1960s, he began walking with a cane. He increasingly spent his summers in East Hampton, New York, his winters on a plantation near Albany, Georgia, and the rest of his time in the St. Louis area. Physical ailments kept him from Churchill Downs and the 100th running of the Kentucky Derby in 1974—a special one not only because of the centennial but also because Olin had a colt in the race. He had named his horse Cannonade because he liked the dictionary definition of the word: "To assault or bombard with heavy cannon or artillery fire." During the race, Cannonade shot out of the pack with a half-mile to go and won by more than two lengths. But the event was perhaps most noteworthy for the fact that it featured a crowded field of twenty-three horses. "There were just too damned many," said Olin, who watched it on television.

For an eighty-one-year-old man interested in horse racing, the Kentucky Derby victory might have served as a satisfying cap-stone to a remarkable career. Olin certainly had led a life of great accomplishment. Just a few years earlier, when Cornell had made him a "presidential councilor"—an honor conferred upon a handful of outstanding alumni—the school gave him an ornate certificate. It described Olin as "one of America's leading indus-trialists," an important financial donor to the university, and a "supporter of veterinary research, conservationist, [and] devel-oper of fine retrievers." He was all of these things, of course. And despite his great generosity over the years to a number of worthy causes, nobody—not even Olin himself—knew that he would yet leave his mark as one of the twentieth century's most influential philanthropists.

CHAPTER TWO

# THE FREEDOM PERSUASION

A FEW DAYS BEFORE A BOARD MEETING of the Olin Corporation in the spring of 1973, John M. Olin made an appointment with Frank O'Connell, the company's vice president for employee relations. "I had no idea what he wanted," said O'Connell, who regarded a summons from the boss as possible trouble. Olin was still honorary chairman of the industrial giant that bore his name. He attended its monthly board meetings and kept an office in a Park Avenue building that had housed the corporation before it moved to Connecticut in 1969. O'Connell had spoken to Olin many times previously, but almost always as he delivered formal reports on labor relations. "I don't think we had ever met one-on-one like this before," said O'Connell.

When they sat down, Olin as usual dispensed with pleasantries and got right to the point. He described the private foundation he had created some years earlier and asked O'Connell to run it for him. "I would like to use this fortune to help to preserve the system which made its accumulation possible in only two lifetimes, my father's and mine," said Olin. The two men spent a few minutes discussing the urgent need to defend capitalism from its enemies. They also talked about how this might be done. "If you ever heard an offer you couldn't refuse, that was it," said O'Connell. In truth, neither Olin nor O'Connell had a clear notion of what to do. Together, however, they would begin to transform the John M. Olin Foundation from an ordinary rich man's charity into a powerful underwriter of ideas.

O'Connell was an unlikely choice for the job. Benefactors who want to hire foundation directors usually seek people with a professional background in philanthropy. Yet Olin deliberately passed over one likely candidate, the fellow who was then in charge of the Olin Corporation's charitable activities, and instead recruited this feisty labor lawyer. A native New Yorker, born on April 4, 1914, O'Connell had come of age during the New Deal, "when everything was stacked against business." By the 1960s, he had developed a national reputation as a resilient negotiator during difficult union talks. "I became a big spokesman for management rights," said O'Connell. "I think Olin saw me as tough. He wanted his foundation's philanthropy to be tough as well."

O'Connell may have been a newcomer to philanthropy, but Olin had two decades of experience behind him. He had established the John M. Olin Foundation at his home in Alton, Illinois, on December 29, 1953, "at 10 o'clock in the forenoon," as the minutes have it. Three people were present: Olin, his brother Spencer, and Gordon Grand, a trusted associate at the Olin Corporation (who eventually became its CEO). One of the foundation's incorporators was John W. Hanes, Olin's business partner, but he was not present. The men agreed to open a bank account at the Illinois State Bank of East Alton. They do not appear to have discussed the foundation's mission in any meaningful way. Everybody seemed to agree that the John M. Olin Foundation would support whatever John M. Olin wanted it to support. Nor did the trustees make any grants. This is perhaps not surprising: These were some of the busiest days of Olin's professional life, as he confronted a succession problem at his own company and prepared for the merger with Mathieson.

Nearly a year passed before the foundation approved its first grant. On December 14, 1954, the board of trustees met in Olin's office in New York City; Olin and Grand were the only two present. They talked about nonprofit organizations the foundation might support. Then they voted ("unanimously," according to the minutes) to make an $18,000 grant to Cornell University. "There being no further business to come before the meeting it was, on motion duly made and seconded, adjourned."

The John M. Olin Foundation would not begin an active program of grantmaking for some time. The board convened in 1955, 1956 and 1957, but undertook no special actions. It was not until the spring of 1958 that the foundation made its second grant: $10,000 to the Cornell University Alumni Fund. The fund received $5,000 the next year and then $10,000 in both 1961 and 1963. The foundation also donated $1,000 to Yale University in 1963.

Up to this point, the John M. Olin Foundation was a conventional rich man's philanthropy. Yet the organization was about to take a step that demonstrated a willingness to use its resources for large-scale social and political goals—a decision that both foreshadowed its ultimate character and contributed to a fascinating subchapter of Cold War history.

The story began on December 29, 1958, when the board approved a $50,000 grant to the Vernon Fund. The purpose of the grant is not described anywhere in the John M. Olin Foundation's records. The only information pertaining to the Vernon Fund is an address: Suite 919 of the Munsey Building, located at 1329 E Street NW, Washington, D.C. The Vernon Fund received another grant of $50,000 on March 17, 1959. According to the minutes from the board of trustees meeting on April 17, "Note was taken that these contributions were made possible by contributions received by the [John M. Olin] Foundation from the Dearborn Foundation in the amount of $50,000 on December 26th, 1958 and $50,000 on March 4, 1959." This pattern then continued, with more grants of $50,000 to the Vernon Fund in June, September, and December of 1959. Four more payments of $50,000 followed in 1960. The next year, the foundation wrote only two checks to the Vernon Fund, though the amount increased to $100,000 each. In each instance, the payment was preceded by a contribution from the Dearborn Foundation.

This money flowing from the Dearborn Foundation to the Vernon Fund dominated the John M. Olin Foundation's activities in the late 1950s and early 1960s. On the second day of 1962, the foundation received another $100,000 from the Dearborn

Foundation, which was disbursed to the Vernon Fund eight days later. In February, the foundation received $100,000 from a new source, the Beacon Fund. Less than a month later, the John M. Olin Foundation gave these monies to the African-American Institute, which was located in New York at 345 East 46th Street. As with the Vernon Fund, the purpose of this contribution was not disclosed. In October, the John M. Olin Foundation received $100,000 from the Tower Fund and two weeks later transferred the cash once more to the African-American Institute. In 1963, the foundation reverted to its previous practice of accepting money from the Dearborn Foundation and transferring it soon after to the Vernon Fund. In total, $1.95 million passed through the John M. Olin Foundation this way, with all of it going to the Vernon Fund except for those two contributions to the African-American Institute. The foundation's final link to the Vernon Fund came on April 22, 1966, when it sent $75,000 to the organization. Then this type of giving came to a complete stop.

The source of all this financial shuffling was the Central Intelligence Agency, which in the 1950s had launched a secret program of trying to combat the influence of communism upon artists, writers, and intellectuals in the Western democracies. This was an urgent cause during the Cold War, and especially during its early years, when the success of the Communist Party in countries such as France and Italy made it possible to think that Marxism might overtake the West through popular elections rather than Soviet tanks. And so the CIA spent millions of dollars on international conferences, high-brow publications, and art exhibits—even a European tour for the Boston Symphony Orchestra and a Russian translation of T. S. Eliot's *Four Quartets*. One of the main recipients of CIA funds was the Congress for Cultural Freedom, which sponsored a number of these and other projects, including a well-regarded culture-and-politics magazine called *Encounter*. Most of the money went to anticommunist liberals and even socialists, because it was felt that they were better able than conservatives to influence people on the Left who felt the allure of Marxism.

Philanthropic foundations played a key role in obscuring the connection between the CIA and its funding recipients, who for the most part did not know about the agency's involvement in their own financing. John M. Olin certainly knew, and he saw it as his patriotic duty to help his country fight the Cold War. Allowing some money to pass in and out of his foundation's accounts was the least he could do. And he was hardly the only participant in this endeavor. According to one estimate, more than a hundred private foundations assisted the CIA in this manner.

In 1967, however, writers for *Ramparts* magazine and the *New York Times* revealed that the CIA had funded the National Student Association and a variety of other anticommunist academic, cultural, and labor organizations. Shortly after the first round of stories broke, the *Washington Post* reported that the CIA was using the Vernon Fund to pass money to the National Education Association and the World Conference of Organizations of the Teaching Profession. The groups were then sponsoring teacher education programs in developing countries. "All available evidence points to the conclusion that the Vernon Fund is a creation of the CIA," said the *Post*. And indeed it was. Once exposed to the public, the CIA's involvement in using American philanthropic foundations to check the spread of communism came to a halt.

John M. Olin's personal giving was kept separate from the foundation's activities during these years. In 1956, Olin gave $1 million to Washington University in St. Louis for the John M. Olin Library. Connie Josse, Olin's longtime secretary, remembered a flurry of check writing every December as the tax year ended. "He would receive requests for money all year long," she said. Ella Cline, another one of Olin's assistants, also took part. "He would set these aside and concentrate on these donations between Christmas and New Year's," she said.

By the mid-1960s, the John M. Olin Foundation increasingly became the primary vehicle of Olin's philanthropy. The foundation's interests also broadened beyond piecemeal grants to Cornell and the shadowy activities involving the Vernon Fund. In 1965, the foundation gave $800,000 to Washington University. The next year, recipients included the St. Louis College of Pharmacy and the Episcopal Church. In 1967, the foundation awarded its largest gift yet: $1 million to Cornell. The board also grew from three to five members, with Olin Corporation lawyer Russell R. Casteel and Olin's son-in-law Eugene F. Williams Jr. joining. (Williams was married to Olin's stepdaughter.)

The foundation's grants continued to reflect Olin's diverse interests. In 1966, the Sport Fishery Research Foundation received $10,000. The next year, Guide Dogs for the Blind and Leader Dogs for the Blind each was given $1,500. Olin himself was becoming hard of hearing during these years, and so the foundation donated $10,000 to the Los Angeles Foundation of Otology. His abiding devotion to conservation resulted in gifts to organizations like the World Wildlife Fund, the International Atlantic Salmon Fund, and the Woods Hole Oceanographic Institute.

Yet 1967 was the year the John M. Olin Foundation showed another flicker of what it was to become. At a meeting on December 20, 1967, the board of trustees approved a $5,000 grant to something called the Educational Reviewer. This was a nonprofit organization attached to the conservative political magazine *National Review*. Founded by William F. Buckley Jr. in 1955 to fill an intellectual void on the political Right, *National Review* went on to serve as a crucial platform for conservative thinkers and writers, including James Burnham and Frank Meyer as well as Buckley himself. It was in the process of becoming one of the most influential publications of the second half of the twentieth century.

One of the Educational Reviewer's main activities was producing *The University Bookman*, a quarterly journal of book reviews edited by Russell Kirk, a columnist for *National Review* who also wrote works of history and analysis from his rural home in Mecosta, Michigan. Kirk was best known as the author of *The Conservative Mind*, which was published to widespread acclaim in 1953 as a response to academics who insisted that American political traditions were wholly liberal. Not so, said Kirk, who described how the neglected legacies of Edmund Burke, John Adams, and many others formed a body of thought that was not only coherent but also preferable to the alternatives. By granting an intellectual pedigree to the American Right, *The Conservative Mind* made it impossible—or at least irresponsible—

for liberals to recycle John Stuart Mill's hackneyed comment about conservatives forming "the stupid party."

*The University Bookman* was sent as a supplement to *National Review* subscribers. The magazine's business staff handled distribution for the *Bookman* and charged for its services. It also became an attractive vehicle for supporting Buckley's enterprise because it was a nonprofit organization that could receive tax-deductible donations. (*National Review* was established as a for-profit corporation under Buckley's ownership in order to avoid the factional conflicts that had doomed *The American Mercury* and *The Freeman*, a pair of earlier right-wing publications.) By no means did all of the Educational Reviewer's revenues find their way into *National Review*'s coffers. Most of them supported Kirk's quarterly and various research projects. John M. Olin surely knew, however, that a gift to the Educational Reviewer helped underwrite one of Buckley's many conservative enterprises. The two men met only twice, and on one of these occasions their conversation revolved almost entirely around horses—a passion of Olin's but not Buckley's. Yet they held each other in mutual esteem and often traded letters.

This gift marked the foundation's first clear foray into the arena of politics and ideas, but Olin himself was no stranger to the machinery of democracy. For most of his adult life, he was a partisan Republican. He did not care for Franklin Roosevelt and he disliked the New Deal intensely. (In a 1981 letter to Ed Feulner of the Heritage Foundation, he complained of "unlimited spending and the rather ill-conceived social adventures which [have] stimulated socialism in our country starting back with the Roosevelt dynasty.") Unlike many other conservatives who opposed FDR, however, Olin was not an America First isolationist: He had been willing and eager to manufacture arms for the United States during the Second World War. Yet he was clearly a man of the Right who aligned himself with the GOP and against Democrats. His brother Spencer became directly involved in politics as national finance chairman of the National Citizens for Eisenhower in 1954. In the early 1960s, Spencer served as the Republican National Committee's treasurer. In between, he was chairman of the National Republican Finance Committee—a position that was offered to him over the phone when, coincidentally, he was hunting elephants in Africa.

John M. Olin did not become as involved in party politics as his brother, though he was a financial supporter of the GOP. He donated to the doomed candidacy of Barry Goldwater in 1964 and four years later backed Richard Nixon, who was perhaps his favorite politician in the country. In 1972, before modern campaign-finance restrictions took effect, he gave $100,000 to Nixon's re-election effort. During the Republican primaries in 1976, he backed President Gerald Ford against Ronald Reagan's insurgency. "He was very much an establishment man," said Ron Crawford, a political consultant who advised Olin. When Jimmy Carter defeated Ford in the general election, Olin was disgusted—and then, four years later, elated at Ronald Reagan's victory. When his foundation's staff sent him a telegram for his eighty-eighth birthday on November 10, 1980, Olin replied in a letter the next day: "It was really an enjoyable day and evening for me surrounded by old and valued friends here. However, the best birthday present I have had was that of last Tuesday when the landslide election restored sanity to our country." (In 1984, the Carter Center sought funding from the foundation for an arms-control project. The board denied the request, noting dryly "Mr. Olin's lack of enthusiasm for Mr. Carter's foreign policy practices while in office.")

Olin's separate interests in education and politics began to converge in the 1960s. He commented in 1962 that he planned to continue donating to Cornell "unless the country goes completely to hell." He believed, further, that there was "a good chance that it may with the present administration"—namely, the one led by John F. Kennedy, a Democrat. Despite this worry, his generous gifts continued. As the decade progressed, however, Olin became more disenchanted with what he saw at Cornell. "I am thoroughly fed up with the activity of the faculty, especially in the arts college," he said. "Certain groups in that college seem to be terribly devoid of soundness. We have little or no trouble from the colleges which represent science such as the engineering schools [and] agriculture." One of his major concerns was university president James Perkins, who had embarked on a project to increase black enrollment. Olin was worried that Perkins' devotion to this cause was allowing admission standards to slip.

Then everything went to hell. Campus upheavals rocked America's most prestigious universities, from Harvard in the East to Berkeley in the West. The worst incident took place in 1968 at Columbia, where protesters occupied five buildings and essentially shut down the school for eight days. The ordeal ended only when the police intervened. The next year, student radicalism came to Cornell. On April 19, 1969, militants affiliated with the Afro-American Society seized control of Cornell's student union, Willard Straight Hall. Brandishing rifles, they issued a long list of demands, including the establishment of an independent black-studies program and the nullification of disciplinary action previously taken against several student vandals. "If we die, you are going to die," they proclaimed. On what was supposed to be a serene parents' weekend, the rebellious students negotiated with fainthearted administrators. Within thirty-six hours, the Afro-American Society had achieved most of its objectives, and its members marched out of the student union holding their guns high. Over the next several days, they threatened violence if the faculty did not approve the administration's agreement. Once more, most of their demands were met.

The incident sabotaged Cornell's image as a serious institution of higher learning and convinced many observers that the liberals running America's universities lacked the courage to oppose left-wing hooliganism. Several prominent professors quit Cornell. Walter Berns resigned within days because the administration refused to respond to threats made against him. Allan Bloom and Thomas Sowell also departed in disgust.

Olin was out of the country as these events unfolded, and so he did not play a direct role in them. Yet they affected him deeply and accelerated his disillusionment with higher education. "It is unfortunate that Cornell is suffering with the impact of such ill-advised demonstrations," he wrote. "In my considered opinion, the real sources of our difficulties with the radical students stems from the fact that education is being offered at too low a price; that is to say, they do not appreciate the opportunity to become educated and they have no sense of direction but are just putting in time." Olin also seemed concerned that recruiting ill-prepared minority students from cities and placing them in an elite university far from home was a recipe for trouble. "My position from the very beginning has been that Cornell is open to all applicants qualified for admission who are able to finance either directly or indirectly their education and that there should be only one standard of educational performance," he wrote. "In my opinion, the departure from these fundamentals has contributed much to the involvement which we now find ourselves in." Elsewhere he expressed his objections to boosting black enrollment if it meant watering down Cornell's entrance requirements, as well as his distress over the prospect that "agitation by the left wingers" might influence the university's investment decisions. At times, he was willing to insert himself directly into campus politics. When a student organization called Radicals for Capitalism approached Olin about funding a twice-monthly newsletter, he gladly helped out.

THE CATASTROPHE AT CORNELL INSPIRED OLIN to take his philanthropy in a bold, new direction. Instead of giving the bulk of his money to hospitals and museums, he would channel his resources primarily toward scholars and activists who understood the principles of market capitalism and were capable of influencing opinion and debate. "My greatest ambition now," he told the *New York Times* in 1977, "is to see free enterprise re-established in this country. Business and the public must be awakened to the creeping stranglehold that socialism has gained here since World War II."

Such pessimism about freedom's prospect was not unusual during the 1970s. Americans were coming to grips with a new and disturbing sense of national limits. A generation after GIs had defeated German fascism and Japanese imperialism, North Vietnam, which President Johnson had labeled a "piss-ant country," chased U.S. troops from Southeast Asia. In the wake of this disaster, many people wondered whether American power might in fact be waning in the face of a militant ideology headquartered in Moscow. Even more disturbing was the feeling that the war had been lost on the streets of America rather than in the jungles of Vietnam. Antiwar protests and violent urban riots had become disturbingly commonplace.

Economic distress further unsettled Americans. Productivity fell off and consumer prices rose. In 1974 and 1975, the real gross national product actually declined. The United States entered a nerve-wracking period of "stagflation"—double-digit inflation and unemployment. The Watergate fiasco sapped national confidence. The "nattering nabobs of negativism," in Spiro Agnew's memorable phrase, were everywhere. A generation earlier, Henry Luce had said that the twentieth century would go down in history as "the American century." Less than three-quarters of the way through, however, it looked to many people as if America's good times were a thing of the past. As one grim saying from the gloomy 1970s put it, "Things will get worse before they get worse."

For Olin, "worse" had a concrete meaning—a panicky departure from the free-enterprise system that had served the United States so well and for so long. He worried that given a choice between the guaranteed opportunities of capitalism and the supposed security of socialism, many people might choose the latter. And he was not the only one who feared such an outcome. In 1975, seven Nobel Prize recipients, including the economists Kenneth J. Arrow and Gunnar Myrdal, condemned capitalism for its obsession with profits and demanded "alternatives to the prevailing Western economic systems." A few months later, *Time* asked a provocative question on its cover: "Can Capitalism Survive?" A long article inside the magazine said that indeed it would, but Olin's own outlook certainly was not rosy. "Socialism is a fundamental impact which has occurred in this country," he wrote to his foundation's board members on August 30, 1979. "I find it difficult to see how it is possible to do very much about this impact in the immediate future." At the same time, however, Olin was becoming increasingly convinced that his foundation might play a small role in turning things around.

Before Olin recruited Frank O'Connell, his philanthropy was largely a product of happenstance. He had a variety of interests that he supported from time to time with gifts of money, but there was no overarching theme to his charitable activity. Politics and ideology were just one aspect of a financial generosity that included grants for everything from Easter Seals to research into blindness. This changed on the day Olin asked O'Connell to run his foundation and concentrate its activities on defending free enterprise. O'Connell may have been an amateur in the world he was entering, but he understood the need to develop a strategy and also began the process of professionalizing the foundation's operations. It turned out to be a much bigger job than either Olin or O'Connell had expected. Both of them had assumed that O'Connell would go on serving as the Olin Corporation's top labor counsel and that the foundation would be just one more activity in his portfolio. After a few months, however, O'Connell grasped the immense challenge that lay before him. "We were talking about saving the free-enterprise system," he said. "You can't do that on a part-time basis." One difficulty was the extensive travel. "If you're going to give people your money to spend, it's a good idea first to meet them in person." This was certainly true. Business leaders who amassed large fortunes often tended to the tiniest details of their companies while giving nowhere near the same consideration to their philanthropy. Olin had resolved to be different.

Before long, O'Connell was running the foundation as its full-time executive director, taking early retirement from the corporation in order to do so. He was very much in favor of defending free enterprise from its foes, but he also realized that he had a lot to learn about how to spend money in the smartest ways possible. "Like many lawyers, I had no formal economics education," said O'Connell. He consulted with philanthropists who were active in the foundation's general field of interest, such as Dick Ware of the Earhart Foundation and George Pearson of the Charles G. Koch Foundation, as well as the staffs of the Sarah Scaife Foundation and the Smith Richardson Foundation. Pearson gave him a collection of books and urged him to start reading. "It was like a home-study course," O'Connell recalled.

One of these books was *The Road to Serfdom,* by the Austrian economist Friedrich Hayek. A bestseller when it was released in the United States in 1945, this slender volume became one of

the most important books of the century. It argued that socialism, which Hayek at that point perceived to be on the march
everywhere, led inevitably to tyranny—but a classical liberalism
that drew its inspiration from eighteenth- and nineteenth-
century intellectuals like John Locke, David Hume and Adam
Smith presented a viable and necessary alternative. Hayek did
not consider himself a conservative (one of his best-known essays,
written in 1960, was titled "Why I Am Not a Conservative") and
was concerned that an outlook rooted in nostalgic traditions
rather than reasoned principles would lack the strength to defeat
the rising specter of collectivism. Yet his ideas resonated with
American conservatives, who were more at home with the classical liberal principles of free markets and limited government
than were European conservatives.

Hayek also understood that defeating contemporary socialism would require a particular kind of combat, which he
described in "The Intellectuals and Socialism," an essay published in 1949. Socialism was a rising force, he wrote, because it
had seduced so many members of the intelligentsia. "It is merely
a question of time until the views now held by the intellectuals
become the governing force of politics," he warned. Unfortunately, "the practical men" who opposed socialism had cut themselves off from the world of ideas. Distrustful of abstraction, they
failed to communicate with scholars who might be inclined to
support their view. This tendency could prove fatal to freedom,
warned Hayek: "It may be that a free society as we have known
it carries in itself the forces of its own destruction, that once freedom has been achieved it is taken for granted and ceases to be
valued, and that the free growth of ideas which is the essence of
a free society will bring about the destruction of the foundations
on which it depends." Instead of counseling despair, however,
Hayek urged his allies "to offer a new liberal program which
appeals to the imagination." He proposed "an intellectual adven-
ture" that would envision "a liberal Utopia." He avoided specifics,
saying merely that his comrades should not confine themselves
to anything "too severely practical" or "what appears today as
politically possible." Hayek conceded his project's grand idealism, and he knew its payoff would not come for years, if at all.

It would be wrong to say that such pleadings immediately galvanized a generation of philanthropists. Yet they did not escape notice, and a handful of minor foundations began to act more or less in accordance with Hayek's recommendations. The William Volker Charities Fund became active in supporting the Mont Pelerin Society, a group of scholars organized by Hayek in 1947 and functioning almost exclusively at elevated levels of theoretical discourse. The Volker Fund later supplied money for the University of Chicago to create a faculty position for Hayek as well as for New York University to hire Hayek's mentor, Ludwig von Mises.

A small network of like-minded foundations and philanthropists became involved in similar projects, helping fund graduate fellowships and giving birth to several organizations that shared a strong libertarian bent, such as the Foundation for Economic Education, the Institute for Humane Studies, and the Intercollegiate Society of Individualists (which changed its name to the Intercollegiate Studies Institute in 1966). George H. Pearson of the Koch Foundation specifically cited Hayek's views as an inspiration. The endowments devoted to free enterprise were puny compared with the name-brand foundations of Ford and Rockefeller. They succeeded at least in kindling Hayek's grand scheme, but they failed to light a fire in the American academy at large. The jobs for Hayek, Mises, and several others were rare exceptions to a set of hard rules that prevented similar scholars from finding their own bases. Throughout the 1960s, as colleges and universities grew increasingly obsessed with race and sex, it became more rather than less difficult for these scholars to gain the professorships that served as gateways to the intellectual salons that Hayek hoped to influence.

The triumph of campus radicalism caused business leaders other than John M. Olin to question how their own philanthropic dollars were being spent. One of the most noteworthy was David Packard, chairman of the Hewlett-Packard Company. On October 17, 1973, in a speech to the Committee for the Corporate Support of American Universities, he sounded an alarm: Businesses should continue supporting higher education, but no longer through unrestricted grants that gave the schools complete control over how the funds were used. "Is kicking ROTC programs off the campus the kind of leadership we need?" he asked. "Should these universities serve as havens for radicals who want to destroy the free enterprise system? Should students be taught that American corporations are evil and deserve to be brought under government control?" At far too many institutions, said Packard, this was actually happening—and unrestricted corporate dollars underwrote much of the problem. "I happen to believe that such hostile groups of scholars are, to a large degree, responsible for the anti-business bias of many of our young people today," he said. The answer was for corporate philanthropists to demand more control over their largesse—and to channel it toward "those areas you believe are educating the right kind of professors."

Packard's comments astonished his listeners. "His speech was clearly an embarrassing disappointment to the committee and to the educators who had assembled," reported the *New York Times*. A few days later, the newspaper mocked Packard's concerns as "a figment of panicky imagination." Moreover, said the *Times*, "higher education owes no *quid pro quo* to any donors." McGeorge Bundy, president of the Ford Foundation, also objected to the notion that corporate philanthropists should take more than a casual interest in what they were financing on campus. "I find no mention in his analysis of the kind of support that includes criticism and even opposition" to free enterprise, he said. To Packard, of course, Bundy was viewing the problem backwards. Colleges and universities were becoming a playground for Marxist academics who reviled capitalism—and who were already receiving well more than their fair share of support.

An alternative to funding scholars on campuses was to support them at research institutions, and this was one of the first places that O'Connell directed Olin's dollars. In 1973, the John M. Olin Foundation made its first donation to a think tank, giving ninety shares of Squibb stock to the American Enterprise Institute, based in Washington, D.C. It was the beginning of a long association—between the foundation and think tanks in

general, as well as between the foundation and AEI in particular. Originally founded in 1938 as the American Enterprise Association, the group focused on free-market solutions to economic
problems. Under the leadership of William J. Baroody, AEA
changed its name to AEI, broadened its interests to include cultural issues, social policy, and foreign affairs, and hired scholars
such as Irving Kristol and Michael Novak. President Nixon was
one of its strongest supporters, and he urged business leaders
to support AEI's work. It is likely that this played a role in the
John M. Olin Foundation's decision to make its initial contributions. At a 1974 dinner celebrating Baroody's twentieth anniversary at AEI, Nixon sent a message praising him for breaking the
"virtual monopoly in the field of ideas." That year, the foundation made its first cash grant to AEI, for $10,000. This amount
increased to $25,000 in 1975 and the foundation has been a reg-
ular and significant supporter ever since, providing more than
$9 million to AEI through 2005.

Another major grant recipient from this period was the
Hoover Institution, on the campus of Stanford University. Its origins reached back to the First World War and the founding of
the Hoover War Library shortly thereafter. Over time, the library's
collection grew and so did Herbert Hoover's personal involvement with it. Hoover was a Republican, but as president he was
not noticeably conservative, and certainly was much less so than
his immediate predecessor, Calvin Coolidge. Yet Hoover became
increasingly conservative as a former president, and during the
1950s he raised significant sums for what eventually became the
Hoover Institution on War, Revolution, and Peace, a think tank
he once described as committed to "the road to peace, to personal freedom, and to the safeguards of the American system."
The John M. Olin Foundation did not contribute to these early
appeals, and Hoover himself passed away in 1964. Yet the foundation became interested in Hoover's legacy, granting $25,000
to the Herbert Hoover Presidential Library Association in 1971.
Gifts of cash and stock followed over the next couple of years.
In 1975, the foundation began its longstanding support for the
Hoover Institution, which was aggressively branching into domestic policy studies, with a grant of $25,000. Ultimately, the John

M. Olin Foundation would commit more than \$6 million to its activities.

Although Frank O'Connell began steering the foundation in these new directions, its giving patterns did not change overnight. O'Connell began to get his sea legs after investigating potential recipients and talking to sympathetic colleagues. In the spring of 1975, he drafted a "Memorandum for Mr. Olin" outlining the foundation's future direction. It was a thirty-page document whose bulk earned it a nickname: the "Fat Memo." Parts of it reflected the despondency typical of conservatives in the 1970s, as O'Connell observed that the United States was moving "ever closer to socialism or some other form of collectivist system." Instead of surrender, however, the memo announced a determination to fight "a battle for men's minds." For more than two decades, the John M. Olin Foundation had lacked a philanthropic vision beyond advancing its benefactor's scattered interests. On the pages of the Fat Memo, it is possible to see the foundation's sharp, new profile. "Our fundamental and overriding purpose," wrote O'Connell, "is to seek to ensure, insofar as it is possible to do so, the revitalization and survival of the free enterprise system." Moreover, O'Connell understood that the battle for the American mind was fundamentally a war of ideas: "Because our aim is the propagation of ideas, our successes will be measured by the degree to which our efforts increase the dissemination and understanding of those ideas."

The Fat Memo focused on specific strategies for developing a philanthropic program "to support such individuals and institutions that are effectively engaged in quality scholarship—teaching, research, writing, and related activities—in Market Economics and the Political Philosophy of Freedom." Agents of the foundation would become talent scouts searching for individuals and organizations, always asking, "What is his reputation (or the reputation of the institution) among other scholars of the freedom persuasion?" Attracting top students was urgent: "The arguments for capitalism and freedom [must be presented] in the idiom of today's youth." Yet the defense of free enterprise ultimately rested on more than classroom seminars. The foundation must support "the production and publication of research

supportive of the philosophy of political and economic freedom." The Fat Memo specifically mentioned the Hoover Institution, the Institute for Humane Studies, and the American
Enterprise Institute, which the memo envisioned as a future rival
to Washington's most influential think tank, the liberal Brookings Institution ("with its enormous resources derived from capitalist philanthropy!"). Publications were crucial as well because
they "contribute significantly to the debate over freedom versus
socialism." The memo listed the *Journal of Law and Economics,
The Public Interest, Reason, The Alternative* (later known as *The American Spectator*), and *Modern Age* as worthy of support.

These were important recommendations, and they marked
the early formulation of a concept that would animate almost
all of the John M. Olin Foundation's grantmaking in the years
ahead. Up to this point, a good deal of conservative philanthropy
was aimed at institutions that appealed to right-wingers but made
little effort to sway the broader public. O'Connell's key insight
was that no battle of ideas could be won by preaching to the
choir. Success required rational persuasion, and this was best
achieved by acting through elite institutions—ones that already
existed, such as America's leading universities, or ones that might
be built up over time, such as the think tanks. After the disaster
at Cornell in 1969, Olin might have been open to the idea that
his philanthropy should retreat from higher education entirely.
But the Fat Memo argued for a renewed commitment, albeit
with some significant differences. Rather than send large checks
to alumni funds or endowment drives, where the monies would
simply subsidize many of the harmful trends taking place on
campus, the foundation would target its giving in ways that cir-
cumvented and confounded campus radicalism.

By the end of 1975—a few months after O'Connell wrote
the Fat Memo—the John M. Olin Foundation began to issue
grants to important groups in the conservative constellation.
These included the Heritage Foundation, which Olin probably
first learned about from Joseph Coors, the brewer who was heavily involved in its creation and growth and a fellow Cornell alumnus. In addition to $10,000 for Heritage, the foundation gave
similar gifts to the Alternative Educational Foundation (i.e., *The*

*American Spectator*), the Center for the Study of Public Choice, the Educational Reviewer, the Foundation for Economic Education, the Institute for Contemporary Studies, the Intercollegiate Studies Institute, and the National Right to Work Legal Defense Foundation. Other recipients included Accuracy in Media ($1,000), the Pacific Legal Foundation ($5,000), the Robert A. Taft Institute for Government ($5,000), and Sidney Hook's University Centers for Rational Alternatives ($2,500). These grants pointed to the incredible diversity of the conservative movement: The Taft Institute invoked the name of an Old Right hero; the Foundation for Economic Education was a product of classical liberalism; and the onetime socialist Sidney Hook was a favorite of the emerging neoconservatives. Fusing them together in various ways were the Educational Reviewer (especially through its connection to *National Review*), the Heritage Foundation, and, increasingly, the John M. Olin Foundation itself.

Conservative groups were by no means the foundation's only beneficiaries or even the largest ones in 1975. The foundation also cut checks for the American Museum of Natural History ($10,000), the Ear Research Institute ($10,000), the Orthopedic Foundation for Animals ($18,672), the Southampton Hospital Expansion Fund ($20,000) and the World Wildlife Fund ($10,000). Yet these were the last gasps of a kind of philanthropy that the foundation was preparing to abandon. Olin and O'Connell had set it on a new course that would characterize its giving for the next three decades.

CHAPTER THREE

# Simon Says

N THE TWILIGHT HOURS OF GERALD FORD'S presidency, John M. Olin was looking for a man to lead his foundation and outgoing Treasury secretary William E. Simon was looking for something to do. Olin was a generation older than Simon and although his mind remained sharp in its eighty-fourth year, his body was becoming frail. "He was feeling mortal," according to George Gillespie, Olin's longtime personal lawyer and confidant. Olin had followed Simon in the news for several years and liked his gusto. Moreover, the two men had met casually as part-time neighbors in East Hampton. Olin made a few discreet inquiries through his contacts in Washington and liked what he learned. A month after leaving government, Simon became president of the John M. Olin Foundation.

Between that moment and his death in 2000, Bill Simon would be the foundation's dominant figure. He was a force of nature—an intense and impatient taskmaster who set ambitious goals for himself and those around him. He wanted to be the best at everything he did, and he threw himself fully into a wide range of activities that included lucrative financial deals, the chairmanship of the U.S. Olympic Committee, and volunteer service as a Eucharistic minister to hospital patients. Despite an almost bottomless reservoir of energy and enthusiasm, Simon kept himself so busy pursuing so many activities that he sometime found it difficult to give his full attention to all of his interests and commitments. With the exception of Olin himself, no

43

one person was more important to the John M. Olin Foundation than William Edward Simon.

He was born in Paterson, New Jersey, on November 27, 1927, to parents he once described as "a couple right out of *The Great Gatsby*," with inherited wealth allowing them to live in a splendor of mansions and servants and European tours that stood in stark contrast to what most other Americans had, especially during the Depression. A chauffeur drove him to Catholic school each day. "I was so embarrassed to be living in wealth when many people were poor and struggling," said Simon, "that I often had my driver drop me off out of sight of St. Joseph's School in Paterson so the other kids wouldn't see me." He was more conspicuous in other ways: "Whenever there was activity in the schoolyard, whenever there was laughter, whenever there was mischief, there was Billy Simon," remembered his second-grade teacher, Sister Julia Agnes Cronin.

Simon's mother died when he was eight years old. After her death, his father's investments failed, making it difficult for the family to go on living as it had. A combination of poor grades and bad behavior made Billy unwelcome at several schools, though he eventually graduated from Newark Academy in 1946. He served in the Army for eighteen months, mostly in occupied Japan. The experience matured him, though he never shed a ferocious temper that later would earn him a memorable nickname, William the Terrible. "When there are jackasses around me, I just get irritated," he told *Fortune* magazine in 1982. "People know I'll chew their hide" if they do not perform. "I'll resolve not to do it again, and I won't—for about two hours."

Simon returned to the United States from Japan in 1948 and soon was a whirlwind of activity. He entered Lafayette College and married Carol Girard, but compiled a middling record. "The charm of academic life eluded me," he once wrote. "I harvested a crop of Cs, ornamented by a few Bs." He received a degree in government and law in 1952 and hoped to go on to law school, but the tuition was more than he could afford. Simon's first child had been born in 1951 and he needed to think of supporting his young family. A friend offered him a job on Wall Street and he began an impressive career in the world of finance.

His rise began at Union Securities. Five years later, he became vice president of Weeden & Company and then joined Salomon Brothers in 1964. He eventually became a senior partner at Salomon and ran its government and municipal bond departments.

By 1972, he was the father of seven children and earning a seven-figure income. Then he received a phone call from Washington. President Richard Nixon had just won re-election and he wanted to meet Simon. At first, Simon thought he was going to become the next housing secretary. But when George Shultz, the secretary of the Treasury, heard Simon's name come up during a conversation about Nixon's second-term appointments, he asked to have Simon by his side. Shultz had come to know him as a regular participant in meetings on bond sales at the Treasury Department and was eager to give him a place in his corner of the administration. Shortly after Thanksgiving, Simon took a job as deputy secretary of the Treasury. A press account described his confirmation as "one of the least controversial major appointments of the Nixon administration." It was perhaps the last time anybody would call Bill Simon uncontroversial.

The hard-driving Simon was well known for putting in long days on Wall Street. The new job in Washington was no less demanding and he put nothing less than everything into it. As deputy secretary, he was in charge of the day-to-day operations of an agency with 125,000 employees and responsible for collecting America's taxes, managing its accounts, and printing its currency. Within a few weeks, Nixon asked him to perform yet another duty: to chair the Oil Policy Committee. This eventually led to Simon becoming head of the Federal Energy Office, the forerunner of the Department of Energy. Not only did he continue to serve as deputy secretary at Treasury, but he was also the nation's "energy czar."

Simon thus became embroiled in the energy crisis, brought on by inefficient regulations and America's heavy reliance on foreign oil. After the OPEC nations announced an oil embargo in the fall of 1973, Simon received much of the blame for rising costs and fuel shortages—not because he had anything to do with these, but because politicians and pundits were eager to identify useful villains. The energy czar, with his horn-rimmed glasses and a penchant for indelicate comments, was suddenly one of the best-known figures in the Nixon administration. Death threats compelled Shultz to assign Secret Service protection to Simon and his family. Bob Hope joked about him on national television: "William Simon is putting in twenty hours a day in his office because he can't get enough gas to get home."

Despite facing enormous pressure to seize control of the country's energy production and distribution, Simon committed himself to the core principles of free enterprise. "There is nothing like becoming an economic planner oneself to learn what is desperately, stupidly wrong with such a system," he wrote. While he came to Washington as something of a conventional Republican business leader, Simon's experience in government, including his tutelage under Shultz, made him a passionate advocate of market economics.

When the oil embargo ended in March 1974, Simon's public image softened as he was hailed for helping the United States weather the storm. A month later, Nixon picked him to replace Shultz as Treasury secretary and he was quickly confirmed. He spent most of his long days trying to fight inflation. He also became a leading advocate of tax cuts and spending reductions, yet the Watergate controversy made it impossible for Nixon to pursue any kind of legislative program, much less a bold one. When Nixon resigned in August, the new president, Gerald Ford, retained Simon. The Treasury chief's blunt rhetoric continued to make him a figure of notoriety loved by some and hated by others. The federal food-stamp program, said Simon to howls of liberal outrage in 1975, was a "well-known haven for chiselers and rip-off artists." He was also criticized for refusing to bail out New York City, whose politicians had brought it to the point of financial collapse. Just as the *New York Daily News* castigated the president with its famous headline, "FORD TO CITY: DROP DEAD," Simon earned his own bad press in the *New York Post:* "SIMON ON U.S. AID: MAKE CITY SUFFER." Despite this level of vituperation, Simon built a loan package that eased the city out of its self-imposed crisis at no cost to American taxpayers.

When Jimmy Carter's election in 1976 ended the Ford administration, Simon rejected pleas that he run for governor of New Jersey the following year, although he understood that it might lead to even greater things. ("I thought perhaps a gubernatorial run in 1977 could set the stage for a presidential run in 1980," he once commented.) Instead, he joined several corporate boards and went on to a successful career as an investor. In the 1980s, he became a pioneer of leveraged buyouts, which allow the purchase of a company by borrowing against its assets. He flirted with the possibility of joining President Ronald Reagan's cabinet in 1980, but ultimately withdrew his name and avoided public office. Yet he maintained a high profile as chairman of the U.S. Olympic Committee, which sponsored the 1984 summer games in Los Angeles.

Ford's defeat distressed Simon. "I became alarmed over the statist, anti-freedom philosophy that was growing like a cancer," he wrote. "I genuinely feared for the future of my country." He was also coming to fear a gloomy prediction made by Joseph Schumpeter, an economics professor who fled the Nazis in the 1930s and became a professor at Harvard. Schumpeter is perhaps best known for describing capitalism as a form of "creative destruction." Like Friedrich Hayek, he believed that capitalism would generate enormous wealth but also weaken the very institutions responsible for its prosperity. Specifically, he worried that an alliance of bureaucrats and intellectuals would lead the lethal attack. Schumpeter had died in 1950, and the fact that Simon became attracted to the late economist's ideas more than two decades later speaks to the growing perception of their relevance. "In Washington," wrote Simon, "I became convinced that Schumpeter was right. America's leading colleges and universities—the training grounds for America's leaders—were increasingly pro-socialist, pro-government regulation, and anti-capitalist in their philosophy, direction, and mission."

Simon certainly did not pore over any of Schumpeter's academic works, but he did come to admire a man who shared many of Schumpeter's concerns and popularized them. This was Irving Kristol, a professor at New York University and a vanguard member of the neoconservative movement taking shape in the

1970s. He could not have been more different from Simon: relaxed rather than frenetic, a thinker rather than a business-man, a Jew rather than a Catholic. Yet the two men formed a pro-ductive partnership. They did not always get along—nobody got along with Simon all the time—but they often brought out the best in each other.

Among his many activities in the 1970s, Kristol wrote a series of widely read articles for the *Wall Street Journal*. One of the most important of these columns appeared in 1975 under the head-line, "Business and the 'New Class.'" Kristol warned that private enterprise must apprehend "the new sociological and political reality in which it is now operating." Most importantly, this involved the birth of "the new class," a group of people "who make their careers in the expanding public sector." They are hostile to the workings of a free-enterprise system "because the market is so vulgarly democratic" and "it wishes to see its 'ideals' more effectual than the market is likely to permit them to be." These ideals include "such issues as environmentalism, ecology, consumer protection, and economic planning." Because the suc-cess of capitalism has led to a postindustrial society in which the new class flourishes, wrote Kristol, "there is a sense in which cap-italism may yet turn out to be its own gravedigger." These were precisely the concerns animating the John M. Olin Foundation.

If Kristol spoke the language of a Trotskyite, that is because he had been one as a young man. Born in 1920, he entered New York's City College at the age of sixteen and began meeting in the cafeteria with fellow radicals, including Daniel Bell, Irving Howe, Melvin Lasky, and Seymour Martin Lipset. During the Sec-ond World War, however, Kristol began a long pilgrimage away from leftism. At first he was a Cold War liberal who harbored especially strong animosities toward communism. In an essay for *Commentary* on whether good liberals should be anti-Commu-nists who oppose the Soviet Union or anti-anti-Communists who oppose the excesses of right-wing red-hunters, Kristol closed with words that made him a figure of great controversy in New York's intellectual circles: "For there is one thing that the American people know about Senator McCarthy; he, like them, is unequiv-ocally anti-Communist. About the spokesmen for American liberalism, they feel they know no such thing." This statement was a hallmark of Kristol's firm belief that while ordinary Americans may not hold advanced degrees, they generally possess more common sense than the people who do.

With each passing year, it seemed, Kristol marched further away from his origins on the Left. After working as an editor at *Commentary,* he helped found and edit *Encounter* magazine in London. At the time, he did not know about the CIA's covert support of *Encounter.* Later on, however, he quipped, "I think it's interesting that the only British magazine worth reading at the time was funded by the CIA, and the British should be damn grateful." Back in the United States in the 1960s, Kristol grew profoundly disenchanted with liberalism's increasingly radical expressions on college campuses. "Tell an American intellectual that he is a disturber of the peace, and he is gratified," wrote Kristol. "Tell him he is a reassuring spokesman for calm and tranquility, and he will think you have made a nasty accusation."

By 1970, Kristol was calling himself a "conservative liberal"— in an article, incidentally, that acknowledged an intellectual debt to Walter Berns, one of the casualties of the student chaos at Cornell University a year earlier. Before long, the adjective became a noun as Kristol became identified with a new moniker: "neoconservative." The word was invented by the left-wing writer Michael Harrington and was meant as an insult. When Kristol's wife, the historian Gertrude Himmelfarb, informed her husband that the words "Tory" and "Whig" also had started out as pejoratives, he decided to embrace the put-down. In one of his best-known witticisms, Kristol defined a neoconservative as "a liberal who has been mugged by reality." The remark both alluded to the social disorder of the times and described the attitudes of a group that was growing disillusioned with liberalism. Despite all this semantic hairsplitting, the trend was clear: Kristol was becoming a man of the Right, and many other intellectuals were following him.

Although the neoconservatives drew much of their inspiration from the same eighteenth- and nineteenth-century intellectuals that Hayek and other classical liberals celebrated, they placed cultural and moral concerns in front of economic ones.

When they summoned the memory of Adam Smith, for instance, they often had in mind *A Theory of Moral Sentiments* (1759) rather than *The Wealth of Nations* (1776), a better-known work that is usually considered Smith's magnum opus. Kristol believed capitalism was worth defending, but it was hardly without its own faults and certainly no sacred doctrine; he famously gave it "two cheers." Social planning and the welfare state received fewer cheers yet. The fundamental problem with them, however, was not that they violated free-market theories but that they failed to work in practice. Their chief legacies were unintended consequences: family breakdown, racial strife, and the demoralization of the poor. Finally, the particular predicaments of the 1970s called for a different response from the one Hayek had proposed a generation earlier. Intellectuals would play a decisive role, Kristol thought, but those who supported free enterprise would have to engage themselves more fully in the concerns of the present day: They would have to do more than chat amongst themselves.

Although Kristol had abandoned the ideology of Trotsky, his apprenticeship on the Left helped him serve the interests of the Right. The newspaper columnist Charles Krauthammer, a personal friend, once called him "the Lenin of the new conservatism—both a theoretician and a builder." In 1979, *Esquire* put a smirking Kristol on its cover and labeled him "The Godfather of Neoconservatism." He had become a fixer—a man with connections in the often-disconnected worlds of academia, business, and journalism. Kristol once advised Jude Wanniski, an author and editorialist for the *Wall Street Journal*, to meet with Jack Kemp, an up-and-coming Republican congressman from New York. "If 'Don Corleone' says you should meet somebody, then you do it," explained Wanniski, who went on to plot the tax-cut legislation that would become known by the last names of its two chief congressional sponsors, Kemp-Roth. Many of Kristol's ideas were expressed on the pages of *The Public Interest*, a quarterly journal he had founded in 1965. Yet its circulation was small and its voice faint compared with the megaphone of the *Wall Street Journal*, on whose pages Kristol attracted a large following that included Simon. "We became chummy, but we weren't friends," said Kristol, who encouraged the Treasury sec-retary's instincts on taxes and budgets.

Kristol's ties to the philanthropic world were growing stronger, too. He understood that as the universities were becom-ing more hostile to intellectuals who were sympathetic to con-servative ideas, these dissident professors increasingly needed to rely on private foundations. In a 1975 letter to Robert Goldwin, an aide to President Ford who served as a conduit between the administration and intellectuals, Kristol highlighted the impor-tance of "the men who head small and sometimes obscure foun-dations which support useful research and activities of a kind that the Ford and Rockefeller Foundations take a dim view of." These foundations—he listed Smith Richardson, Merrill, Scaife, Earhart and Lilly—were "unbeknownst to it, being helpful to this Administration, to the Republican party, and to conserva-tive and moderate enterprise in general."

By 1976, Kristol's ideas on business, education, and philan-thropy were having a profound effect on Simon and his public rhetoric. In a speech to the Public Relations Society of America on February 18, the Treasury secretary called special attention to comments that Richard A. Riley, the president of the Firestone Tire and Rubber Company, had made several months earlier: "the term 'free enterprise' is dead." These words, coming from the leader of a large American corporation, astonished and angered Simon. "I shudder to think how many other business leaders share in that counsel of despair," he said. "If *they* give up, who is left to uphold economic freedom?" At the end of his remarks, Simon devoted a few words to a topic that would receive an increasing amount of his attention in the future: "One way to ensure our free-dom is through education." He urged the members of his audi-ence to "counsel your bosses and your clients to take a close look at the teaching policies of those schools and foundations being considered for corporate gifts. Find out if the subjects of that gen-erosity are really assisting in the fight to maintain our freedoms or if they're working to erode them—and urge that judgments be made accordingly. Otherwise the largesse of the free-enterprise system will continue to finance its own destruction."

With Simon developing this kind of public profile, it is no surprise that John M. Olin contacted him about leading his foundation. "Toward the end of 1976, John approached me with his concerns over the state of the union, concerns that mirrored my own," recalled Simon.

> John knew that human freedom is an indispensable ingredient in the advancement of the human race. He knew that economic freedom and human rights are inseparable—that you can't have political and social freedom unless individuals are free to engage in the peaceful exchange of goods and services and ideas. He knew that collectivism is the antithesis of freedom, and that it always leads to stagnation, decline, and the stifling of the human spirit. He was resolute about using the resources at his disposal to advance the cause of freedom in the battlefield of ideas, and about using his foundation to fight encroachments on our basic liberties.

At a special meeting of the board of the John M. Olin Foundation, in New York City on February 21, 1977, Olin announced his desire to resign as president and be replaced by Simon. The board approved this plan, changing its bylaws to create a chairman-of-the-board position for the foundation's benefactor. The board itself grew to include not only Simon but also John Hanes, a director of the Olin Corporation and Olin's closest friend, as well as John J. McCloy, a New York lawyer who had served as U.S. high commissioner in Germany following the Second World War and then as president of the World Bank. Other board members were Eugene Williams, a St. Louis businessman who was married to Olin's stepdaughter, and George Gillespie, who was Olin's personal lawyer. (Three months later, the board would expand again with the election of Walter F. O'Connell, another one of Olin's business partners—and no relation to Frank O'Connell.) Olin said he chose Simon to head the foundation "because his fundamental thinking and philosophy are almost identical with mine." Simon, for his part, said he agreed to take over "because I learned in conversations with Mr. Olin that he and his associates shared utterly my own views regarding the virtues of the free enterprise system and the traditional American values of individual political freedom and the responsibility which it represents. They also shared my concern over the grave threat which has increasingly been posed to those institutions."

By 1977, the foundation was giving away more than $1 million annually. In addition to the American Enterprise Institute, the Hoover Institution, and the Institute for Humane Studies, a program in law and economics at the University of Miami attracted special interest, as did plans to produce a television series on the virtues of free enterprise, hosted by Milton Friedman. (This was *Free to Choose,* though it did not have this name at the time.) At Simon's second board meeting, on May 26, the new president began to exert his influence. He noted that the foundation had assets of $10 million. With $6 million in new money from John M. Olin plus investment income, he figured the foundation would enjoy assets of as much as $20 million over the next five years. Then he proposed a five-year budget to distribute $3 million annually. Olin himself expressed some misgivings. What if stock prices declined? After considerable debate, the board decided to hand out $2 million in 1977 and $3 million the next year.

The foundation also retained Irving Kristol as a consultant, paying him a monthly stipend for his advice. This was the first direct financial link between the foundation and America's leading neoconservative, but by no means the last. Starting in 1983, Kristol would occupy the John M. Olin Distinguished Professorship of Social Thought at New York University, and between 1988 and 1999 he would be a John M. Olin Distinguished Fellow at the American Enterprise Institute. Pulling Kristol directly into the foundation's orbit at this early date as a consultant represented part of Simon's efforts to professionalize the foundation's operations, a step that Olin himself had begun when he hired Frank O'Connell several years earlier. Even with O'Connell as executive director, however, the foundation resembled an ad hoc organization during its pre-Simon years. That began to change when the former Treasury secretary took charge. The staff slowly began to expand, and Simon insisted that it prepare extensive written material on grants the foundation was considering. These were called "board books" and were often as thick as telephone directories. Prior to the trustees' debate on their contents, the board books appeared before a steering committee that made specific recommendations. This advice was almost always followed, in part because of the meticulous preparations but also because it would have taken a large effort by an individual board member to mount an effective challenge. These practices made the foundation more efficient as an institution and allowed Simon to exert his authority over both its staff and his fellow board members. The steering committee remained a fixture at the foundation until the early 1990s, when enough trustees were attending it routinely that they formed a quorum for the entire board.

Within a few months of leaving government, Simon found himself in high demand as a public speaker. In October 1977, he addressed the National Chamber Foundation and described a troubling set of circumstances: "Where we are, in my judgment, is well past mid-point on the way to losing our economic and political freedoms." Because his audience consisted of people from the world of business, Simon wanted to tell them what they might do to fix the problem. He focused on a fundamental predicament in corporate philanthropy: Too many businesses were giving their money to individuals and organizations opposed to free enterprise, such as public-interest law firms led by the likes of Ralph Nader, who believed it was their duty to assault corporate America with a torrent of litigation. "Capitalism has no duty to subsidize its enemies," Simon said. One of the biggest problems involved donations to colleges and universities. "The greatest threat to the free pursuit of truth comes from the radicals on the Left. They are the ones who have tilted many of our universities and colleges toward the Marxist teachings," he said. "Perhaps no other country in history has given greater liberty to those who would destroy that liberty, just as no other society in my memory has reached such heights of prosperity for its people and yet has raised an entire class of men and women who are hostile to the very institutions that make that progress possible."

Yet the situation was not hopeless. "There are a growing number of scholars and intellectuals who do believe in freedom—who do understand the nexus between economic freedom and political freedom, the link between capitalism and democracy—and also know the intellectual job that needs to be done," said Simon. "I believe that they must be sought out and they must be supported, for this fight over the hearts and minds of the American people is the most critical one we face in trying to preserve the institutions of our civilization."

Several commentators suggested that Simon run for president, and although he was flattered at the suggestion and surely thought he was up to the job, he probably understood that his odds of success were slim. And although he wanted to see the Republicans defeat Carter in 1980, he was beginning to think less about political tactics and more about long-term strategic goals. His ideas took shape in a book called *A Time for Truth*. Simon actually had started thinking about the book when he was in the Nixon administration. In 1975, he had published an article in *Reader's Digest* entitled "Big Government and Our Economic Woes." The next year, he was the subject of a very favorable profile in the same magazine, written by William Schulz. At a lunch in New York, Simon met with Schulz as well as *Digest* founder DeWitt Wallace and editor Hobart Lewis. Wallace suggested that Simon write a book. At first, Simon was dismissive. Back in Washington the following day, however, he called Schulz to say he wanted to do it.

Simon knew he would need help. He was accustomed to working with professional writers—he had speechwriters at Treasury and had received assistance with his article for *Reader's Digest*. Kristol arranged for Edith Efron, a libertarian-leaning writer who had worked for *TV Guide,* to assist with the writing. *A Time for Truth* was partly a memoir that recounted Simon's battles in government over the energy crisis and New York's financial plight. Yet it was mostly a loud call to restore lost freedoms—a forward-looking book that aimed to become for a new generation what Barry Goldwater's classic *The Conscience of a Conservative* had been for an older one. "We are careening with frightening speed toward collectivism and away from individual sovereignty, toward coercive centralized planning and away from free individual choices, toward a statist-dictatorial system and away from a nation in which individual liberty is sacred," he wrote. The pages of *A Time for*

*Truth* were replete with bracing observations and forthright opinions. Simon described "liberal ideology," for instance, as "a hash of statism, collectivism, egalitarianism, and anticapitalism, mixed with the desire for the *results* of capitalism. This murky conceptual mess renders even the most innately brilliant men stupid."

The most important ideas in *A Time for Truth* came in its final chapter. "What we need today in America is adherence to a set of broad guiding principles, not a thousand more technocratic adjustments," he wrote. He briefly laid out these principles in his trademark way. The young Billy Simon who was embarrassed to have a chauffeur was no more. "The concept that the absence of money implies some sort of virtue should be repudiated," he wrote. "Poverty may result from honest misfortune, but it also may result from sloth, incompetence, and dishonesty." He believed it was essential to distinguish between the deserving poor and the undeserving poor—and one of the main problems of government and elite society was its complete refusal to do so.

The solution to America's dilemma, he said, was to begin challenging the prevailing assumptions of the professors, bureaucrats, and media leaders. "What we desperately need in America today is a powerful counterintelligentsia," he wrote. "A powerful counterintelligentsia can be organized to challenge our ruling 'new class' opinion makers—an intelligentsia dedicated consciously to the political value of individual liberty, above all, which understands its relationship to meritocracy, and which is consciously aware of the value of private property and the free market in generating innovative technology, jobs, and wealth. Such an intelligentsia exists, and an audience awaits its views."

Just as Frank O'Connell had turned to military metaphors in writing his "Fat Memo" to John M. Olin several years earlier— he had called for "a battle for men's minds"—Simon was now demanding a war of ideas. "Ideas are weapons—indeed, the only weapons with which other ideas can be fought," he wrote. "If we are to fight the 'New Despotism' effectively and respect the very individual liberty for which we are fighting, we can only do it by building up the influence of the counterintelligentsia, whose views, if known, would command a respectful hearing in the marketplace of ideas."

The counterintelligentsia did not have to be created from scratch because it already existed, albeit as "an impoverished underground." The vital task was to identify and assist its members. "They must be given grants, grants, and more grants in exchange for books, books, and more books," wrote Simon. This would begin to correct the problem that Simon had identified in his speech to the National Chamber Foundation:

> The problem is that the existing counterintelligentsia has comparatively little access to that broad market of ideas. The reason for that is shocking: There are few voluntary institutions in America today that are organized to finance intellectuals who fight for economic, as well as political, liberty. Most private funds—inevitably from business itself—flow ceaselessly to the very institutions which are philosophically committed to the destruction of capitalism. The great corporations of America sustain the major universities, with no regard for the content of their teachings. They sustain the major foundations which nurture the most destructive egalitarian trends. And with their advertising, they sustain the mass media, which today inevitably serve as a national megaphone for every egalitarian crusade. In the last analysis, American business is financing the destruction of both free enterprise and political freedom.

Simon did not meditate long on why this was so. He suggested that most businessmen were more interested in "short-range respectability" than "long-range survival." In other words, they viewed corporate philanthropy as a way of rounding off the hard edges of capitalism and also an opportunity to buy off their critics. Yet Simon believed that businesses should not feel remorseful for their profit-driven activities, because they formed the backbone of American prosperity. The very worst thing they might do—and which in fact they were doing—was to finance the activities of those who would undermine the principles of free enterprise, as if they were applying salves to a guilty conscience. "America's universities are today churning out young collectivists by legions, and it is irrational for businessmen to support them," he wrote.

These ideas soon made their mark on the John M. Olin Foundation itself. At a meeting on January 26, 1978, the board outlined the foundation's objectives: "The influence of scholarly writing upon others (and not just other scholars) is highly significant in both the academic and the political processes. Such writing assists our friends (in the academy and politics) and, if it does not *persuade* our opponents, it at least gives them intellectual obstacles to overcome."

Upon publication in the spring of 1978, *A Time for Truth* zipped onto the bestseller list and stayed there for twenty weeks. By the end of the year, some 200,000 copies of the hardcover were in circulation. Herbert Mitgang of the *New York Times* called it "one of the best-selling treatises on conservative economics ever published."

In retrospect, it is not hard to understand the book's enormous appeal. Simon had been one of the best-known members of the Nixon administration. He was exceptionally good at expressing his views and attracting attention to them. He put into plain words many of the things ordinary Americans felt but did not know how to say. Moreover, Milton Friedman wrote a preface and Friedrich Hayek contributed a foreword. Although Simon found the experience of authorship grueling—"I got so sick of it that I didn't want to see another piece of paper," he once complained—the result was immensely satisfying. The book was clearly being read and appreciated by both a popular and an influential audience. Simon received celebratory notes from the likes of Supreme Court justice William Rehnquist and golfer Arnold Palmer. "I think it catches the mood of the moment," Simon said a few months after his unexpected run on the bestseller lists. And he was right. As the malaise of the 1970s progressed, a growing number of people were ready to hear Simon's pleas to revive the spirit of free enterprise.

A critique in *The Economist* called *A Time for Truth* "stimulating," "entertaining," "instructive," and "important." Curiously, however, the reviewer believed that Simon's call to develop a counterintelligentsia was a bit of pie-in-the-sky idealism: "Some of his pleas to his fellow businessmen—for example, to spend lavishly on pro-capitalist propaganda—have the familiar unpractical note of the innocent from Wall Street still reeling from his first encounter with skullduggery in Washington."

It was true that Simon's entreaties did not reverse harmful trends in corporate philanthropy. Yet it was in precisely this area of supporting the counterintelligentsia that William Simon would make his most lasting mark in the final two decades of his life, as president of the John M. Olin Foundation.

CHAPTER FOUR

# "ECONOMICS TO LAWYERS?"

I N THE OPENING PAGES OF *A Time for Truth,* Bill Simon described the drudgery of testifying on Capitol Hill hundreds of times before legislators who refused to understand that Congress itself was the source of so many national problems. "Most of these hearings were an abysmal waste to time," he wrote. "Nonetheless, I patiently complied with the Congressional invitations. I never neglected an opportunity to offer these gentlemen carefully documented evidence of their own historic irresponsibility." Quite often, this irresponsibility grew from economic illiteracy. "I was entirely committed to the Dickensian view that in the economic realm 'the law is a ass'—and in Washington, that was philosophical heresy," wrote Simon.

It may have been a philosophical heresy in the marbled halls of federal power, but during these same years it was becoming the gospel truth at the John M. Olin Foundation. A few months after accepting Olin's invitation to run his foundation in 1973, Frank O'Connell learned of a new discipline emerging from the University of Chicago Law School. Despite its unassuming name, the "law and economics" movement was beginning to extend its influence beyond the shores of Lake Michigan and change the shape of legal education everywhere. Its premise was simple: The lessons of modern economics should be applied to legal rules and procedures. O'Connell became aware of this idea largely through discussions with Henry Manne, a Chicago-trained professor who was then in charge of planning a new law school at the University of Rochester.

O'Connell drove to Rochester to meet with Manne, who gave him a copy of his prospectus for a center dedicated to law and economics. O'Connell took it home, examined it, and became enthusiastic. Here was exactly the sort of thing the foundation should support, he thought. On his next trip to St. Louis, he described the law and economics movement to John M. Olin and suggested that the foundation invest in it. Olin, however, was far from convinced. "What the hell is a lawyer doing teaching economics?" he asked. Like so many others, he also believed that when it came to economics, "the law is a ass."

Yet Olin kept an open mind. He looked over Manne's prospectus plus a few other materials. The next time O'Connell traveled to St. Louis, Olin said he had decided to support the law and economics movement. "Men like Olin are successful because their first hunch is so often right," O'Connell observed. "But Olin also was able to change his mind based on his reading of the facts, something that few men at his age and level of accomplishment are capable of doing. He was utterly convinced that law and economics was important."

The John M. Olin Foundation invested more of its resources in law and economics than any other single area, with the total value of its grants ultimately topping $68 million. Of all the foundation's activities, this was perhaps its most significant. Unlike many of the projects that the foundation would embrace following Olin's death, this is one that Olin himself realized was important and he remained convinced of its potential until the end of his life. At the 1981 tribute dinner held in Olin's honor, for instance, Manne was one of the featured speakers. When Manne finished his remarks, Olin grabbed him by the sleeve and pulled him over to Richard Nixon. "This man is teaching economics to lawyers," he told the former president. Nixon was polite but puzzled: "Economics to lawyers? Hmmm." To him, it was a foreign concept.

The core idea of law and economics is that laws must be evaluated as much for their consequences as for their dispensation of justice. (For this reason, some have described it as a "consequentialist" philosophy.) That may sound like common sense, but it was a revolutionary concept shortly after the Second World

War. Before law and economics arrived on the scene, most legal scholars analyzed how rules and cases distributed wealth between parties. Their overriding concern was "fairness." Law and economics scholars did not believe this was sufficient. They evaluated rules on the basis of their underlying incentive structures and sought to understand how government regulations and court decisions influence behavior. This school of thought "explicitly considers legal institutions not as given outside the economic system but as variables within it, and looks at the effects of changing one or more of them upon other elements of the system," according to the *Encyclopedia of Law and Economics.* "Legal institutions are treated not as fixed outside the economic system but as belonging to the choices to be explained." Rather than a modest attempt to examine the areas where laws obviously affect economic activity—rules governing taxation and business organization, for instance—law and economics is an ambitious program that scrutinizes virtually every field of legal activity. As Richard A. Posner put it in his landmark book, *Economic Analysis of Law,* "Economics turns out to be a powerful tool of normative analysis of law and legal institutions—a source of criticism and reform."

The intellectual roots of law and economics stretch back to David Hume and Adam Smith in the eighteenth century and continue through to Oliver Wendell Holmes in the nineteenth and twentieth centuries. "For the rational study of the law the black-letter man [i.e., a legal fundamentalist] may be the man of the present, but the man of the future is the man of statistics and the master of economics," wrote Holmes. The modern law and economics movement began to take shape in the 1950s at the University of Chicago, where Aaron Director was an economist on the law-school faculty. Friends had tried to find a place for him in the economics department, but the guildlike exclusiveness of the professoriate prevented the hiring of a man who did not have a Ph.D., no matter how brilliant he was. The law school, however, maintained a slot for an economist. It became available just as Director was leaving government service. He came aboard and immediately tried to make sure that Chicago's law students understood rudimentary economics.

Today, it is widely accepted that law students ought to have a broad understanding of that critical subject. In Director's day, however, legal economics was confined to a few narrow fields, most notably antitrust regulation. Even there, the rules of monopoly often made little economic sense, according to Director, who believed that antitrust laws hurt corporations without protecting consumers from price fixing. His students included Robert Bork, who went on to become a federal appeals court judge, an unsuccessful Supreme Court nominee, and, from the late 1980s to the late 1990s, the occupant of the John M. Olin Chair in Legal Studies at the American Enterprise Institute. Richard Posner, whose prolific work has helped propel law and economics into the forefront of modern legal scholarship, also studied under Director, as did Henry Manne.

Connecting antitrust law to economics was an obvious link. The importance of the law and economics movement, however, is that it did not limit itself to this single area. In 1958, the University of Chicago began publishing the *Journal of Law and Economics,* which would become a venue for bold and influential thinking. One of its earliest offerings was "The Problem of Social Cost," by economist Ronald Coase, who succeeded Director at the law school. "When I came to the University of Chicago," Coase once explained, "I regarded my role as that of Saint Paul to Aaron Director's Christ." Coase had been an important figure as early as the 1930s, but it was his later scholarship that played an essential role in popularizing law and economics—and especially a groundbreaking idea that has become known as the "Coase Theorem." In a world of perfect information and no transaction costs, said Coase, resources will be allocated in a way that maximizes wealth. In other words, if people bargain among themselves without interference, they will generally arrive at an efficient distribution of resources.

Coase offered an illustration. Suppose that a railroad track runs by a farmer's field and that sparks from the locomotive destroy a portion of the farmer's crops—a common hazard in the nineteenth century. Suppose also that the train company could install a $100 device to keep the sparks from flying, but the sparks themselves do only $50 worth of damage to the crops.

In traditional legal thinking, one party to the conflict must suffer its entire cost—either the train company must purchase the device or the farmer must absorb the losses. Whatever the outcome, there's a clear winner and a clear loser. Coase, however, pointed out that there's a more efficient possible outcome. The railroad company could pay the farmer $60 for the right to emit sparks, thereby saving itself the full cost of a $100 device. The farmer approves of the result as well, because he makes $60 from a piece of land that is capable of producing only $50 worth of crops. The dispute is resolved, and everybody comes away with a pretty good deal.

In "The Problem of Social Cost," Coase presented a powerful methodology for applying economics to the law outside the cramped confines of antitrust regulation. It took a group of popularizers, however, for his ideas to realize their full potential. In 1968, Gary Becker wrote an influential article on the economics of criminal behavior. Manne applied the insights of economics to corporate law so successfully that today the field of corporate-law scholarship is a branch of the law and economics movement. A few years later, Posner released the first edition of *Economic Analysis of Law*, a vital book in the effort to popularize law and economics. Other leaders in the field have included William Baxter, Guido Calabresi, Frank Easterbrook, Daniel Fischel, and Douglas Ginsburg. Together, these scholars showed how to apply economic analysis to virtually every corner of the law. They did it through the power of their own scholarship as well as classroom instruction to a cadre of promising students who would go on to notable careers as lawyers, professors, and judges.

At first, the only place in the academy where law and economics held sway was at the University of Chicago. This began to change in the 1970s, as scholars associated with other institutions began to see the field's tremendous importance and as Chicago graduates joined the faculties at other institutions. One of these was Henry Manne, who was devising a curriculum for a new law school at the University of Rochester in the early 1970s. Although his scholarship had a great impact, Manne made his most lasting contribution as an organizer. He was determined to expose students to law and economics thinking, but that was not his only idea. "I also wanted to teach economics to law professors," he said. "I believed this would be a good way for the new school to make its mark in legal education." With corporate and foundation support, Manne started a pilot program in 1971 called the Economics Institute for Law Professors. For three and a half weeks during the summer, a class of twenty-five participants studied economics with a group of distinguished teachers. Manne immediately knew he was on to something. Unfortunately, fundraising for Rochester's law school did not go well. It appeared as though there would be no law school after all, and Manne would have to make his mark elsewhere.

Manne circulated a prospectus describing the advantage of finding a permanent home for the Economics Institute for Law Professors at an established law school. One of these made it into the hands of Frank O'Connell, and soon the John M. Olin Foundation was investing in the project. In 1974, as Manne was establishing the Law and Economics Center at the University of Miami, the foundation donated $100,400. Larger amounts followed in later years. "Your support," Manne wrote to Olin some years later, "was an entrepreneurial act comparable to funding a large and risky new enterprise.... Without your financial and moral support of the Law and Economics Center, my own aspirations and ambitions would have come to nothing." Olin's consistent aid helped Manne expand his program to include fellowships for students with graduate degrees in economics. Manne also created programs for educating judges—and this would be his true legacy, although it did not become apparent for a number of years. Interest in the seminars was high from the start, however. Many judges understood that their own knowledge of economics was deficient and that this was a serious handicap in the world that Coase, Becker, and Posner were creating. The John M. Olin Foundation regarded Manne's program as one of its premier projects. At a board meeting in 1979, Olin himself wondered whether it might be replicated at other schools.

Keeping one program functioning at a single school proved to be enough of a challenge. The realm of academics is full of contentious politics and petty turf battles, and by 1980, the administration at Miami was making Manne feel unwelcome. He knew he would have to go elsewhere. Olin approached the president of Cornell about the possibility of moving the Law and Economics Center to Ithaca, and the matter was handed over to the law school. Manne paid a visit, and although he was not enthusiastic about returning to a colder climate, he certainly understood the attraction of giving the LEC an Ivy League imprimatur. Ultimately, however, the Cornell faculty prevented the move. The decision dismayed Olin, who viewed it as further confirmation of his alma mater's decline. In a letter to Cornell president Frank Rhodes, he wrote of "the very disappointing experience with left-wing attitudes in the Law College" and said the situation "needs very very serious study and correction."

Blocked at Cornell, Manne turned his attention to the law school at Emory University. He retained the John M. Olin Foundation's full support the whole time. Both Manne and the foundation hoped the Law and Economics Center would find a permanent home in Atlanta and flourish there. Emory may not have been as prestigious a school as Cornell, but perhaps it was good enough. Before long, Manne's program was developing a reputation around campus for its sharp students. In one memorable incident, Jimmy Carter visited Emory and about a dozen Olin Fellows were invited to have lunch with him. As they introduced themselves, Carter snapped: "Do you have to be white to be a John M. Olin Fellow?" The students themselves were nervous about meeting a former president, and so they did not respond to Carter's baiting question. A few more minutes passed, and Carter posed his question again: "Do you have to be white to be a John M. Olin Fellow?" This time, Bruce Johnson, one of the students, spoke up: "Well, I haven't seen any black presidents lately."

Yet even as the Law and Economics Center began to gain prestige at Emory, trouble was brewing. In 1981, foundation board member George Gillespie expressed his concern that many of Manne's Olin Fellows were entering private law practice rather than the academy, and those who chose to become professors were not able to secure appointments at the nation's best law schools. The LEC was suffering in another way as well. At Miami, it had enjoyed outstanding facilities. At Emory, however, Manne was forced to rent conference space and had little room for growth. Setting about to correct this problem, he located a building off campus and took advantage of the center's nonprofit status to negotiate a purchase price at just a fraction of the building's true value. The John M. Olin Foundation became excited at the prospect of helping Manne set down roots, and in 1982 the board indicated its willingness to spend $1.5 million, provided that Emory put up $1 million. The new building would become the headquarters of the renamed John M. Olin Center for Law and Economics. A deal appeared imminent as Manne and Emory president Jim Laney attended a steering committee meeting at the foundation's offices in New York City.

The meeting, however, was not a success. Confusion arose over why the building was not on campus. Laney had assumed that the foundation's support was contingent upon accepting the off-campus site. But this was not true: Simon said that the foundation would pay for an on-campus building if that was what Emory preferred. Suddenly it seemed that nobody could agree on where the building should be located. Simon blamed Manne for the mix-up and the foundation lost confidence in Emory's administration. Instead of becoming one of the John M. Olin Foundation's most significant grants, the entire deal collapsed.

In 1983, the John M. Olin Foundation decided conclusively that it would try to attach the Olin name to a law and economics center at a place other than Emory. "Efforts should be made to identify one of the top dozen or so law schools in the United States ... [for] a law and economics program similar in scope to that which had been offered at the University of Miami Law School and Emory University Law School for students who might be known as John M. Olin Fellows," say the minutes for the board meeting on March 31. "The trustees emphasized in the course of their discussions the desirability of emphasizing both the quality of the institution—law school and economics department—and the quality of the students and faculty." The board also voted to fund Manne's current group of Olin Fellows and then discontinue payments thereafter.

Manne left Emory in 1986 to become dean at George Mason University's law school in Virginia, and he took the Law and Economics Center with him. Its first home at GMU, fittingly, was in a converted department-store building. The center published newsletters and sponsored conferences that helped those at work in this emerging field to keep track of what others were doing. Despite the problems with Manne in Atlanta, the John M. Olin Foundation supported the LEC at George Mason from the start, with $63,000 in 1986, followed by a long string of six-figure gifts.

The education of judges eventually became the center's dominant activity. Hundreds of federal judges took advantage of LEC courses. A typical seminar involved more than twenty hours of lectures over a six-day period, plus about five hundred pages of required reading. The faculty changed from program to program, but it always featured top-notch scholars, including more than half a dozen Nobel laureates. "A lot of judges graduated from law school thirty years ago," said F. H. Buckley, director of the center. "They had no training in economics and no training in numbers—if they liked numbers, they would have become doctors." The LEC sought to make better judges by encouraging its program participants to apply the insights of law and economics to their jurisprudence. Supreme Court justice Ruth Bader Ginsburg attended two LEC seminars and sent a letter of thanks: "For lifting the veil on such mysteries as regression analysis, and for advancing both learning and collegial relationships among federal judges, my enduring appreciation." By the end of 2004, the LEC had trained more than 1,300 judges.

The LEC's programs were seen as so effective that other groups began to mimic them—never quite as well, but not without consequence. The Foundation for Research on Economics and the Environment (FREE), another recipient of John M. Olin Foundation funding, sponsored its own courses and enrolled scores of federal judges. "The impact of these seminars was made clear in 1993," claimed the National Committee for Responsive Philanthropy, a liberal watchdog group. In a property-rights case, *Sweet Home v. Babbitt,* circuit judge Stephen Williams sided with a two-to-one majority in allowing the government to prohibit timber companies from certain activities deemed threatening to endangered species. Two weeks later, Williams attended a FREE seminar in Idaho. When he returned, his panel reheard the case and Williams switched his vote.

Left-wing critics pointed to the *Sweet Home* case as a nefarious example of an impressionable judge doing harm because he was exposed to law and economics, and they lobbied to neuter FREE and the LEC through legislation. In 2000, Democratic senators Russ Feingold of Wisconsin and John Kerry of Massachusetts proposed a bill that would have stripped the organizations of their ability to educate judges. The senators said that corporations with interests before the courts should not finance educational programs for judges, but their real interest lay in unplugging one of the most important tools the law and economics movement has for disseminating its ideas. (In fact, grants from the John M. Olin Foundation and similar sources were more important to FREE and the LEC than corporate dollars.) Every organization of federal judges criticized the proposed legislation, as did Supreme Court chief justice William Rehnquist. The bill was defeated. Its backers continued to press for restrictions, however, and they could always count on the solid support of liberal editorial pages.

Despite this controversy, law and economics continued to have an enormous impact on legal education. Even its critics could not help but admire its growing influence. In 1986, Bruce Ackerman of the Columbia Law School told the *Wall Street Journal* that law and economics was "the most important thing in legal education since the birth of Harvard Law School." By the end of the decade, every major law school offered at least some economics training to its students. Courses ranging from bankruptcy to torts were taught from the perspective of law and economics. "Few developments in legal analysis are broad enough or important enough to change the face of legal education. But the law and economics movement ... has profoundly affected the way we think and talk about law," wrote Michael McConnell in 1987. Its influence continued to grow into the 1990s and beyond. "Law and economics has become a part of the legal establishment," wrote Larissa MacFarquhar in the *New Yorker* in 2001.

As the law and economics movement matured, many of its adherents took positions in the government and won nominations to the federal bench. The notion that laws should be analyzed not just for their fairness but also for their economic consequences began to spread. Judges became increasingly sensitive to the behavioral incentives they created through their rulings. Supporters of the movement pointed to dozens of important accomplishments, from an antitrust field full of economic analysis to the computation of damages in personal injury and commercial lawsuits. Law and economics also was crucial in the drive toward deregulation as well as the relatively recent belief that new regulations should not be imposed without first conducting a cost/benefit analysis. Perhaps most noteworthy was that Coase and Becker won Nobel Prizes in economics. When Coase received his award, Simon sent him a letter of congratulations. Coase responded with a handwritten note: "You should not forget that without all the work in Law and Economics, a great part of which has been supported by the John M. Olin Foundation, it is doubtful whether the importance of my work would have been recognized. So I give you a special thanks."

Scholarship in the field thrived, with the John M. Olin Foundation making much of it possible. The foundation focused on nurturing the movement at a dozen elite law schools. Many of these programs were themselves named after the foundation's benefactor. Funds went toward faculty research, academic conferences, student fellowships, public lectures, and legal journals—each of them essential to the manufacture and promotion of ideas. Its earliest support, appropriately enough, went to the University of Chicago, beginning in 1977. Student fellowships were one of the most impressive features of this partnership. Starting in 1985, John M. Olin Fellows won clerkships to the Supreme Court at a rate of roughly one per year. Others went on to become law professors. "The Olin student fellowships mean that the very best students in the nation focus their attention on law and economics," said a 1991 grant application from Chicago.

"They set the tone for conversation and debate with their fellow students inside class and out."

The law and economics program at Chicago also helped underwrite dozens of important articles and books. One of the most significant was *Takings,* by Richard Epstein (even though he was not a pure law and economics consequentialist). Published in 1985, his book built upon the takings clause of the Fifth Amendment to the Constitution: "... nor shall private property be taken for public use without just compensation." Epstein argued that the government should reimburse property holders when new regulations lower the value of their private property. This helped establish the legal logic of an emerging property-rights movement and formed the basis of a Supreme Court decision ordering South Carolina to pay a beachfront landowner for damage done to him by a law that stopped him from building homes in an area that was suddenly declared environmentally sensitive. The government had not taken the property through an eminent domain proceeding—a case in which it clearly would have had to compensate the owner—but its aggressive restrictions represented a difference without a distinction. The Court recognized this, thanks to the judiciary's newfound appreciation of economics in general and Epstein's work in particular.

One of the best-known law and economics scholars, at least to the public, may be John R. Lott Jr., whose 1998 book, *More Guns, Less Crime,* transformed one of America's most contentious debates. A fixture on the op-ed pages and a frequent presence on TV talk shows, he was dubbed by *Newsweek* "the gun crowd's guru." Lott's central claim, based on a rigorous analysis of FBI statistics, is that concealed-carry laws deter crime by raising the cost of criminal behavior. The bad guys have to worry about whether their potential victims are armed, and this in turn makes committing crimes a less attractive option than it would otherwise be. In short, ordinary citizens are made safer when they have access to guns. These conclusions were controversial, even among some scholars who were sympathetic to the perspective of law and economics. Yet there is no doubt that Lott became an influential figure. He did most of the work for his book as an Olin

Fellow at Chicago. "There's no doubt the foundation helped make my work possible," said Lott, who later took a position at Yale Law School and then the American Enterprise Institute. Gun-control advocates have tried to suggest that Lott is a pawn of the gun industry, on the questionable grounds that because he was an Olin Fellow, and because the John M. Olin Foundation's endowment came in part from Olin Corporation stock, and because the Olin Corporation manufactured guns and ammunition, he therefore is not impartial on the topic of firearms. When Democratic congressman Charles Schumer of New York leveled the charge in a letter to the *Wall Street Journal,* Simon called it "an outrageous slander." In truth, the foundation had nothing to do with selecting Lott for the Chicago fellowship. (And the Olin Corporation had no connection whatsoever, of course.) As with all John M. Olin fellowships at Chicago and elsewhere, decisions about appointments and research topics were made by program directors at the schools— not by foundation staff.

Over the years, the John M. Olin Foundation tried to advance law and economics thinking at law schools other than Chicago and placed a premium on those regarded as the best in the country. Henry Manne's Law and Economics Center, for instance, was seen as a worthwhile investment, but was based at good schools rather than great ones. A confidential staff evaluation of the John M. Olin fellowship program prepared for the board in 1983 made the point: "Judging by the test scores and the graduate institutions attended, the students are very good but not truly exceptional. They come from good institutions, and have very respectable test scores. But few come from the very best institutions." A couple of the very best institutions were in fact represented—Yale and the University of Virginia—but they were outnumbered by the likes of Georgia State, SUNY-Binghamton and Texas A&M.

This fact clashed with the John M. Olin's growing interest in swaying public opinion by focusing on elite institutions. In the 1970s, the foundation had supported academics at small liberal-arts schools like Berry, Harding, and Hillsdale Colleges. By the end of the decade, however, the board was questioning this strategy. The matter came up directly at a meeting on July 5, 1979. Shouldn't the foundation invest its resources at more noteworthy colleges and universities? Olin said he thought supporting these traditional recipients remained worthwhile. Others were less certain. A memo prepared for the trustees that November said these were "decent schools, but they are not academically respectable in terms of influence on public policy." Moreover, "the work of these schools, however laudable in its intentions, makes little or no difference in the hearts and minds of Americans as regards attitudes towards free enterprise, nor do their faculties, alumni, and students tend to influence the climate of opinion.... Over the years our hull has acquired a few barnacles and it may now be time to scrape down the hull." There was clearly a strong sentiment for the foundation to establish beachheads at the nation's elite schools. This sentiment did nothing but grow.

In 1985, an unexpected opportunity to gain a foothold in the most prestigious law school in America presented itself. The importance of Harvard Law School is difficult to overstate: At the dawn of the twenty-first century, five of the nine Supreme Court justices had attended it, along with nine senators, 28 percent of the managing partners in top-fifty law firms, and 16 percent of America's law-school professors (with an even higher percentage at first-tier law schools). In the 1980s, however, it was a deeply troubled institution whose faculty was bitterly divided over its future direction. At the heart of the controversy was a group of scholars devoted to Critical Legal Studies, which viewed the law as an oppressive tool of the ruling class. Relations between the "Crits," as the CLS professors like to call themselves, and more traditional scholars grew rancorous. Whereas Yale had kept the Crits at arm's length—they were not able to secure tenure—Harvard welcomed them. "This is the Rome of Critical Legal Studies," declared a jubilant Duncan Kennedy, the leader of the group. The newcomers were so aggressive, they made it impossible for the school to hire anybody for a tenured job for several years. One professor, former deputy solicitor general Paul Bator, announced that he was leaving Harvard for the presumably more friendly confines of Chicago. This was unheard-of: once ensconced at Harvard Law School, professors almost never left. But Bator, who had spent twenty-six years in Cambridge, had seen enough. "Serious and productive non-left scholars do not want to be at an institution devoted to guerilla warfare," he said. "The Harvard Law School is the only educational institution I know where it is considered a symptom of right-wing extremism to be in favor of rigorous standards of scholarly excellence." Law and economics had not penetrated the curriculum the way it had at Chicago, and the entire movement was ostracized. "It was ludicrous. Almost nothing was more politically incorrect," said Stephen Shavell, an economist at the law school. "Students would hiss in the classroom. The climate was simply unbelievable."

These disputes might not have gained wide notice but for Duncan Kennedy's unguarded advocacy of Crit ideology in a magazine for law-school alumni, which garnered further attention when Calvin Trillin cited it in a long story on Harvard Law's troubles for the *New Yorker*. Kennedy's disdain for capitalism and his dedication to Marxism were so complete that he encouraged young graduates to become fifth columnists and undermine their corporate law firms from within. Recent Harvard alumni, he wrote, should engage in "sly, collective tactics" in order to "confront, outflank, sabotage, or manipulate the bad guys." The "bad guys," of course, were the senior lawyers who had been irredeemably corrupted by the evils of capitalism. "Young associates should think of it as a requirement of moral hygiene that they defy the people they work for, and do it at regular intervals," wrote Kennedy.

Alumni were outraged. Was this what their contributions to Harvard Law School were supporting? Were they expected to hire young students trained in the art of corporate sabotage? The law school knew it had a significant problem on its hands— and Harvard's problem was the John M. Olin Foundation's opportunity. George Gillespie, a key member of the foundation board and a Harvard Law graduate, got in touch with Phil Areeda, a member of the law-school faculty whom he had known when they were both students. Gillespie had gone on to work in private practice at one of New York's finest law firms, Cravath, Swaine

& Moore, which handled John M. Olin's personal legal business. Areeda, however, had served in the Eisenhower administration and then joined the faculty at Harvard Law, where he became an authority on antitrust law. He was also a conservative who had little patience for the Crits.

Gillespie arranged for Areeda to visit the foundation's board, and the group discussed the possibility of beginning a law and economics program. Harvard president Derek Bok, always on the lookout for new sources of funding and eager to allay the concerns of irritated alumni, embraced the foundation. Ultimately, the John M. Olin Foundation awarded a multiyear grant of $1 million to the new Program in Law and Economics. Shavell was put in charge. "We viewed it as a modest amount of money," he said. "It was clear the foundation was happy with Chicago but decided to see if something good could happen at Harvard. Well, something good did happen."

The John M. Olin Foundation's support kept growing. It sponsored student and faculty fellowships, prizes for papers, and seminars. Bill Simon became one of Harvard's biggest backers. "He came to one of our events in 1995," said Shavell. "It turned out that we both liked Tom Clancy novels. We really hit it off." The foundation eventually spent more than $18 million on law and economics at Harvard—more than it spent on any other single program of any kind in its history. A turning point came in 1997, when the foundation pledged $6 million and Harvard rechristened the program as the John M. Olin Center for Law, Economics, and Business. "When the foundation began supporting us in 1985, Harvard Law School was by many accounts an embattled institution known more for its hostility to than its study of economics and business," wrote Dean Robert Clark in 2002. "Now law and economics faculty comprise over 25 percent of our entire full-time faculty, making it the largest research constituency at the Law School.... Through Olin's support, the discipline of law and economics has come to represent a substantial portion of a Harvard legal education." Indeed, the economic analysis of the law found a place within the Harvard curriculum. By 2005, the number of Harvard faculty whose interests could be defined within the area of law and economics had jumped to

23, from just 6 in 1985. The John M. Olin Fellowships for students became springboards to prominent clerkships, but most impressive were the 48 students who had obtained academic positions, including 21 at top-ten law schools such as Berkeley, Chicago, and Michigan.

At Yale University, the John M. Olin Center for Studies in Law, Economics, and Public Policy produced similarly strong results. Its director, George Priest, was the John M. Olin Professor of Law and Economics, and he became a leading figure in the field. By 2005, there were 65 fellows who had taught at law schools, including some of the best in the country, 11 Supreme Court clerks, 121 federal appeals court clerks, and 76 federal district court clerks. Starting in 1985, the foundation provided this program with more than $11 million.

The John M. Olin Program in Law and Economics at Stanford Law School was no less successful. "This is undoubtedly one of our top programs in Law and Economics," said an evaluation by the foundation's staff in 2003. In the early 1980s, Stanford was home to a modest law and economics program supported by a handful of corporate contributors. "We ran it on a shoestring," said A. Mitchell Polinksy, who was the program's director from 1979, when he left Harvard to join the Stanford faculty. He also knew it could grow much larger. As a close friend of Shavell's since their days as graduate students at the Massachusetts Institute of Technology, Polinsky knew what the John M. Olin Foundation was doing at Harvard Law School. His dean, Paul Brest, learned about it as well and suggested that they introduce themselves to the foundation. A meeting in Manhattan was arranged. It was the start of a long relationship. The foundation's first grant, for $871,000, came in 1987. More followed, including gifts worth more than $1 million apiece in 1999 and 2001.

Many of the academic trends paralyzing Harvard were present at Stanford as well, though in much weaker forms. "We had a contingent of critical legal scholars here, but everything was more civil," said Polinsky. "We debated rather than shouted." Over time, the influence of the Crits receded. In 2004, about a quarter of the Stanford law professors were associated in some way with law and economics. "The foundation made it easy for

us to hire," said Polinsky, who remained in charge of the program throughout the period of the foundation's support. "The
resistance to hire people diminishes when you have the resources
to do it." And the success of law and economics at Stanford made
it easier for scholars trained there to find jobs on other campuses. Veterans of the Stanford program won appointments at
Harvard, Penn, Columbia, Berkeley, USC, Cornell, Northwestern, Texas, Wisconsin, and elsewhere. "The impact these former
students will have through their own research and teaching will,
I believe, create extraordinary value for the John M. Olin Foundation by leveraging its investment in Stanford's program," wrote
Polinsky in a 2003 grant proposal. Dean Paul Brest's successor,
Kathleen M. Sullivan, concurred: "The work of the Foundation
in promoting study, research, and dissemination of information
on law and economics has been so wide-reaching and influential that having the Olin name connected to an institution's program brings instant credibility to the work of its scholars."

Perhaps inevitably, in the two or three decades following
the advent of the Coase Theorem, scholarship in law and economics became more academic. "Much of the earlier work in
law and economics was written in ordinary English and was acces-
sible even to readers who did not have any strong economic background," wrote Richard Epstein in a 1990 evaluation of the John
M. Olin Foundation's programs. "The modern material is different. There is far less interest in defending the boundaries of law
and economics against external attack, and far more interest in
doing technical work within the field." Specialization was coming to define the discipline. "Much of the material is hard to follow even by people who do have some economics training," wrote
Epstein. "While the overall level of economic sophistication on
[law] faculties has grown, there is probably a greater gap between
the cutting edge of research on the one hand and the knowledge of the ordinary law professor on the other." In one sense,
this was merely a symptom of success. Yet Epstein pointed to further challenges. "There are conspicuous barriers between what
is done and understood by law and economics types . . . and the
rest of the legal academic world," he wrote. Several areas
remained relatively untouched by law and economics thinking,

including antidiscrimination law, family law, labor law, and legal history—but these pockets of resistance probably could not hold out forever.

By the late 1980s, professors who were interested in law and economics but were not on the faculties supported by the John M. Olin Foundation often found themselves isolated from their colleagues-in-arms. Harvard, Yale, and Stanford were very good at graduating students who found jobs at other schools. One problem for many of these young scholars, however, was their separation from the law and economics programs that were responsible for so much intellectual ferment. "These people would go teach at schools like Iowa State, where they had almost nobody to talk to about their scholarship," said Polinsky. "They needed a way to communicate with the law and economics community."

In the late 1980s, a group of leading law and economics scholars tried to address the problem by founding the American Law and Economics Association. They first convened at George Mason University, at the invitation of Henry Manne, who by now was recognized not only as a leading scholar in the field but also as one of the movement's great organizers. The John M. Olin Foundation provided ALEA with seed money—a grant of $152,750 in the final days of 1989. "These funds were necessary and crucial," said Harvard's Shavell, a founding member of the group. "We didn't know of any other financial sources." Law and economics was becoming so popular that an academic association was probably inevitable. "But it might have taken some real time to happen," said Shavell. "Moreover, the number of academics generating the demand for the ALEA was itself a partial product of Olin support." The group began by hosting an annual conference and creating a membership directory, and then grew. In the late 1990s, a grant of $143,468 from the John M. Olin Foundation made it possible for ALEA to begin publishing the semiannual *American Law and Economics Review*. The association also saw sister organizations arise in Australia, Europe, and Latin America. The movement's increasing diversity—not just regionally but also intellectually and in just about every way imaginable—has made law and economics more difficult to compartmentalize. "Thirty years ago one person, in one book, could map most of the terrain of law and economics," wrote Richard Posner in the foreword to the *Encyclopedia of Law and Economics*. That is no longer so.

Despite this general success, not every one of the John M. Olin Foundation's forays into law and economics achieved positive results. Attempts to support the movement at Duke and Penn, for instance, were disappointments. At Duke, the foundation thought it saw untapped potential in Jerome M. Culp Jr., a black law professor who had graduated from Chicago and Harvard and directed the John M. Olin Program in Law and Economics from 1989 to 1993. Yet in a 1992 speech, he revealed himself as beholden to the racial politics that were incapacitating higher education everywhere. Chief Justice William Rehnquist, asserted Culp, had "reintroduced the story of white supremacy to the Supreme Court." There was no direct connection between these words and the foundation ending its support of law and economics at Duke—though the foundation came to view Culp's remarks as the symptom of a larger problem.

Although the movement is often seen as a "conservative" force in legal education, there is nothing intrinsically conservative about it. "Law and economics imposes an intellectual constraint," said F. H. Buckley of the LEC. "Liberals can do it, but you have to be a certain kind of liberal." One of the founding fathers of law and economics, Guido Calabresi, was a liberal Democrat. (In 2004, he compared the political rise of President Bush to that of Hitler and Mussolini.) At its core, law and economics is utilitarian because it strives to obtain the greatest good for the greatest number of people, putting its faith in market decisions rather than governmental directives. "The economist," wrote Posner in 1972, "cannot tell society whether it should seek to limit theft, but he can show that it would be inefficient to allow unlimited theft." No true conservative would argue that efficiency is the soul of the law and not all law and economics scholars agree on where to draw the line between politics and markets. A much-discussed paper by Steven Levitt of the University of Chicago and John Donahue of Stanford University linked the declining crime rate of the 1990s with legalized abortion—in other words, crime fell because a disproportionate number of future criminals never made it out of the womb. The study was controversial and its methodology criticized. Yet it clearly came out of the law and economics field. It also served no conservative purpose, at least insofar as conservatism has been associated with pro-life politics.

Yet law and economics did emerge from the classical liberalism that so many modern conservatives embraced, and it probably represented the best hope for injecting the ideas of the Right into legal education. This was true in large measure because transforming attitudes in constitutional law—surely high on any conservative's legal to-do list—was seen as an impossible task. Whereas constitutional law involves subjective judgments, law and economics is seen as a more objective discipline. By forcing all participants to submit themselves to a neutral methodology, it offers a much better fit for law schools that are riddled with anticonservative sentiment, as well as scholarly shelter for conservatives pursuing careers in the academy.

Whatever its limitations, law and economics did much to advance the interests of conservatism. Because of its emphasis on consequences, it became a powerful analytic tool for people worried about the growth of government and an unchecked judiciary. Social conservatives found it helpful in policy debates surrounding divorce and school choice. Moreover, there was simply nothing like it from the other side. As John Brigham of the University of Massachusetts observed in his book *The Constitution of Interests,* "While law and economics is transforming the way American law is taught, practiced, and decided, the left has failed to respond.... Where the right has supplanted, the left has critiqued."

The supplanting remains far from complete. As with most precincts of higher education, liberals continue to rule the law schools. Yet law and economics has weakened their reign, thanks in part to the John M. Olin Foundation's use of its financial resources to help an idea find a home in America's best universities. Significantly, the origins of the foundation's interest in law and economics lead back to Olin himself. Whereas he empowered his foundation to make important decisions after he died—including decisions whose specific purposes he could only dimly foresee during his lifetime—support for law and economics began with him in the 1970s and remained a mainstay of the foundation's activities until the very end. In its last years, the board of the John M. Olin Foundation affirmed this legacy and gave away $21 million in final grants to the various law and economics centers it founded and financed. Many people, both inside and outside the foundation, regarded the heavy investment in law and economics as perhaps the foundation's most important project.

# CHAPTER FIVE

# Legal Eagles

A T THE BEGINNING OF 1979, Bill Simon and the board of the John M. Olin Foundation recognized that their most important project for the year might not involve a grant, but rather finding a replacement for Frank O'Connell. The foundation's first and only executive director was preparing to retire. At a minimum, his successor would have to pick up where O'Connell was planning to leave off and manage the day-to-day affairs of the foundation. Yet everybody also was hoping to hire a dynamic young person who would become a powerful promoter of the conservative counterintelligentsia. Moreover, Simon was eager to install his own man into such an important post.

One of O'Connell's final assignments was to help identify suitable candidates. The name of William J. Bennett surfaced. At the time, Bennett was affiliated with the National Humanities Center in North Carolina. He visited with O'Connell on what Bennett took to be an interview, and it is interesting to wonder what would have happened if he had wound up in the job. Simon, however, had a different candidate in mind. A year earlier, neither he nor anybody else at the foundation had heard of Michael Joyce, but they quickly became impressed with the energy and vision Joyce had brought to the Institute for Educational Affairs, an organization that the foundation had started a year earlier in concert with several of its philanthropic allies. Joyce seemed like the perfect man for running the John M. Olin Foundation's operations. He was young, hardworking, and committed to the foundation's principles. He was also fiercely intelligent. Yet there was a problem. The foundation had played a role in bringing Joyce to the IEA only a few months earlier. Asking him to leave so soon was bound to raise eyebrows.

For this reason, Olin himself brought up the matter at a board meeting. He wondered whether hiring Joyce was the right thing to do. Then John Hanes, his longtime business associate and fellow board member, asked a question: "Is Mike Joyce the best man for the job?" Everybody including Olin believed that he was. "The foundation should seek out the best," said Hanes. "We should just hire him." That seemed to settle the matter for Olin. "Hanes put his mind at ease with just a few words," said O'Connell. This was the kind of influence Hanes had on his old friend—and it led to what was perhaps the most consequential personnel decision in the foundation's history, with the possible exception of Simon's agreeing to serve as its president two years earlier.

Born in Cleveland on July 5, 1942, Joyce attended Catholic schools and then Kent State University, where he hoped to play football. Injuries kept him off the field, and after two years he transferred to Cleveland State University, where he graduated with degrees in history and philosophy. For the next five years, he taught history and coached football at St. Edward High School. At a teacher seminar, Joyce encountered Raymond English of the Education Research Council of America, which was producing high-school textbooks for the publisher Allyn & Bacon. English persuaded Joyce to leave the classroom and become a researcher at ERC, where he quickly rose to the position of assistant director. His responsibilities included fundraising, which introduced him to philanthropic foundations. With the encouragement of his employer, who wanted to boast of Ph.D.s on staff, Joyce took summer courses at Walden University and earned a doctorate in the philosophy of education. In 1975, he learned that the new Morris Goldseker Foundation in Baltimore was looking for a director. His over-the-transom application won him the job.

Joyce hailed from a family of Democrats. Like others in his generation, however, he began to have second thoughts about the 1960s. He voted for Democratic presidential candidate Hubert Humphrey in 1968 but could not bring himself to support George McGovern in 1972. "I was a liberal who was reading Irving Kristol in the *Wall Street Journal*," said Joyce. "I also started looking at *Commentary* and *The Public Interest*, reading Michael Novak and Nathan Glazer." Joyce did not realize it at the time, but he was a neoconservative—a liberal who was having doubts about the Great Society and the government's ability to rectify social ills. Working at the Morris Goldseker Foundation, he observed the problem firsthand. "In Baltimore, I could see how well-intended programs set out to achieve impossible ends, and what kind of wreckage they created through unintended consequences," said Joyce. "It was a huge disappointment."

Joyce was a dynamic figure, an intellectual among activists and an activist among intellectuals. He understood how the world of ideas influenced the real world, and he would display a knack throughout his career for bringing the two together in creative ways. "He reads *everything*," said George Gillespie. Anybody who met him almost instantly saw his enormous potential. After he had spent three years in Baltimore, conservative philanthropists pulled him into their orbit with an offer in 1978 to head the Institute for Educational Affairs. By accepting the job in New York, Joyce took his first concrete step toward becoming one of the most influential members of a burgeoning conservative movement.

IEA's mission is described on the pages of *A Time for Truth*, where Bill Simon excoriated businesses for subsidizing the enemies of free enterprise. He and Irving Kristol thought a new organization composed of conservative foundation leaders and corporate philanthropists might help both groups do a better job of identifying worthy grant recipients and coordinating resources. "We decided to form a partnership that would bring together businessmen and right-thinking intellectuals in common cause," said Simon. They intended to locate and support "intellectuals open-minded and sensible enough to understand that business should be managed by hard-nosed professionals, rather than by, as Irving [Kristol] put it, the editors of *The New Left Review*." The more important part of the equation, however, involved leveraging corporate dollars. "We wanted to persuade businessmen to make the commitment to compete and win on the battlefield of ideas, as well as to support their friends rather than foes in this battle," Simon explained. When corporations engaged in charitable giving, he and Kristol essentially wanted them to act more like the John M. Olin Foundation.

They could have persuaded corporations to donate money to the foundation. This was a legal option, but not a realistic one. A separate entity would have much more success tapping these sources. Moreover, private foundations were not allowed to provide grants directly to individuals. This was a role for public charities—independent, nonprofit organizations that could accept funds from the John M. Olin Foundation and other donors and give them away to other groups or individuals. The Institute for Educational Affairs was seen as the solution to both these problems. It would receive contributions from corporations and then disburse them to deserving scholars. It would bridge the gap between the foundation and academic communities.

Within a year of Simon's joining the John M. Olin Foundation, plans for IEA were well under way. O'Connell organized a meeting between directors of several right-minded foundations, including Earhart, JM, Scaife, and Smith Richardson. Kristol, who attended, remarked, "There are scholars who know what needs to be done. We must find the means of getting aid to them."

Simon would serve as its chairman, Kristol as its vice chairman, and Leslie Lenkowsky, director of research at the Smith Richardson Foundation, as its secretary and treasurer. The board of the John M. Olin Foundation strongly supported the concept of the Institute for Educational Affairs, but worried about its bland name. After hearing a progress report at a meeting on January 26, 1978, the board gently suggested "that a more felicitous name might be selected which would be perhaps more descriptive of the broad intended gauge of the new foundation's activities." Yet the foundation approved a grant of $100,000, and the name stuck. Kristol, for his part, liked that its initials were the same as the Institute for Economic Affairs, a London-based think tank that would influence Margaret Thatcher's government in Great Britain during the 1980s.

One of IEA's first priorities was to hire someone to manage its day-to-day operations. Michael Joyce had come to the attention of Lenkowsky at a Council on Foundations conference, where they had participated in a panel discussion together. "I was immediately impressed with Mike," said Lenkowsky. "I thought he would be ideal for IEA." Joyce started in September 1978, but he worked there for only nine months before joining the John M. Olin Foundation as its executive director.

The Institute for Educational Affairs never really took off in the ways its creators had hoped. Its goal of marshalling corporate philanthropy in the service of scholars who favored free enterprise produced results that Simon once described as "mixed, at best." The institute did attract support from the likes of David Packard, as well as business leaders from Contel, Motorola, Chase Manhattan, and other companies. Yet it became clear that most corporate philanthropy was driven by pragmatism rather than principle. Companies were more interested in sidestepping controversies that could lead to consumer boycotts than they were in defending ideas, even when the ideas they were asked to defend involved the importance of capitalism in a free society. Occasionally, businesses were able to band together and fund meaningful initiatives—Milton Friedman's *Free to Choose* documentary attracted both corporate and foundation money—but by and large they were wary of becoming too wrapped up in grantmaking programs that critics might accuse of having a political dimension. Moreover, when they did give to universities and public-policy groups, the gifts benefited liberals far more than conservatives. This led to a theory among IEA's supporters that perhaps the problem was not the corporations themselves but public-affairs officers who pursued their own ideological agendas. And it was true that many of these individuals were liberals who viewed conservative ideas as provocative. But the problem was more complicated than that. "It turned out the companies knew exactly what they were doing: avoiding controversy at all costs, and trying to quiet their critics with hush money when necessary," said Joyce.

Despite IEA's failure to realize its main goal, the organization did achieve several notable accomplishments. For several

years, it was a wellspring of ingenuity for conservative philanthropy—and one of its most significant initiatives was its decision in early 1982 to join the John M. Olin Foundation (which
at the time was giving IEA $100,000 each year) in funding a new
group called the Federalist Society. Few would dispute that these
coordinated gifts allowing the Federalist Society to hold its 1982
conference represent one of the foundation's most far-reaching
acts of philanthropy.

THE ROOTS OF THE FEDERALIST SOCIETY may be found in the
friendship of three undergraduates at Yale University in the late
1970s. Steven Calabresi, Lee Liberman, and David McIntosh
were allies at the Yale Political Union, a campus debating society. They were also energized by the presidential campaign of
Ronald Reagan in the spring of 1980, when they graduated from
Yale. As they entered law school in the fall—Liberman and Mac-
Intosh at the University of Chicago and Calabresi at Yale—they
found themselves disgusted by law-school liberalism. "We had
seen a lot of left-wing politics as undergraduates, but the politics of the law schools were worse than anything we had seen earlier," said Calabresi, whose uncle was the law and economics
scholar Guido Calabresi. "It felt like an island that was completely
oblivious to what was happening around the rest of the country."
    Although separated by distance, the three friends remained
in touch—not just complaining about law-school liberalism, but
plotting their moves to counter it. What was needed, they
thought, was a conservative alternative to the National Lawyers
Guild, a left-wing membership group that coordinated legal
activism. No comparable conservative organization existed. And
even though the political climate at Chicago was much more
conservative than elsewhere, Liberman and McIntosh struggled
to secure funds from the Chicago administration for a group of
about twenty-five members. In 1981, the student association
grudgingly gave them $170, but insisted that the money be spent
on "the discussion of ideas." Liberman and McIntosh decided
to call themselves the Federalist Society as a way of honoring the
Federalist Papers and the principles of the American founding.

Meanwhile, Calabresi was organizing his own Federalist Society at Yale. In January 1982, his group sponsored a debate on *Roe v. Wade,* but it was not considered a success. "Our speaker made a good argument, but he seemed to lose the audience," recalled Calabresi. A second event, two months later, provided a much-needed spark. Richard Epstein, who was then a young scholar at the University of Chicago, gave a speech on *Lochner v. New York,* a Supreme Court ruling that said the state could not limit the number of hours that bakers worked. Epstein made a broad case against business regulations. It was a controversial view, but Epstein persuaded many in his crowd and at least stimulated the rest. "He did a brilliant job," said Calabresi.

All the while, Calabresi, Liberman, and McIntosh were promoting the idea of a national conference at Yale. They called it "A Symposium on the Legal Ramifications of the New Federalism" and wrote a detailed proposal. It began with a statement of purpose:

> Law schools and the legal profession are currently strongly dominated by a form of orthodox liberal ideology which advocates a centralized and uniform society. While some members of the legal community have dissented from these views, no comprehensive conservative critique or agenda has been formulated in this field. This conference will furnish an occasion for such a response to begin to be articulated.

The proposal said nothing about starting a permanent organization, though it did mention the benefit of assembling "top law students" at a conference because it presented an "educational opportunity" and would "encourage debate on the meaning of federalism in law schools throughout the nation."

The two Federalist Societies at Chicago and Yale went on to make contacts with sympathetic students at Harvard and Stanford. One of the leaders at Harvard was Spencer Abraham, a Michigan native who edited the *Harvard Journal of Law and Public Policy.* He, too, had experienced political barriers to winning funds for his publication. As a friend of Irving Kristol's son William, however, Abraham had access to the world of conservative philanthropy. He contacted Michael Joyce at the John M.

Olin Foundation, and Joyce immediately recognized the opportunity not only to help a group of students pursue their worthy goals but also to establish a beachhead at several of America's top campuses. This was exactly the terrain on which the foundation hoped to fight its battle of ideas. In March 1982, the foundation pledged $6,000 to the *Harvard Journal of Law and Public Policy*. That same month, the Institute for Educational Affairs announced that it would give $15,000 "for support of a Symposium on Federalism sponsored by the Chicago and Yale Federalist Societies, the Harvard Journal [of] Law and Public Policy, and the Stanford Foundation for Law and Economic Policy." Years later, Irving Kristol would call this "the best money we ever spent at IEA."

The Federalist Society may owe its existence to this seed money, but a mistake in *National Review* also played a crucial role. In the issue dated April 2, 1982, the magazine announced the formation of an organization it described as "a group of conservatively inclined law students, with chapters at Yale, Columbia, and Chicago." This was an error. The Federalists had virtually no presence at Columbia, and they certainly did not have anything resembling "chapters." At best, they were a loose collection of students—affinity groups not organized in any meaningful way. Yet *National Review*'s notice did get a few important facts right: The Federalist Society was planning a conference at Yale Law School for the weekend of April 23–25. The magazine also published a mailing address. The result was unexpected but welcome: Law students from more than a dozen schools sent letters to inquire about attending the conference and starting their own campus chapters. "When we started the Federalist Society, we didn't know we were starting the Federalist Society," said Liberman.

The conference featured an all-star list of speakers. Robert Bork delivered the keynote address. At the time, Bork was on the District of Columbia Court of Appeals and not yet a household name as an unsuccessful nominee for the Supreme Court. He was also one of the main attractions at the conference, which he got off to what a correspondent for *The American Spectator* called "a rather awkward start" with an address declaring federalism all but dead. Harvard professor Charles Fried, who would become solicitor general in Reagan's second term, spoke next and was more optimistic as he addressed what conservatives might expect from a revived federalism. Other prominent speakers included Walter Berns, Ted Olson of the Department of Justice, Judge Richard Posner, future Supreme Court justice Antonin Scalia, and Judge Ralph Winter. Another future Supreme Court justice, Stephen Breyer, was scheduled to speak, but a death in his family forced a last-minute cancellation.

The conference drew about two hundred participants, including roughly seventy from out of town. Most were law students, and they came from as far away as California, Colorado, and Louisiana. Much of their travel was subsidized by the grants from the Institute for Educational Affairs and the John M. Olin Foundation. The overall turnout was especially good considering that end-of-the-semester finals loomed for just about everyone. The *New York Times* even printed an article on Bork's speech, citing "an unusual criticism" of the Supreme Court "by a sitting federal judge."

The conference was meant primarily to function as an intellectual exercise, as the titles of the conference papers indicated: "Toward an Economic Theory of Federal Jurisdiction" (Posner), "Constitutional Conventions and Constitutional Arguments: Some Thoughts about Limits" (Grover Rees III), and so on. The prospectus for the conference talked about the importance of articulating conservative ideas, but it said nothing about organizing conservative activists. And yet this became the conference's main legacy. Years later, few people in attendance would remember exactly what any of the speakers said. Instead, they would remember being present at the creation of a vital organization.

One of the speakers did address the importance of activism. "Our need is to get in-depth, conservative organizations on as many campuses as possible," said Morton Blackwell, who was then an aide in the Reagan White House. "There are about 200 law schools in America. If the Federalist Society, which is obviously philosophically conservative, is going to have a major impact across the nation, it must go far beyond the number of campuses represented here today."

As it happened, several of the students used the conference as an occasion to discuss forming a national organization and starting chapters. Lee Liberman and David McIntosh had spent a sleepless night prior to the event working on a primitive computer to produce a five-page pamphlet that described how to create conservative student groups on law-school campuses. In the months to come, they had more conversations and meetings. One of their early decisions was to merge the names of the Chicago and Yale Federalist Societies with the *Harvard Journal of Law and Public Policy*. This union produced the Federalist Society for Law and Public Policy Studies, as the organization continues to be formally known today.

Liberman and McIntosh soon wrote a more complete guide on how to establish campus chapters. They highlighted the importance of sponsoring evenhanded debates rather than pontificating lectures: "You are more likely to convince people of your viewpoint if they feel the other side has been given a fair hearing." They also distributed a fifteen-page outline of their plans for expanding the Federalist Society over the next three years. This document was aimed at potential funders, such as the John M. Olin Foundation. The Federalists' primary goal was to build on a nucleus of law students and recent law-school graduates to become "an effective national conservative legal network." They proposed recruiting professional lawyers in dozens of cities and arranging them into local chapters, where they would make contacts with one another and begin to influence the activities of the American Bar Association. On campus, the Federalists would continue to organize themselves around debates between guest speakers and "the local liberal professors who imply that theirs is the last word." Although these chapters would enjoy a large amount of autonomy, the national organization would support them and offer advice: "Specific programs such as debates on Critical Legal Studies at afflicted campuses can help spread ideas developed at our national symposium or in other arenas." The society hoped to have twelve thousand members and an annual budget of nearly $1 million by 1987. "Despite the ambitious nature of what we have described, prospects for success are excellent because we are filling an obvious need," wrote Liberman and McIntosh. "Many conservative resources are expended creating organizations which duplicate each other. The potential here is enormous because no such organization exists."

One of the first steps was to hire Eugene B. Meyer as executive director. The son of longtime *National Review* editor and writer Frank Meyer, he was a bit older than the original Federalist triumvirate of Calabresi, Liberman, and McIntosh. Meyer had been working in Washington, D.C., with an anti-tax group and on Capitol Hill, but he knew the Federalists individually from his own days as a Yale student. He had even attended the 1982 conference as what he called "a warm body"—a friend of the organizers who was there to help guarantee a respectable turnout. And even though he did not possess a law degree, Meyer would guide the Federalist Society through a remarkable period of fast expansion.

Before long, the Federalist Society had a swelling membership and a healthy budget. By October 1983, it had raised a total of $103,000; of this, $66,000 came from the John M. Olin Foundation and the Institute for Educational Affairs. "The Olin Foundation was absolutely number one in terms of foundation support," said Calabresi, who became chairman of the Federalist Society. "Olin has been indispensable."

The foundation's most significant contribution was probably the creation and support of the John M. Olin Lectures in Law series, which the Federalist Society describes as its "cornerstone" program "to bring substantial discussion of traditional legal principles to our nation's top law schools." Because law-school administrations and student governments cannot be relied upon to bring conservative and libertarian speakers to campus, the Federalist Society stepped in with this service, which it offered continuously from 1983. "I don't think it is an exaggeration to say that students being graduated by the top law schools today are more familiar with, and have more sympathy for and certainly more understanding of conservative ideas than other recent graduates simply because they have heard some of these ideas put forward articulately," said a Federalist Society document dated May 1984. Over the years, thousands of law-school students attending events sponsored by the Federalist Society have

listened to talks by the likes of Supreme Court chief justice
William Rehnquist and associate justices Anthony Kennedy and
Antonin Scalia as well as former attorney general Edwin Meese
and special prosecutor Kenneth Starr. Many speakers have come
from the law and economics discipline, while others, such as Russell Kirk and Walter E. Williams, have had no special background
in legal affairs. One of the most popular formats was a debate
between a liberal and a conservative on some question of law.
"Early on, we discovered that debates between lesser-known figures outdrew speeches by better-known figures," said McIntosh.
"In addition, a neutral audience will discount what conservatives
have to say unless there's someone there to challenge them. It's
in debates that the strength of conservative ideas really comes
through." A successful campus lecture sponsored by the Federalist Society also delivered an important byproduct: increased
student interest in the activities and ideas of the society as well
as an opportunity for the local chapter to grow in size and
influence.

For all its success at the nuts and bolts of building a successful organization, the Federalist Society remained attached
to the intellectual enterprise its founders had laid out in the
prospectus for their 1982 symposium at Yale. The Olin speakers
were a part of this mission, as were the group's annual conferences, which never turned into the career-counseling sessions
that dominate so many other professional gatherings. By the late
1980s, it had become impossible to ignore what the Federalist
Society was accomplishing. President Ronald Reagan hailed the
group at one of its 1988 conferences. "The Federalist Society is
changing the culture of our nation's law schools," he said. "You
are returning the values and concepts of law as our founders
understood them to scholarly dialogue and, through that dialogue, our legal institutions."

Over the course of two decades, the Federalist Society
received more than $5.5 million from the John M. Olin Foun-
dation to support programs encouraging limited constitutional
government, individual freedom, and the rule of law. Other foundations also became involved in helping the group, but the Olin
money mattered most. "I don't know if the Federalist Society

would have come about in some other way, absent the John M. Olin Foundation's support," said Eugene Meyer. "It might not exist at all."

BY THE EARLY YEARS OF THE twenty-first century, the Federalist Society had become an impressive member of the academic and legal establishment, counting more than 30,000 members and boasting an annual budget of more than $4 million. Its core program of assisting conservative law students remained in place, with student chapters at about 150 law schools, or roughly four of every five accredited law schools in the country. These student groups continued to import conservative and libertarian speakers from an impressive roster whose names include U.S. Court of Appeals judges Edith Jones and Alex Kozinski, plus professors like Harvey Mansfield of Harvard and government officials such as Bradley Smith of the Federal Election Commission. "This is our main program," said Meyer. "Our ultimate goal is to develop lawyers who believe in the rule of law, properly understood."

The Federalist Society also had about sixty lawyers' chapters, based mainly in large cities. They provided professional lawyers with the opportunity to discuss topics lying outside the obligations of their day jobs (for example, corporate attorneys with an interest in constitutional law), attend lectures by prominent judges and intellectuals, and network with one another. Many of these lawyers also belonged to one or more practice groups, which worked to infuse Federalist Society principles into every area of law. The Federalist Society also administered the John M. Olin Fellowships in Law, a program that allowed young legal scholars to spend a year writing books and law-review articles, which are essential requirements for securing tenure-track jobs at top-ranking law schools. In 2003, the foundation staff noted proudly that of the seventeen people receiving fellowships since 1997, eleven had obtained tenure-track positions, three worked in the Bush administration, and two others appeared to be poised for similar success.

Over the course of two decades, the Federalist Society became an essential counterweight to the American Bar Association, a supposedly mainstream and nonideological legal organization that nevertheless lobbied against the death penalty and for abortion rights. The ABA once enjoyed quasi-official status in the screening of federal judicial nominations. Controversy over its institutional bias erupted in 1987, when several ABA evaluators deemed federal judge Robert Bork "not qualified" for an appointment to the Supreme Court. In 2001, representatives of the ABA attended "Stop Ashcroft!" meetings sponsored by left-wing groups trying to defeat the nomination of John Ashcroft as attorney general. The ABA denied that it either supported or opposed Ashcroft, but these protests could not erase a dubious history of activism. The Federalist Society's careful monitoring, through publications such as *ABA Watch,* helped convince the Bush administration to quit asking the ABA to rate its candidates for judicial nominations.

Even critics have felt compelled to acknowledge the Federalist Society's success. The liberal *Washington Monthly* called the group "quite simply the best-organized, best-funded, and most effective legal network operating in this country." The *Washington Post* seemed to concur when it examined the Federalist Society's role in helping the Bush administration fill its ranks in the spring of 2001: "The numerous appointments of Federalist members and their success in influencing policy are testament to two decades of organizing and aggressive efforts to promote a conservative vision of the law and public policy." In a report to the board of trustees in 2003, the staff of the John M. Olin Foundation gave the group a glowing review: "All in all, the Federalist Society has been one of the best investments the Foundation has ever made."

Vice President Dick Cheney spoke at the Federalist Society's national lawyers' convention in 2001: "You have changed the debate, while gaining the respect of people across the ideological spectrum. The Federalist Society has been a model of thoughtful, reasoned dialogue. You've helped bring a spirit of civility to Washington, D.C. Even more remarkably, you've managed to bring it to some of the law schools. Your spirit of honest, fair-minded debate hasn't always prevailed.... But against great odds, this organization has become one of the most influential in the world of law and public policy. I commend you for it." The Federalist Society's influence grew to the point where

Democratic senators attending confirmation hearings routinely interrogated Republican nominees to federal posts about their ties to the group. ("There are many members of the Federalist Society in our administration," cracked Cheney in his address. "We know that because they were quizzed about it under oath.")

In 1999, a professor at Georgetown decided to found a liberal version of the Federalist Society. Peter J. Rubin dubbed his group the Madison Society for Law and Policy, and he paid a kind of tribute to what the Federalists had achieved: "One of the things about the Federalists that is admirable is that it's one of the few focuses of intellectual ferment on law school campuses in America." (The Madison Society has since changed its name to the American Constitution Society because the group's organizers did not want to associate themselves with a slaveholder.)

There was a chance that the Federalist Society might have gone in a different direction. When its founders were still thinking about what their new organization might become in the aftermath of their first conference in 1982, they considered having it assume the functions of a public-interest law firm that litigates to establish legal precedents. The Federalist Society's eventual decision to debate ideas rather than enter the world of public-interest law did not diminish the perception among many conservatives, including those at the John M. Olin Foundation, that they needed to engage in litigation that had political ends—a strategy that had worked wonders for the Left.

Legal-aid societies in the United States date back to the nineteenth century, with groups devoted to settling disputes between landlords and tenants and preventing the exploitation of immigrants. Before the 1960s, however, these efforts were funded privately. With the advent of the Office of Economic Opportunity and the Legal Services Corporation, millions of federal dollars began to flow annually into the coffers of lawyers who saw the courts as a tool for expanding the welfare state, enacting regulations, and weakening federalism. They correctly believed that activist judges could help liberals achieve political goals they were not able to realize at the ballot box.

Conservatives understood the utility of public-interest law firms almost immediately. In 1968, the National Right to Work

Legal Defense Foundation began helping workers fight off com-
pulsory unionization. In the early 1970s, aides to then-Governor
Reagan in California became frustrated with lawsuits that threatened to block welfare reform. Business leaders were dispirited
by environmental litigation that delayed the construction of the
Alaska oil pipeline and similar development. These irritations
led to the incorporation of the Pacific Legal Foundation in 1973.
Its early successes prompted the creation of the National Legal
Center for the Public Interest in 1975, followed by even more
groups. By the late 1970s, several fledgling organizations had
sprouted. Almost by accident—but also because of the PLF
model—most of them focused on a particular region rather
than having a national focus.

   The John M. Olin Foundation took an interest in these
groups from the start. A memo distributed to the board on January 26, 1978, lists public-interest law as a major area of interest:

> Purpose: To break the monopolistic hold which Ralph Nader and oth-
> ers have established in the public mind on the concept of "The Public
> Interest" and where it lies and who its defenders are; to engage in litiga-
> tion in opposition to the anti-freedom, doctrinaire approaches of the
> special interest groups of the Left. (The risk that this will increase the
> already excessive amount of litigation which goes on—primarily at the
> instance of "reformers" who aim at "legislating by litigation"—is a cal-
> culated one, which, it is felt, must be undertaken not only for defensive
> purposes, but also to educate the public as to "the other side of the story"
> and the true effects of much of the interventionist regulation and liti-
> gation which the public is led to believe is to its benefit.

The memo specifically cited the Pacific Legal Foundation and
the National Legal Council for the Public Interest as worthy of
support. Later that year, the foundation distributed $65,000 to
public-interest law firms—slightly more than 2 percent of its
budget. It gave $10,000 to both the PLF and the NLCPI. It also
donated to the Plains Legal Foundation (Kansas), Mountain
States Legal Foundation (Colorado), Southeastern Legal Foundation (Georgia), and Southwestern Legal Foundation (Texas).

   Although Bill Simon was enthusiastic about these groups
and their potential, other conservatives questioned their

effectiveness. Michael Joyce in particular was concerned about the uneven quality of these regional firms. In a report to the board in 1979, Joyce said he believed that the Pacific Legal Foundation was the best of the bunch but several of the others were more interested in winning minor cases than in taking chances on much larger ones that might establish helpful precedents. George Gillespie shared many of these worries as well.

At about the same time, the Sarah Scaife Foundation hired Michael Horowitz, then an attorney in private practice, to write an analysis of conservative public-interest law firms. He produced a devastating critique that influenced conservative grantmaking for years. The fundamental problem, Horowitz said, was that the firms lacked strategic vision. Their regional character removed them from the epicenter of national power, in Washington, D.C. He understood that conservatives aimed to decentralize authority. "Still, in maintaining its regional orientation, the conservative public interest law movement has essentially confused wish with reality," wrote Horowitz. "It is in being more effective in Washington that the conservative public interest law movement can more effectively erode the power of its agencies."

Horowitz did not stop there. His hard-hitting indictment argued that the firms spent too much time filing amicus briefs intended to show their donors, who were unsophisticated in the arcane ways of the law, that they were "doing something." The firms were more interested in chalking up minor courtroom victories than in altering the shape of American legal culture. Moreover, they frequently behaved not as "public-interest" law firms, but as outsourced corporate attorneys who did the bidding of their business backers. This led to accusations from liberals that the conservative groups merely performed corporate work with funds raised through tax-deductible donations—that is, they were basically vehicles for tax avoidance. Horowitz believed that a number of high-minded people worked for these firms, but he also thought they ceded the moral high ground whenever they focused on the interests of business. All of these problems were compounded by yet another factor: "The quality of staff attorneys at most conservative public interest law firms is appallingly mediocre." Changing this would require the firms to weaken their ties to the business community and to strengthen them with the academic and intellectual worlds.

The Horowitz report was not widely distributed, but the Scaife Foundation made sure that it got into the hands of its philanthropic allies. The staff and board of the John M. Olin Foundation read Horowitz's appraisal with great interest, and its impact was felt almost immediately. The foundation did not retreat entirely from supporting public-interest law firms. But it became much more selective with its investments.

The most spectacular case to involve a conservative public-interest law firm came when General William C. Westmoreland sued CBS in 1982 over a television program that accused him of trying to manipulate military intelligence during the Vietnam War. He was represented on a pro bono basis by the Capital Legal Foundation, a Washington, D.C.-based firm that had started receiving support from the John M. Olin Foundation in 1980. Simon knew and liked "Westy," as he called the general, and held the mainstream media in contempt for its pronounced liberal bias. He was eager to see Westmoreland fight back. (Another member of the board, George Gillespie, was less enthusiastic, partly because CBS was a client of his law firm, Cravath, Swaine & Moore.) The John M. Olin Foundation never earmarked grants for Westmoreland's litigation; its support of Capital Legal was always for general expenses, and the group did pursue other cases. Yet the Westmoreland dispute was clearly the occasion for increased support, and in 1983 the foundation awarded a grant of $45,000 to Capital Legal, as well as three more worth $50,000 apiece the following year. Combined with funds from other con-servative philanthropies, as well as thousands of dollars in small donations from disgruntled veterans, Capital Legal and West-moreland enjoyed solid financial backing. In the court of pub-lic opinion, they made impressive gains. The controversy surrounding the suit became an obvious embarrassment to the entire news industry, whose political prejudices came unmasked. "CBS almost certainly misled viewers," concluded veteran reporter Stephen Klaidman in the *New York Times*. At the same time, the legal result was a disappointment. Shortly before the trial went to jury in 1985, Westmoreland accepted a settlement from CBS in the form of a weak statement. Capital Legal and its president, Dan M. Burt, came under withering attack for agreeing to a bad deal. The legacy of the Westmoreland case may not have been a courtroom victory for the general, but it indisputably made the public more cynical about the news media's claims of objectivity—and arguably helped lay the groundwork for the public's swift rejection, two decades later, of Dan Rather's election-year assertions about President George W. Bush's military record.

Throughout the 1980s and into the 1990s, the John M. Olin Foundation remained deeply wary of supporting public-interest law firms. (The Capital Legal Foundation, for example, received its final grant in 1986.) Even as the public-interest law firms shifted away from their regional emphasis and began to specialize in discrete subject areas, the foundation remained cautious. As a memo to the board observed in 1992:

> Staff is well aware of the Board's reluctance to make new grants for conservative public interest law organizations, and well aware of the good reasons for this reluctance. The bright hopes of ten years ago that conservatives could create effective counterparts to the liberal groups that have taken their policy agendas to the courtroom, such as the American Civil Liberties Union and the Sierra Club, have produced more disappointments than successes. The loose network of law firms has not been conspicuously effective, well-organized, or stable.

These words were written in the context of a grant proposal from the Institute for Justice, a public-interest law firm founded in 1991 by two veterans of the conservative public-interest law movement, Clint Bolick and Chip Mellor. The John M. Olin Foundation began to support IJ almost from the start, and eventually gave more than $1.5 million. Over the next decade, IJ went on to fight a variety of legal battles for economic liberty and property rights. It showed a special talent at winning positive media attention for its clients, and this helped shape public opinion on key topics. IJ's signature issue was school choice. The group was instrumental in securing the Supreme Court's *Zelman* ruling, which in 2002 declared that a school-choice program in Cleveland was constitutional. A good case can be made that this was the most important legal victory ever achieved by a conservative public-interest law firm, even though its primary effect was to create the conditions for a political success that the school-choice movement had not yet realized.

Other efforts were equally ambitious but less successful. In 1989, Michael Greve founded the Center for Individual Rights to match clients with attorneys looking for appealing pro bono cases. The John M. Olin Foundation was attracted to this new approach, and over a little more than a decade it spent nearly $2 million on CIR activities. The firm became involved in several important cases—including a few that went before the Supreme Court—on the rights of professors accused of sexual harassment, on the ability of religious groups to participate in publicly funded activity, and on attempts to make "gender violence" a federal issue. Its greatest hope, and the one that most appealed to the John M. Olin Foundation, was the chance to win a Supreme Court decision on racial preferences. CIR litigated successfully against an admissions policy at the University of Texas. When a pair of CIR-sponsored cases involving the University of Michigan made their way to the Supreme Court, it appeared as though CIR was possibly on the verge of a great victory for colorblind equal opportunity. But when the ruling came down in 2003, it permitted colleges and universities to continue using race as a factor in their admissions policies.

Compared with what the John M. Olin Foundation spent on other legal issues—most notably, the law and economics centers at top universities—its investment in the public-interest law firms was small. But at more than $11 million, it was not insubstantial. Although the foundation was always careful and sometimes skeptical about supporting these groups, it maintained an abiding interest in them and hoped they would succeed. Parlaying its investment in them with its support of the Federalist Society, the foundation changed America's legal landscape.

# CHAPTER SIX

# A NEW BEGINNING

OHN M. OLIN WAS JUST TWO months shy of his ninetieth birthday when he died at his home in East Hampton, New York, on September 8, 1982. His remains were cremated and scattered, leaving no gravesite for one of the twentieth century's most notable Americans. His memorials took different forms, and they began to appear almost immediately as both friends and strangers evaluated his life. "Nation's Loss," proclaimed the headline to an editorial in the *Alton Telegraph,* his hometown newspaper. He earned a tribute from the Senate: "John Olin was one of the most articulate spokesmen in the nation for the free enterprise system during his long and fruitful life," said Senator Barry Goldwater. "John gave of himself to insure that our free enterprise system would survive.... He was one of that group of rugged individualists who always put principle and honesty above all else." Bill Simon penned an obituary for his friend in the *East Hampton Star:* "John Olin was truly one of God's noblemen and everything he touched he made brighter and better."

Within two weeks of Olin's death, his nineteen-page will was filed with the St. Louis County Probate Court. Much of the estate's value came from hundreds of thousands of shares of stock in the Olin Corporation, which then held the 195th position on the Fortune 500 list. Olin also owned stock in Baker International, Exxon, and Squibb. The will included gifts of money and property to relatives as well as more than two dozen individual bequests to former friends and employees. Most of the estate, however, was split between Olin's widow and his foundation. By the end of 1982, the foundation's assets had jumped from $12 million to $64 million. The will also stipulated that the foundation would receive a second large infusion of cash upon the death of Evelyn Olin.

Olin's death brought enormous change to the John M. Olin Foundation. Although Simon was never anything but an assertive force, he and the other members of the board had often deferred to the man who had made their philanthropic activities possible. The infusion of new cash, of course, provided the foundation with the means to give away more money—a lot more. In 1982, the final year of Olin's life, the foundation made grants worth nearly $2.4 million. This figure would increase every year through 1990, when the foundation disbursed $19.5 million.

Yet the John M. Olin Foundation changed in other ways as well, as it developed a broader understanding of its own objectives. Its interests moved beyond the strict confines of free enterprise, which had animated so much of its giving in the 1970s. This transformation was becoming apparent in the final years of Olin's life, and it continued well into the 1980s, as neoconservatism influenced the foundation's grantmaking. Simon and his staff became convinced that the ranks of the counterintelligentsia needed to include figures other than economists who subscribed to the classical liberalism of Friedrich Hayek and Ludwig von Mises. The defense of capitalism, they believed, would also require noneconomic arguments rooted in culture and morals. They came to see themselves as advocates not just for free enterprise, but for a free society. Markets were a key part of the equation, though not the only part. Equally important were representative government and cultural institutions. Thus the counterintelligentsia would grow to encompass scholars and organizations interested in the traditional humanities, religion, and foreign affairs. They would also engage more directly in the rough-and-tumble of public policy, as opposed to the rarefied abstractions of theory.

It was an auspicious moment to begin such an endeavor, as the early 1980s marked a time of rebirth for the ideas that John M. Olin spent his final years supporting. The election of Ronald

Reagan in 1980 was seen as a triumph not just of Republican politics, but also of conservative ideas—the very ideas that the John M. Olin Foundation had been underwriting for years. "Though it is difficult to assess the full impact of the dozen major conservative foundations on Mr. Reagan's election or the nation's shift to the right, the foundations have obviously helped spawn and nurture writers, thinkers and economists whose provocative ideas are now part of the conservative landscape," said the *New York Times* in an article published on the day of Reagan's first inauguration. "There is a sense now that the work we've been doing all along, the studies we've been supporting, have reached a kind of fruition with Ronald Reagan's election," said Michael Joyce. "The ideals we've been supporting have filtered down into public opinion."

One of the most effective conduits for these ideals had been the Heritage Foundation, a conservative think tank founded in 1972. Its main financial backers were the beer magnate Joseph Coors and the Pittsburgh philanthropist Richard Mellon Scaife. John M. Olin was an early supporter as well, though his first contributions took the form of personal checks rather than foundation grants. At the end of 1975, as he went about his year-end flurry of charitable giving, Olin sent $10,000 to the Heritage Foundation. He doubled his gift to $20,000 in 1976 and increased it again to $30,000 in 1977. These contributions made Olin one of the Heritage Foundation's top donors—still nowhere near the support that Coors and Scaife were giving it, but significant nonetheless. In 1978, Olin stopped sending money personally and let the John M. Olin Foundation take over with a grant of $50,000. This amount increased to $100,000 the next year. "Heritage is quicker to the act than the very scholarly AEI," said a staff report in 1979. Whatever the reasons behind the giving, the Heritage Foundation appreciated every penny. "To come in at six figures for an upstart group when Jimmy Carter was president and the possibility of electing Ronald Reagan seemed far-fetched—that really mattered," said Heritage president Ed Feulner. Over the next twenty-five years, the John M. Olin Foundation would contribute nearly $10 million to the Heritage Foundation.

Fresh out of government, Bill Simon had joined the board of the Heritage Foundation in 1977. The trustees met several times a year and Simon's attendance was far from perfect. When he was there, however, he could dominate the discussion. In the fall of 1979, Simon and another board member, Jack Eckerd, reflected upon their experience working for President Nixon and described what senior officials in a new administration would want from the Heritage Foundation. If Jimmy Carter was defeated in 1980, they observed, a new GOP president would have only a few weeks between the election and his inauguration. This transition period was crucial for hiring personnel and establishing policy principles that would guide the government. Feulner recalled the last time a Republican administration had succeeded a Democratic one, in the winter of 1968–69. "Republicans were briefed by Democrats, the very people whose jobs were at stake and who had a vested interest in maintaining the status quo," he said. Conservatives did not want that to happen again, and so Simon and Eckerd urged the Heritage Foundation to ensure that there was an alternative. Acting upon this suggestion, Feulner and his staff began planning for what would become one of the most influential publications ever produced by a think tank: a thick volume called *Mandate for Leadership*. It laid out more than two thousand specific policy proposals to improve the economy, strengthen national defense, and limit the growth of government. It was a big risk for a young think tank—an expensive undertaking that would have come to naught if Carter had been re-elected. But the gamble paid off with Reagan's victory and his administration's acceptance of many of the ideas described in *Mandate for Leadership*. Significantly, nearly two dozen contributors to the book found jobs in Reagan's government.

Simon was not one of them. He had advised Reagan's presidential campaign and even was mentioned as a possible running mate—he filled out some initial paperwork that might have led to his nomination, but nothing resulted from it. Simon's name also came up for various posts in Reagan's cabinet, including a possible return to the Department of the Treasury. Yet none of these discussions led to anything either, in large part because Simon's wife objected to spending more years in Washington with her husband putting work before family. Simon did agree to lead the National Productivity Advisory Committee, but this was not a major obligation. Had he accepted a job with the government, of course, he would have been forced to cut his ties to the John M. Olin Foundation. By not taking this step, Simon was able to remain intimately involved in the foundation's growth during the 1980s.

Joyce, however, did enter the fray. He authored a section of *Mandate for Leadership* on the National Endowment for the Arts and the National Endowment for the Humanities, accusing the NEA of being more concerned "with politically calculated goals of social policy than with the arts," and saying that the NEH was supporting scholars outside their fields of expertise. This assessment—labeled "controversial" by the mainstream media—generated a significant amount of additional publicity for the Heritage Foundation's opus. It also led to Joyce's joining the Reagan transition team and helping the new administration make appointments to the NEA and the NEH, something he did on a volunteer basis and without taking a leave from his work at the foundation. Two of his confidants during this period were William Bennett of the National Humanities Center and Samuel Lipman, a concert pianist and a music critic for *Commentary*.

Bennett would go on to become something of a household name as secretary of education, drug czar, and a bestselling author. Yet he first earned public notice as head of the NEH, the very agency he had helped Joyce critique for the Heritage Foundation. Reagan nominated him for the post in the fall of 1981. Although it looked good in hindsight, the decision to choose Bennett was highly controversial among conservatives at the time. He had supported Reagan's candidacy, but was still a registered Democrat. Many on the Right remained suspicious of these so-called Reagan Democrats, whom they welcomed as members of a voting bloc but not so readily as leaders inside a conservative administration. Moreover, a large number of conservatives had their own favorite for the humanities slot: Melvin E. Bradford, an English professor at the University of Dallas.

Like Bennett, Bradford had a background as a Democrat. Yet the two men came from wholly different strands of the party.

Whereas the Brooklyn-born Bennett was an Irish-Catholic brawler, Bradford was a tall and courtly native of Texas. He had supported George Wallace for president before switching his allegiance to the GOP in 1976. He also belonged to a southern academic tradition that continued to frown on Abraham Lincoln more than a century after the Civil War. Indeed, Bradford viewed Lincoln as the founding father of big government—a radical politician who unjustly trampled on the rights of states. In one of his writings, he compared Lincoln to Adolf Hitler.

The question of who would head an agency with a budget of $152 million may seem a small thing, but many academics viewed the NEH as their own bailiwick within the federal government and they policed its grant decisions and its leadership with great care. The case of Bennett versus Bradford split the conservative counterintelligentsia in two. Figures associated with the more established wing of the conservative movement, such as William F. Buckley Jr. and Russell Kirk, tended to favor Bradford. The neoconservatives sided with Bennett. This internecine conflict was fought primarily behind the scenes, but it occasionally spilled into public view on the pages of the *Washington Post* and elsewhere. "There is opposition to me," complained Bradford, "from the Northeast and from neoconservatives—Irving Kristol, Norman Podhoretz, Bill Simon, Michael Joyce."

Despite Bradford's accusation, Simon's part in the dispute was minimal. Joyce, however, played an important role in diminishing Bradford's chances. Even after he had left the Reagan transition team, the White House personnel office continued to consult with him on the NEA and the NEH. Joyce knew Bennett from his days at the Institute for Educational Affairs, which made him, at least initially, more pro-Bennett than anti-Bradford. When Bradford's views on Lincoln came to his attention, however, he grew deeply troubled. "He had gone overboard in print," said Joyce. "We were afraid that his nomination would cause embarrassment to a president who was born in Illinois, the Land of Lincoln. You can be sure that Reagan's enemies would have used confirmation hearings to make an issue of Bradford's writings." Joyce quietly spread the word among his allies within the administration as well as conservatives who already had announced their support for Bradford. At an event in New York, Joyce discussed the matter with Buckley, Feulner, and Kristol. The four of them agreed that Bennett was the best choice. They slipped into an empty room and phoned the office of White House counselor Edwin Meese, who was one of the president's most trusted aides. Meese was not available, so they discussed the matter with his assistant, T. Kenneth Cribb. "The issues they raised really helped Bennett," said Cribb.

Bennett ultimately secured the nomination, assumed the job at the NEH, and began his career as a public official. This was a watershed moment for neoconservatives—a demonstration of their emerging clout but also a source of resentment. At the time, Bennett was by no means the most significant neoconservative in the administration; that honor probably belonged to Jeane Kirkpatrick, the ambassador to the United Nations. Yet it was Bennett's success—or, perhaps more accurately, Bradford's failure—that exposed a fault line in the Reagan coalition. A number of longstanding conservative leaders believed that the growing influence of neoconservatives amounted to a denial of birthright. "For years conservatives had wandered in the wilderness, but now, just as they were about to reap the reward for their suffering, a set of 'Johnny-come-latelies' were taking the lion's share," grumbled Paul Gottfried and Thomas Fleming, who specifically identified the John M. Olin Foundation as a victim of a neoconservative insurgency. Pat Buchanan put it more colorfully in a 1991 column: "Like the fleas who conclude they are steering the dog, [the neoconservatives'] relationship to the movement has always been parasitical."

Bill Simon certainly was no neoconservative—and he said so in a private letter to Buchanan. There was in fact nothing distinctively "neoconservative" about the John M. Olin Foundation's funding patterns, which included support for William F. Buckley Jr.'s *Firing Line* television program, social conservative Phyllis Schlafly's Eagle Forum, and many other recipients. Yet the foundation was becoming increasingly identified with the neocons, and not entirely without reason. Joyce both qualified for the label and accepted it, as did several other key staffers. All of them, including Simon, had been listening to the advice of Kristol for several years, in addition to supporting him. The paleoconservatives—as the Bradford wing of the conservative movement took to calling itself—often spoke of the neoconservatives as somehow seizing control of important institutions such as *National Review,* the Heritage Foundation, and the John M. Olin Foundation. It would be more accurate to say that the conservative movement as a whole adapted to the neoconservatives and even absorbed them, in the grand tradition of the "fusionism" that Frank Meyer and others had espoused in the 1960s as they confronted philosophical differences between conservatives and libertarians. Like metals that combine to forge a stronger alloy, the mixture of older conservatives who had supported Barry Goldwater and newer ones who were joining the Reagan bandwagon both broadened the movement and made it better able to govern in the 1980s and beyond.

Samuel Lipman was another neoconservative in Joyce's circle, and he was also an old friend of Hilton Kramer's, a distinguished art critic for the *New York Times* who wrote a front-page article on the NEA, the NEH, and Joyce shortly after Reagan's victory. Kramer and Lipman were frustrated with the Left's domination of the art world. "We thought it was ridiculous for conservatives to be so separated from the arts," said Kramer. They decided the time was right for a magazine that bridged the gap. It would be conservative in its politics and modernist in its aesthetics, taking its inspiration from T. S. Eliot's literary review *The Criterion,* which published four times a year in London between 1922 and 1939. Theirs would be called *The New Criterion.*

Lipman was a quintessential New York intellectual and he contributed mightily to *The New Criterion's* identity, but he was something else as well: a masterful organizer. He immediately began lining up support. Joyce was among his first contacts, as well as his most important one. In 1981, the John M. Olin Foundation approved a grant of $100,000 for the venture. With additional funding from Scaife and Smith Richardson, *The New Criterion* was born. The first issue appeared in September 1982.

While Lipman focused on dollars and cents, Kramer concentrated on writing and editing. The first issue included an editorial statement that made a case for *The New Criterion's* unique

perspective. Most criticism, said the magazine, "is either hope-
lessly ignorant, deliberately obscurantist, commercially compro-
mised, or politically motivated.... Almost everywhere [criticism
has] degenerated into one or another form of ideology or publicity or some pernicious combination of the two." This, in turn,
has coarsened "the way the arts and the humanities are now studied in our universities" and "it plays a role in the way government
agencies, private foundations, and corporate sponsors dispense
funds for cultural projects." *The New Criterion* declared its affinity for capitalism ("the greatest safeguard of democratic institutions and the best guarantee of intellectual and artistic freedom
... that the modern world has given us"), scoffed at the notion
of "the life of art in the United States as existing under some
kind of dire political threat from big business," and bristled at
suggestions that it was wrong "for corporate patrons of the arts
to evince the least curiosity about the social implications of the
artistic programs they are invited to sponsor."

This final point echoed Simon's critique of corporate philanthropy in *A Time for Truth*. Although Simon probably never
read an issue of *The New Criterion* from cover to cover, he was one
of the magazine's strongest supporters. He was especially
impressed with the boldness Kramer had demonstrated in aban-
doning the *New York Times*. Kramer had risen to the height of his
profession and enjoyed great prestige in the art world. And yet
he chose to give it up. The move baffled many of his friends and
did nothing to pacify his enemies. "The political passion behind
*The New Criterion*, at least in its first issues, seems mostly to be
resentment of intellectuals who think differently from Hilton
Kramer," sneered Alfred Kazin in the *New York Review of Books*.
"The 1960s may be over for most of its young people but they
are not over for Kramer, who views most of our cultural defects
as survivals of a defunct radicalism."

As the cultural establishment heaped scorn on *The New Criterion*, Simon found himself cheering for Kramer and Lipman.
He admired people who took chances, and he recognized that
Kramer especially was taking the chance of a lifetime. The bond
between Simon and Kramer helped *The New Criterion* flourish
under the foundation's steady support. It also did not hurt that

they were in regular contact—for about a year, *The New Criterion* shared office space with the foundation. "We couldn't afford our own quarters," said Kramer.

Unlike several other journals with close ties to the John M. Olin Foundation, *The New Criterion* never published a revelatory article that forever changed the ways Americans thought about a particular subject. Yet this is not to suggest that it failed, or that the foundation's total investment of $3 million was ill advised. Quite the contrary. *The New Criterion* created space for conservative writers to discuss topics that could not be crammed into news magazines and did not belong in publications devoted to policy minutiae. In doing so, it helped conservatives, sometimes blindly loyal to hidebound traditions, come to terms with twentieth-century modernism and at the same time develop a language for rejecting the extreme relativism of an academy saturated with postmodernism. It also provided established figures such as Kramer and Lipman with a meaningful forum and helped launch younger talents. Erich Eichman, who was *The New Criterion*'s managing editor in the 1980s, went on to an influential career as a books and arts editor at the *Wall Street Journal*. His successor, Roger Kimball, used the same job as a platform for his own writings, which made him one of the most important cultural critics on the Right. Among the many writers who benefited from *The New Criterion* was Heather Mac Donald, who began writing for it in 1992 and used its pages as a springboard for her widely recognized work in *City Journal*, a publication of the Manhattan Institute (which ultimately employed Mac Donald as a John M. Olin Fellow).

Publications such as *The New Criterion* were one of the John M. Olin Foundation's favorite ways to spend money. From a budgetary standpoint, they were never an enormous part of the grants program. Yet they were incredibly effective at spreading ideas and promoting talent. The foundation staff tended to favor them more than the board did. The trustees sometimes wondered how low-circulation magazines specializing in certain topics could have sweeping effects. In a 1990 memo to the board, the staff explained: "Journals are excellent vehicles for reaching opinion leaders and policymakers across the country at a relatively low cost. They provide a perspective on contemporary issues and events which is not reflected in the mainstream press. They are necessary forums of debate and discussion, and important training grounds for young writers and journalists." The memo also pointed out that these were the venues in which some of their top scholars published their best work and found audiences outside the academy.

One of the favorite forums for these scholars was *Commentary* magazine, started in 1945 and published monthly by the American Jewish Committee. Under the editorship of Norman Podhoretz, it became a leading voice of neoconservatism in the 1960s and 1970s. "The list of important conservative writers who have not appeared in *Commentary*'s pages would be very brief, while the list of compelling new writers or ideas brought to the world's attention by *Commentary* would be both long and impressive," said a staff evaluation toward the end of the foundation's life. For many years, the John M. Olin Foundation did not fund *Commentary* (though it did support many who wrote for it). Starting in 1990, however, it made annual grants whose total value eventually approached $1 million.

As *Commentary* flourished and *The New Criterion* was getting off the ground in the early 1980s, the John M. Olin Foundation continued to support its preferred groups, from the American Enterprise Institute and the Heritage Foundation in Washington to the Hoover Institution at Stanford University and Henry Manne's law and economics program at Emory University. A number of academics obtained assistance as well, including George Stigler, a University of Chicago professor who won the Nobel Prize for economics in 1982. Another favorite was Murray Weidenbaum, whose Center for the Study of American Business at Washington University in St. Louis examined the costs of government regulation, and who served as Reagan's first chairman of the Council of Economic Advisors. John M. Olin's name was attached to professorships at Carnegie-Mellon University, Fordham Law School, and the Colorado School of Mines as well as student and graduate fellowships at Harvard, Yale, UCLA, and New York University. Academic publications such as the University of Chicago's *Journal of Law and Economics* and George Mason

University's *Journal of Labor Research* received help. So did more popular magazines, such as *National Review* and *The American Spectator.*

Yet the foundation's overall giving actually declined during these years (when special grants for the John M. Olin Center for Law and Economics at Emory University are removed from the equation). In 1980, the foundation gave away $3.2 million. This figure slipped to $3 million in 1981 and fell to $2.6 million in 1982. After Olin's death, the board continued to meet, but discussions about investment strategy tended to dominate. With the exception of high-priority programs, the foundation made few grants until the spring of 1983. This was partly the result of holding applicants to stricter standards, which led to ending support of organizations that were judged to be ineffective. But the pause also arose from a determination to take stock and plot a future course.

Joyce spent the weeks following Olin's death writing a memo entitled, "Report to the Trustees on the Future Direction of the Grants Program." Numbering forty pages, it was a bit longer than Frank O'Connell's "Fat Memo" of seven years earlier, and so it came to be known informally as the "Fatter Memo." Joyce's collaborator in this project was James Piereson, who had joined the foundation as a program officer the previous year. Their document began by reaffirming Olin's desire "to support work intended to strengthen the American system of free institutions." At a time when the Ford Foundation and other organizations were drifting from their donors' principles, the Fatter Memo insisted that the John M. Olin Foundation remain true to its original mission. "This mandate has guided the Foundation to its present position, and it provides a sound basis for continued growth and improvement," wrote Joyce and Piereson.

At the same time, they suggested that the foundation do more than simply promote free enterprise as such. John M. Olin's philanthropy was devoted to "strengthening the work of political institutions, moral values, and philosophical principles" that make free enterprise possible in the first place. This was a subtle point, but also a significant one: It signaled the foundation's desire to place more emphasis on projects that fell outside the immediate sphere of economics. *The New Criterion* was an obvious example of this, and an indication that the foundation was moving in this direction before Joyce and Piereson put the notion to paper. The desire sprang in large part from one of the central insights of the neoconservatives: Left-wing attacks on free enterprise were not exclusively economic in origin. They were based as much on cultural and moral assumptions—a preference for community over individualism, harmony over competition, and equality of results over equality of opportunity. Thus, the "battle for men's minds" that Frank O'Connell had advocated in the Fat Memo would have to include a broad-based defense of all the cultural and moral girders that made a commercial civilization possible. It would be a gross exaggeration to call the Fatter Memo a neoconservative manifesto, yet it did reveal that the insights of Irving Kristol would inform the foundation's progress as the number and value of its grants increased.

The bulk of the Fatter Memo actually dealt with programmatic strategies—the nuts and bolts of effective philanthropy. Most of the key recommendations would animate the foundation's philanthropy for the rest of its existence. The first suggestion was one of the most important: favoring large grants over small ones. "Large grants to a few organizations appear to be a more effective use of the Foundation's resources than small grants to a large number of organizations," observed Joyce and Piereson, defining small grants as those worth less than $25,000. A foundation "with a clear sense of priorities," they wrote, was particularly well suited to this approach. And so they advised "that the foundation move away from small grants to a large extent, and focus its support on fewer projects of high quality, which requires substantial grants to maximize impact."

A second proposal addressed whether the foundation should underwrite general operations or specific projects. "General support grants give the recipient maximum flexibility in their use; project support gives the Foundation greater leverage over the way in which its funds are used," said the Fatter Memo. The lesson was obvious: Small grants of general support to large organizations would give the John M. Olin Foundation the least amount of leverage. "Small grants are the most effective when they are earmarked for projects, and the general support grants are most effective when they are large enough to make a real difference to the organization receiving them," argued the memo. It went on to recommend "that general support grants be limited to organizations whose institutional purposes match our own and which are of very high caliber; that smaller grants be earmarked for projects, and that small grants for general support be made infrequently and, if at all, only for special reasons."

Next, the Fatter Memo said the foundation should become more active in determining how its grants are used. "Currently the Foundation still tends to operate by sitting back and waiting for proposals to arrive, discussing and evaluating them, and then selecting the best ones as recipients of grants," it said. "Here the staff functions like a 'bank teller,' merely cashing checks or, perhaps, like a loan officer, saying 'yes' to the qualified and 'no' to the unqualified." The memo proposed a different model: "the 'venture capitalist,' who seeks new and more productive investments for his funds." Instead of supporting existing organizations that knocked on the door, the John M. Olin Foundation would be present at the creation of new entities. "Here the Foundation is in on the project from the start and can have a role in selecting the personnel, the location or the institutional affiliation, and the program of the new enterprise," wrote the authors. The foundation was already doing something like this with Henry Manne's law and economics program, of course, but Joyce and Piereson wanted to pursue this strategy more aggressively.

The central recommendation of the Fatter Memo may have been that the John M. Olin Foundation should not assume a "merely passive role" in the world of philanthropy—it should be "taking initiative" rather than "sitting back." Joyce and Piereson noted that the foundation's accomplishments were not limited strictly to grantmaking, because the staff gave personnel advice to the Reagan administration as well as nongovernmental organizations, wrote articles for influential publications, and appeared on television programs. The foundation also supported many of Simon's public endeavors.

ONE OF THESE SIMON-LED PROJECTS—and one of the foundation's most important activities during the 1980s—did not involve "sitting back" or even a substantial gift of money, but rather a contribution of ideas, personnel, and other resources to the Lay Commission on Catholic Social Teaching and the U.S. Economy. Chaired by Simon, this ad hoc group banded together in 1984 as America's Catholic bishops went about releasing a series of statements on political issues. Many Catholic conservatives were deeply frustrated with the bishops for a 1983 pastoral letter that had urged nuclear disarmament—and, in an obvious but unspoken subtext, opposed the military buildup and foreign policies of President Reagan during the Cold War. A letter from American bishops does not carry the same moral weight as a formal church teaching, but it is certainly significant in shaping opinions.

When Simon learned that the bishops were planning to issue a new pastoral letter addressing the U.S. economy, he decided not to let the bishops go unchallenged. Taking a cue from the Second Vatican Council, which had encouraged the laity to offer advice on matters in which they had special expertise, Simon contacted several friends and together they raised enough money to underwrite the establishment of the Lay Commission.

One of Simon's earliest phone calls went to a man who would make an intellectual donation rather than a financial one. Michael Novak was a prominent Catholic thinker and a prolific author who had begun his career on the Left. He had penned a regular column for *Commonweal,* railed against the Vietnam War, and written speeches for liberal Democratic presidential candidate George McGovern in 1972. In the mid-1970s, however, he began to drift rightward, joining the American Enterprise Institute in 1978 and publicly announcing his support for Reagan in 1980. It was the classic path of a neoconservative—a journey that outraged his old political allies and endeared him to his new ones.

During this conversion experience, Novak read Simon's book, *A Time for Truth.* "It was the first libertarian book that really sang for me," he said. "I didn't agree with everything in it, but

I liked it and sent Simon a fan letter saying so." Novak soon entered the orbit of the John M. Olin Foundation. At the behest of Kristol, he joined the board of the Institute for Educational Affairs, where he came into regular contact with Simon. (From 1985 to 2003, Novak received more than $1.3 million from the John M. Olin Foundation for research and administrative assistance.)

Novak had already exerted a positive influence on the bishops' pastoral letter about the nuclear arms race, according to many conservatives. He had obtained an early draft of what the bishops were writing and proposed several changes to it. He also went public with many of his criticisms: The April 1, 1983 issue of *National Review* was given over to a long Novak essay, "Moral Clarity in the Nuclear Age." When the bishops' letter at last appeared in final form, the Left claimed it as an important victory. But Novak insisted that for all its faults, it could have been much worse. "The last draft got off the nuclear freeze and individual weapon systems," said Novak. "It wound up being a setback for the peace movement, which had expected something else." The bishops, in his view, were swayable.

Yet debating the arms race was just a sidebar to Novak's main activity during the early 1980s, when he devoted most of his energy to formulating a theological defense of capitalism — a project that resulted in his 1982 book, *The Spirit of Democratic Capitalism*. So when Simon sought a vice chairman for the Lay Commission who understood both Catholicism and economics, Novak was an obvious and ideal candidate.

Simon and Novak expected the pastoral letter to be disappointing: The bishops had previously backed consumer boycotts over labor disputes and, refusing to learn the lessons of the Great Society, endorsed massive government spending on the poor. Simon and Novak decided to produce a document that emphasized economic growth over income redistribution as the best way to improve humanity's material condition. Their goal was not to debunk the bishops but to present an alternative to their ideas. "The commission will give lay Catholics who have a practical understanding of economic affairs an opportunity to contribute their hard-won experience and knowledge in applying religious values to the economic issues of our day," said Simon in May 1984, when he announced the Lay Commission's formation.

The commission itself consisted of more than two dozen members, including businessman J. Peter Grace, former secretary of state Alexander Haig, and writer and activist Clare Boothe Luce. Simon and Novak were not the group's only connection to the John M. Olin Foundation: current trustee George Gillespie and future trustee Peter Flanigan were also on the commission, and Michael Joyce served as Simon's personal assistant. The Lay Commission was formally housed within a small organization called the American Catholic Committee, a nonprofit group headed by commission member James J. McFadden that allowed the commission to receive tax-deductible contributions, including a $10,000 gift from the John M. Olin Foundation. Novak did most of the drafting in Washington and much of the commission's other work was conducted in New York.

The employees of the John M. Olin Foundation, in fact, essentially served as the Lay Commission's staff. On paper, everything was run from the office of the American Catholic Committee. In reality, much of the work was run from offices of the foundation. Between July and September, the commission sponsored six hearings featuring sixty-five people testifying or submitting written comments. The members of the commission also gathered privately several times to discuss Novak's progress.

The Lay Commission did not want to fight a rearguard action, merely responding to what the bishops were saying and doing. Instead, it aimed to produce a stand-alone document that would present a separate vision for Catholics in a capitalist society. It also hoped to influence the bishops' internal discussions. As both the bishops and the commission were drafting their documents that summer, a small delegation from the Lay Commission—consisting of Simon, Novak, Joyce, and Grace—flew out to Milwaukee for a face-to-face meeting with Archbishop Rembert Weakland, a prime mover behind the pastoral letter and one of the most liberal Catholic leaders in America. The conversation inevitably turned toward the content of the two documents, and Weakland brought up a matter that concerned him deeply: plant closings. "I listened patiently to their side," said Weakland to his

biographer, "and granted that I might be called a socialist for
what I was saying." Simon and Grace wanted Weakland to understand that capitalists did not enjoy shutting down factories or lay-
ing off workers, but sometimes they had no other choice. As it
happened, Joyce had picked up a local newspaper at the airport
that morning and read an article on the archbishop's plan to shut
down a parochial high school. He raised the issue by way of anal-
ogy. "The devil made me do it," said Joyce years later. "I think I
scored a debating point, even if I didn't make a friend."

The Lay Commission scored many more points in November, when it released its report to the public after the polls had
closed on Election Day and shortly before the bishops made the
first draft of their pastoral letter public. The report was called
"Toward the Future" and subtitled "A Lay Letter." At 106 pages
in its final form, the letter was a sophisticated commentary on
economic matters that combined a firm appreciation for free
enterprise with references to Biblical parables and papal encycli-
cals. Its fundamental point was that Catholic notions of justice
had already found fertile ground in the United States and its tradition of liberty. "Both Catholic social thought and American
institutions are directed against tyranny and poverty, the ancient
enemies of the human race," said the report. The U.S. economy,
it said, "has freed millions of families from poverty, given them
an unparalleled domain of free choice, taught them virtues of
cooperation and compassion, and unloosed upon this earth an
unprecedented surge of creativity, invention, and productivity."
Government may have the proper ends in mind, but that does
not mean it knows how to deliver. "A democratic capitalist regime
seeks to empower others, not to manage all things," said the commission. "We who are laypersons have learned through our own
experience, however, how precious are the liberties which encourage economic creativity, and how easy it is to stifle those liberties through neglect, indifference, excessive state entanglement,
imprudent regulation, a decline in capital formation, and the
unwise monetary, fiscal, and credit policies of government." The
report went on to defend entrepreneurship, the profit motive,
and multinational corporations, while also advocating a strong
role for labor unions in a free society.

*Former president Richard Nixon talks to William E. Simon as John Olin looks on at a 1981 dinner. In a toast, Nixon called Olin "one of the best and most loyal friends and one of the finest human beings that any of us could know."*

*Olin served as president of his foundation until 1977, when he asked William E. Simon to succeed him. Olin remained chairman of the foundation's board of trustees until his death in 1982.*

*William Simon had been secretary of the Treasury in the Nixon and Ford administrations. Hard charging and sometimes abrasive, he was also a bestselling author, successful investor, and president of the U.S. Olympic Committee.*

*Frank O'Connell was John Olin's personal attorney and the first executive director of the John M. Olin Foundation. O'Connell helped set the course of the foundation as an indispensable underwriter of conservative causes until his retirement in 1979. He is shown here in 1999.*

*James Piereson left a career in academia to join the John M. Olin Foundation as a program officer in 1981. He became executive director in 1985 and held that job under the foundation ceased operations two decades later.*

*Heritage Foundation president Ed Feulner greets John Olin in 1981. Olin was an early patron of Feulner's conservative think tank. The John M. Olin Foundation contributed nearly $10 million to Heritage between 1975 and 2005.*

*Michael Joyce (shown here in the center, to the right of Olin) was the John M Olin Foundation's executive director from 1979 to 1985. He guided the foundation through its most creative period and was a major force in neoconservatism later on as head of the Bradley Foundation.*

*John Olin was such a highly regarded outdoorsman that* Sports Illustrated *put him and his wife, Evelyn, on the cover of its November 17, 1958 issue.*

Even though the results from the presidential election were coming in almost simultaneously, the Lay Commission's report received prominent attention from journalists eagerly anticipating the first draft of the bishops' letter. The *New York Times* gave it especially good coverage, even printing excerpts from the document. The report's success on the public-relations front was due in no small part to its intellectual seriousness—there was no way anybody could ignore such a substantial statement of faith and principle. And the commission's statement was disseminated widely, with a copy mailed to every parish in the United States. When the bishops finally released the first version of their own letter, a few days after the Lay Commission had spoken, many of the news articles observed that the bishops did not represent the views of all Catholics.

The bishops' first draft confirmed all of the Lay Commission's fears. It labeled the federal welfare system "woefully inadequate," endorsed limits on personal income and family wealth, and called for an "experiment in economic democracy." Novak was quick to respond. "Taken together," he wrote in the *Washington Post*, these "unabashedly statist" positions "often read more like the platform of a political party than like a moral statement." Simon was equally critical in his memoir, *A Time for Reflection:* "The letter made a gargantuan leap and concluded that the American economic system is in direct conflict with morally responsible behavior—a conclusion that flies in the face of history and common sense," he wrote. "It escaped me how one can practice Christian compassion to the poor merely by submitting to the demands of Caesar's tax gatherers. . . . There is no fundamental conflict between the goals of the Church and the principles of a free and just economic system."

Journalists enjoy stories full of conflict and drama, and the Lay Commission's report probably had the effect of drawing more attention to the bishops' letter than the bishops would have received on their own. But the alternative was much less attractive: no special attention for the idea that Catholics can support capitalism without seeking absolution for their sins. And the Lay Commission may even have had an effect on the bishops' own deliberations, because there were important differences between what the draft letter said in the fall of 1984 and what the completed document stated two years later. The pastoral letter in its finished form, for example, did not include the phrase "economic democracy." The liberal Catholic commentator John C. Cort deemed this "a failure of nerve on the bishops' part"—and he blamed its elimination on Novak and the Lay Commission.

To be sure, the pastoral letter of 1986 was an expression of left-wing economic thinking. Even as many members of the Lay Commission considered it an improvement over the draft letter, none of them came close to embracing it. Indeed, the Lay Commission issued a new booklet, "Liberty and Justice for All," that criticized the bishops' document and its "serious intellectual defects." Simon continued to sound the themes that had motivated him to form the Lay Commission in the first place: "Private economic initiative, and not the state, is the source of wealth in our country," he told the *New York Times*. "In a world in which poverty is the rule and prosperity the exception, our bishops would do well to study the causes of prosperity." Ten years later, Joyce offered his own reflections on the pastoral letter and his profound disappointment with what the bishops had said. "Is it not the tragedy of our time that good and learned men sit in committee and produce a program that invokes precisely the misconception of a single institution, a central government, that can guarantee, as rights, the requisites of a meaningful human life?" he wrote. "This is the same all-powerful central government that has degraded life on earth throughout the twentieth century."

When Pope John Paul II issued his encyclical *Centessimus Annus* in 1991, many members of the Lay Commission regarded it as a powerful validation of their work. Although the Pope was hardly uncritical of capitalism, he also recognized how much economic good it could do—and seemed to prefer its substantial benefits to the obvious inadequacies of collectivism. There is no clear evidence suggesting that the Lay Commission's first report had any influence on the encyclical, but it may be worth noting that Archbishop Weakland seemed as displeased by it as the Lay Commission members were pleased.

The Lay Commission was by no means the John M. Olin Foundation's only foray into the subject of religion. In 1984, it began supporting the Center on Religion and Society, started by Richard John Neuhaus in Manhattan just as his seminal book *The Naked Public Square* was being published. Neuhaus was a Lutheran minister who had been an antiwar activist in the 1960s, but by the 1980s was a committed neoconservative who believed that faith deserved a central role in democratic life. "The naked public square is the result of political doctrine and practice that would exclude religion and religiously grounded values from the conduct of public business," wrote Neuhaus. "It is a perverse mindset that insists that the relationship between church and state must always be one of conflict and confrontation." The consequences of leaving the public square naked, he warned, are grave: "Where there are no transcendent sanctions, positive and negative, there is no final inhibition against evil."

The book became an enormous success, which Neuhaus attributed in part to the philanthropies that helped finance its marketing. Between 1983 and 1988, the John M. Olin Foundation provided the Center on Religion and Society with $350,000. Then Neuhaus became involved in an ugly break with his parent organization, the Illinois-based Rockford Institute. Neuhaus had complained about opinions expressed in *Chronicles,* the institute's monthly magazine and a bastion of paleoconservative thinking. Rockford and Neuhaus agreed to sever their ties, but wrestled over who would receive certain monies that already had been pledged. The dispute turned so bitter that several Rockford trustees physically evicted Neuhaus and his staff from their New York offices, and the incident became a legendary chapter in the annals of conservative infighting.

The John M. Olin Foundation continued to support Neuhaus at his new organization, the Institute on Religion and Public Life. The first in a series of annual grants began in 1989, and the foundation's total level of support eventually approached $2 million. During these years, Neuhaus converted to Catholicism, became a priest, and launched *First Things,* a monthly magazine on religion, politics, and culture that was to become his group's main activity. Its essays on everything from just-war theory to the threat of judicial activism received wide notice and praise. "*First Things* is simply the deepest, best written, and least compromising journal of religion in the entire English-speaking world and probably the best in any language," wrote Novak to the John M. Olin Foundation in 2004, after the foundation solicited his views. George Weigel, a biographer of Pope John Paul II who occupied the John M. Olin Chair in Religion and American Democracy at the Ethics and Public Policy Center, concurred: "As my own work and writing have become more 'globalized' in recent years, I've become ever more aware of the utter uniqueness of *First Things*—not just in the United States, but in the world. There simply is no other journal regularly addressing issues of the moral and cultural foundations of political and economic freedom in such depth."

MOST OF THE JOHN M. OLIN FOUNDATION's philanthropy was secular, of course. Yet its support of Novak, Neuhaus, Weigel, and others intersected with different elements of its grant program. As the Lay Commission and the bishops argued over society's obligation to the poor and the desirability of an expanded welfare state, for example, the John M. Olin Foundation was funding social-science research into these very subjects. One of its favorite think tanks was the Manhattan Institute, started in the late 1970s by British businessman Antony Fisher, an intellectual entrepreneur involved in founding think tanks in several countries, including the Institute for Economic Affairs in London and the Fraser Institute in Vancouver, British Columbia. His partner in the New York venture was future CIA chief William Casey. Initially, Ed Feulner had agreed to run the new think tank—then called the International Center for Economic Policy Studies—but the opportunity to become president of the Heritage Foundation presented itself and he decided to accept that job instead. So the Manhattan Institute slipped into the hands of William Hammett, a brilliant but mercurial libertarian who became a prominent impresario of ideas. One of the organization's early successes was George Gilder's book on supply-side economics, *Wealth and Poverty*. It became a bestseller in 1981 and was often described as a handbook of Reaganomics.

Yet the Manhattan Institute remained a humble operation. "The 'institute,' barely four years old, consisted of half a dozen souls crammed into an office dingier than a movie private eye's, seven flights up in a sorry, use-the-stairs, the-elevator's-broken building," said Tom Wolfe at a 25th anniversary dinner. Despite these humble conditions, the think tank would go on to have an impact on public policy, especially in New York City, where it became an important influence on Mayor Rudy Giuliani as he fought crime and welfare dependency. One of its most influential products was *City Journal,* a quarterly publication devoted to urban issues. The Manhattan Institute's goal of promoting free-market ideas was right in line with aims of the John M. Olin Foundation, which began supporting the organization in 1977. In all, the foundation's total support for the think tank amounted to more than $6.3 million.

The most significant single gift to the Manhattan Institute may have been a $25,000 award in support of a book on welfare policy by an obscure social scientist named Charles Murray, who wrote an article for *The Public Interest* that caught Hammett's eye. "It was a classic case of philanthropic entrepreneurship," said Murray, who did not imagine his article might become a book until he received an unexpected phone call from the Manhattan Institute's chief. Hammett proposed that Murray turn his article into something longer, Murray accepted, and the partnership resulted in a landmark book, *Losing Ground: American Social Policy, 1950–1980.* Murray was exactly the right author, coming to the project with a firm grasp of social science and a solid understanding of how welfare programs really operated. And the tone of *Losing Ground* was perfect: Rather than taking a perverse delight in the failure of government to alleviate the suffering of the poor, it approached the subject with heartfelt regret and unyielding resolve. "When [social policy] reforms finally do occur, they will happen not because stingy people have won, but because generous people have stopped kidding themselves," wrote Murray.

When the book came out in 1984, it immediately sparked a contentious debate on welfare reform. Liberals savaged it in editorials and columns. In a cover story, *The New Republic* asked: "Is Charles Murray a fraud?" The *New York Review of Books,* a bastion of left-wing commentary, printed a cartoon of Murray to make him look like a robber baron. For all their fulminations, however, the book's critics could not wish away its central insights. In a 10th anniversary edition of *Losing Ground,* Murray wrote a passage that was remarkable because it was true: "It is now accepted that the social programs of the 1960s broadly failed; that government is clumsy and ineffectual when it intervenes in local life; and the principles of personal responsibility, penalties for bad behavior, and rewards for good behavior have to be introduced into social policy."

The John M. Olin Foundation was not the book's only patron. The Smith Richardson Foundation also kicked in $25,000 to promote *Losing Ground* upon its publication. "The amounts of money were small, but they were critical to me," said Murray. They were also critical to the future of welfare. A dozen years after Murray proposed ending welfare, President Bill Clinton signed a law to do something very much like that. Although the Arkansas Democrat was no fan of Murray, he did acknowledge that Murray "did the country a great service."

SCHOOL CHOICE WAS ANOTHER AREA in which the foundation made an early investment and later witnessed a handsome payoff—perhaps not as concrete or conclusive as the welfare reforms of the 1990s, but clearly important and possibly in ways that may yet be realized. Milton Friedman originally brought school choice to the foundation's attention. In 1980, he urged it to support the Education Voucher Institute, a Michigan-based organization that was trying to promote market reforms in public education. At first, the John M. Olin Foundation was skeptical. The steering committee labeled school choice "controversial and untried" and chose not to make an award. Then Friedman pressed Bill Simon directly, and the foundation agreed to chip in $25,000, followed by another $25,000 in 1982. Still, the concept of vouchers often seemed more like a libertarian fantasy than a realistic reform.

As the decade advanced, however, the plight of the public schools worsened—and market solutions looked increasingly attractive. In 1989, the John M. Olin Foundation received a proposal from the Brookings Institution to support the work of two

Stanford University political scientists, John E. Chubb and Terry M. Moe. Although it had not previously given much support to the liberal think tank, the foundation sensed an opportunity. "When I saw Chubb's name on the proposal, I recognized him as a very good political scientist teaching at a top-level institution," said Piereson. Moreover, the proposal spoke of using markets to understand and improve education. For Piereson, it was an irresistible mix. "We were interested in getting these ideas ensconced at liberal places," he said. "A Brookings Institution publication carries weight with Democrats and moderates. It can't be written off as conservative propaganda." The John M. Olin Foundation donated $50,000 to the project.

The result was *Politics, Markets, and America's Schools*. Published by Brookings in 1990, it became one of the most influential books on elementary and secondary education ever written. Chubb and Moe's achievement was to turn an intellectually appealing theory into an argument backed by extensive empirical data showing that public schools, shackled by bureaucratic and political meddling, were incapable of performing as well as private ones. Using exhaustive data provided by the Department of Education, the authors concluded that the problems plaguing public education were so fundamental that solving them would require a totally new set of institutions that took advantage of free markets and parental choice. "Reformers believe the source of [educational] problems is to be found in and around the schools, and that schools can be 'made' better by relying on existing institutions to impose the proper reforms," wrote Chubb and Moe. "We believe existing institutions cannot solve the problem, because they *are* the problem—and that the key to better schools is institutional reform."

By "institutional reform," Chubb and Moe meant school choice. Their arguments were persuasive on their own terms, but *Politics, Markets, and America's Schools* mattered more than it might have otherwise because of the Brookings Institution's liberal credentials. In other words, it came from the sort of place that was not supposed to favor such a remedy. Yet Paul E. Peterson, who was then the director of research at Brookings, backed the project from the start. "I remember visiting the Olin

Foundation with a portfolio of our projects," he said. "When I began describing this one, their eyes just lit up." *Politics, Markets, and America's Schools* also benefited from appearing the same year that Wisconsin approved a groundbreaking school-choice program for students in Milwaukee, an event that focused national attention on a key reform. The addition of Peter Flanigan to the John M. Olin Foundation board of trustees in 1990 provided further incentive. The board's final new member, he was committed to the cause of school choice and encouraged the foundation to stay involved.

The John M. Olin Foundation's most important foray into school choice during the 1990s was its support of the Program on Education Policy and Governance, based at Harvard's Kennedy School of Government. Its director was Peterson, who had left Brookings, and its mission was to evaluate alternatives to the traditional forms of government-run education—and so it became active in providing sophisticated assessments of charter schools, private contracting, and school-choice programs in Milwaukee, Florida and elsewhere. Peterson's program held conferences, issued books, and published scores of research papers. It also helped develop a cadre of talented graduate students who were interested in studying and promoting fresh ideas about education reform. The John M. Olin Foundation supported it with a total of $2.6 million. Separately, the foundation gave $575,000 to *Education Next*, a quarterly journal edited by Peterson and published by the Hoover Institution.

IT IS SIMPLE FOR PHILANTHROPISTS to give away money, but challenging for them to give it away effectively—and that is especially true when a foundation has a mandate to spend its entire endowment within a single generation. "We are at a time when we'll be moving up from spending $3 million toward spending $10 million a year, and it is not easy if you want to do it well," said Joyce in a 1983 interview with the *New York Times*. In fact, the foundation needed four years from the time of Olin's death to reach that mark. In 1983, it distributed $4.9 million in grants— more than twice the amount from the previous year but still less than 7 percent of its total assets. The value of its grants rose to

$7.2 million in 1984 and $8.6 million in 1985. During this period, the foundation received a good return on its investments. Despite the steady increase in spending, the size of its endowment grew. At the end of 1982, the foundation's assets were worth more than $64 million. Three years later, they had grown to more than $90 million. Then, in 1986, the foundation gave away more than $10 million for the first time.

Three decades earlier, the Council on Foundations had been created to support philanthropists facing the challenges of growth and other dilemmas. It offered advice and assistance to member organizations on everything from assembling a board of directors to running an international grants program. Yet like so much in the foundation world, liberals controlled it and they influenced everything it did. The John M. Olin Foundation had belonged to the council for several years, and it was a bumpy relationship.

In 1980, Irving Kristol—then a director of the Olin-supported Institute for Educational Affairs and still a close advisor to Simon and Joyce—spoke at the council's annual gathering. His message was jarring. "I think the foundation world today is suffering from the sin of pride," he said. Kristol disputed the notion that nonprofit groups formed a "third sector" of American life distinct from government and business. "Foundations are creations of the private sector," he said. "You're not *above* the private sector, by God, you're *in* it." He was concerned that too many people in the foundation world had other ideas, and he saw the council's departure from New York in 1979 as a troubling development. "I really am a little sorry," he said, "that the Council on Foundations has decided to set up headquarters in Washington. I think that's the wrong signal to the foundation world. Foundations should not be an adjunct to government. Foundations should be an adjunct to their own, private sector." He went on to offer the example of Meals on Wheels, established by communities to provide food to the elderly and bedridden. "This was a marvelous program," said Kristol. Then Congress heard about it, passed legislation with too many regulations, and essentially took over and bureaucratized a charitable activity that the private sector was performing adequately and without producing better results. "There is clearly a tendency of government, in the name of the welfare state, to expand the conception of the welfare state so far as to be bureaucratically paternalistic," he said. "I think foundations should combat this tendency, not encourage it."

Simon agreed with these sentiments. "Just because foundations are encouraged by tax policy does not mean that they are public institutions," he said in a 1983 interview with *Foundation News*. "Private schools are encouraged by tax policy, and so are owner-occupied houses. So it doesn't make any sense to me to claim that foundations are public institutions."

Despite this difference in philosophy, the John M. Olin Foundation wanted to have a seat at the council's table. Joyce became involved in various committees and the foundation participated in council events. Yet it quickly became a case of familiarity breeding contempt. Simon himself railed at the agenda for the council's 1983 conference. "There were many programs that were organized to attack the institutions of our society; that were simply pleas to the faithful to confirm their prejudices," he said. "Conference literature for the panel on 'Nuclear Disarmament: The Grassroots Movement of the 1980s' said the panel would look at 'what's been accomplished and what's been left on the agenda'; not exactly an objective appraisal of the pros and cons of disarmament."

The John M. Olin Foundation might have tolerated the Council on Foundations if it merely displayed a liberal bias in its conference programming. Yet the council had other ambitions. In 1980, its board of directors approved an eleven-point statement on "Recommended Principles and Practices for Effective Grantmaking." Two years later, it voted to require that all of the council's members sign it.

Much of the document was innocuous, with its humdrum advice to obey tax rules and publish annual reports. Yet the guidelines also said that foundations should "serve the needs and interests of the public." Moreover, they said, "it is important that grantmakers be alert and responsive to changing conditions in society and to the changing needs and merits of particular grantseeking organizations." The statement went on to encourage a "diversified staff and board members." The diversity it endorsed, however, was not a diversity of professional experience or expertise so much as a form of affirmative action. "In view of the historic under representation of minorities and women in supervisory and policy positions," said the council, "particular attention should be given to finding ways to draw them into the decision-making processes."

The board of the John M. Olin Foundation balked at submitting itself to the Council on Foundations or any other external authority. "We believe it is improper to require subscription to any set of principles and practices, for to do so is to require trustees to cede judgment and to relinquish in part their responsibilities, especially to the donor, with whose wishes such principles and practices might sometimes conflict," wrote Joyce in a letter to council president James A. Joseph in 1984. "Such an obligation threatens to rob the foundation community of its traditional independence and diversity, on which the vitality of the philanthropic community depends."

Joyce's objections were not merely theoretical but also substantive. "We believe the Recommended Principles and Practices are informed by a philosophy which cannot be implemented and which, if it were ever widely accepted, would undermine foundations' very reasons to exist." He laid out the John M. Olin Foundation's concerns in some detail, and they are worth reading at length because they express a certain vision of philanthropy:

> The document treats "the public" as a single body composed, to be sure, of various constituencies, and it strongly implies that each individual foundation should be responsive to this public and its constituent elements. In other words, each foundation is treated as analogous to the state itself, responsive to the public, and representative of its various constituent groups. On this reading, each foundation should constitute itself so that it can respond quickly to the changing needs and requirements of the entire society.
>
> This is a seriously mistaken understanding of the responsibility of foundations to the public and of their relationship to the state. Foundations are private, not public, institutions. They cannot function like governments. The responsibility of meeting the public interest is in the

hands of government, not private foundations. Government has provided the tax exemption for charitable institutions in the belief that charitable activities can be better carried out by private organizations than
by government itself. The government recognized, when it took this step,
that there are many different kinds of charitable activities that may be
carried out by many different kinds of organizations. The public interest is served not by each individual organization, but by the diversity of
organizations and purposes that come into being as a result of the general encouragement provided by the tax exemption.

We believe it is wrong, then, to assert, as this document does, that
each individual foundation must serve the general public or the public
interest. Such a responsibility is not implied by the tax laws, nor in any
event could it be carried out in a manner that would preserve foundations in their present form. The responsibility of foundations to the law
is specific; the purposes they may serve consistent with the law are broad
and elastic. To assert that each foundation must serve the public interest is to invite someone to define that public interest, and then to force
every foundation into that defined role. More importantly, the claim
deprives foundations of their legitimate reasons for existence: If, like
government, they must serve the public interest, there is no reason why
their funds should not be disbursed by government itself, which is well
set up to discharge the public interest.

Joyce concluded his letter by saying that the John M. Olin Foundation would not be renewing its membership. It never rejoined.

Yet the foundation was, of course, deeply interested in the
business of philanthropy and eager to associate with groups that
shared its values. In the 1970s, staff members participated in the
Grantmakers Roundtable, an informal gathering led by Leslie
Lenkowsky of Smith Richardson. When Lenkowsky joined the
Institute for Educational Affairs in 1985, he revived the group,
and by 1991 it had become an independent organization called
the Philanthropy Roundtable. It aimed through a program of
conferences and publications to encourage philanthropists to
advance freedom, opportunity, and personal responsibility in
their giving. A chief goal was to enlist newly created foundations
in this mission, and the group experienced steady growth—boasting more than five hundred affiliates in 2005. "The Philanthropy
Roundtable is an extremely important organization in the enterprise of philanthropy," said an evaluation prepared for the John

M. Olin Foundation board. "The Roundtable has become a potent alternative to the Council on Foundations, which is steeped in the thinking of the liberal establishment." Over the years, the John M. Olin Foundation supported it with grants worth nearly $1 million, and members of the staff were heavily involved in its activities from the start.

One of them was Mike Joyce, except that his own connection to the Philanthropy Roundtable, including service as the chairman of its board, came after he had left the John M. Olin Foundation for another job. In 1985, Rockwell International purchased the Allen-Bradley Company, based in Milwaukee, for $1.65 billion. As a result of the transaction, the Lynde and Harry Bradley Foundation, established more than forty years earlier, saw its assets jump from less than $14 million to more than $290 million almost in an instant. "The Foundation had operated for years without a paid staff, without an office of its own, and with administrative expenses in the range of $1,500 a year," wrote John Gurda in *The Bradley Legacy*. "Now it found itself among the 20 largest foundations in the country."

That meant the Bradley Foundation would have to reinvent itself. Much of its giving had focused on activities in Wisconsin and more particularly in Milwaukee. After the Rockwell sale, the board of directors promised that this tradition would continue, but they also intended to participate in public policy and the world of ideas. "The principles Harry believed in gave us the strongest economy, the highest living standard, and the greatest individual freedom in the world. We felt it was our task to do everything we could to preserve those principles," said Italo Andrew "Tiny" Rader, an Allen-Bradley executive who served as the foundation's chairman of the board. W. H. "Bill" Brady, the board's vice chairman and other leading figure, agreed. As Brady told John Gurda, "It is not government, it is not dictators or presidents or generals or popes who rule the world. It's ideas."

Rader and Brady knew they would have to hire a creative and energetic leader to head the foundation, and so they went to the one place where they knew they could find one: the John M. Olin Foundation. "I had never heard of Allen-Bradley before," said Joyce. "At first I thought they meant Milton Bradley, the toy company." That confusion was soon cleared up, as Rader and Brady made clear the direction in which they hoped to take their reborn foundation. "We've got money, and we want to do what you did at Olin," Rader told Joyce. "We want to become Olin West."

After working at the John M. Olin Foundation for six years, Joyce resigned and moved to Wisconsin. One of the foundation's program officers, Hillel Fradkin, went with him. For more than fifteen years, Joyce led the Bradley Foundation as its president, taking many of the ideas and principles he developed in New York and applying them in Milwaukee with Bradley's substantial resources. He was a major force in the school-choice movement, as well as a pioneer in welfare reform, faith-based initiatives, and the development of "compassionate conservatism."

Joyce retired from Bradley in 2001, and although he probably will be most remembered for this service in Milwaukee, his legacy at the John M. Olin Foundation is perhaps no less important. From 1979 to 1985, he was its top intellectual strategist. He played a critical role in broadening the foundation's mandate, elevating its aspirations, and improving its understanding of how ideas shape public policy. As a manager, he established internal procedures for dealing with grant proposals and board meetings that would remain in place through the remaining years of the foundation's lifespan. Michael Joyce may not have been as well known as Bill Simon or Irving Kristol, but he was without a doubt one of the most important conservatives in philanthropy as well as one of the most important conservatives in the United States.

CHAPTER SEVEN

# AMERICAN MINDS

THE QUESTION OF WHO WOULD SUCCEED Mike Joyce as executive director of the John M. Olin Foundation was really never much of a question at all. Yet the board appointed a three-member panel to review the matter and make a suggestion. It consisted of Joyce, Irving Kristol, and Ed Feulner. "We met over lunch in New York and we didn't have much to discuss," said Feulner. "The choice was obvious." They submitted their recommendation to the board, which affirmed it at a meeting on November 1, 1985. James Piereson would take over.

Four years earlier, Piereson had been an assistant professor of political science at the University of Pennsylvania, and he was thinking about quitting the academy. Born on October 4, 1946, in Grand Rapids, Michigan, Piereson grew up there and in the nearby town of Rockford. He attended Michigan State University on an Evans Scholarship, a program created by golf champion Chick Evans to assist former golf caddies like Piereson, and remained in East Lansing for his doctorate. Jobs at Iowa State and Indiana followed, and then he arrived at Penn in the fall of 1976. "Jim had a genuine interest in students, and a genuine ability to teach," said Frank Luntz, a Piereson student, who went on to become one of the country's best-known political pollsters. "He was the first professor who treated me like a peer. And in the classroom, he never revealed his political leanings."

Yet Piereson did have political leanings, and he enjoyed talking about politics with one of his colleagues, William Kristol, the son of Irving. Their offices were next door to each other. They became fast friends, taking meals together several times a week and attending basketball games. They often discussed the plight they shared as untenured members of the faculty. "We assistant professors were a persecuted and pathetic lot," said Kristol. By the early 1980s, it was becoming apparent to Piereson that he was no shoe-in for a tenured position. Another friend of his, Mark Blitz, had been turned down. "The senior professors were split into factions," said Piereson. "Only candidates from the outside, who had no factional affiliation, could get hired into tenured jobs. And I certainly wasn't eager to go through some horrible battle, getting shot at from all sides, in a process that's basically secret."

Moreover, Piereson was losing his interest in academic life. Like others in his generation, he responded to the excesses of campus radicalism by moving to the right, and by the late 1970s he regarded himself as a neoconservative. Kristol and Blitz introduced him to Leo Strauss and Straussian thought. Piereson went on to read books and articles by Martin Diamond, Harry Jaffa, and Harvey Mansfield. He began to read *The American Spectator* and *The Public Interest*. Then he started writing for both of them. He also became familiar with the Intercollegiate Studies Institute and wrote an article for one of its publications, *The Political Science Reviewer*. "The university was not a hospitable place for someone with my views," he said. "The 'diversity police' were taking over, and they believed the university as an institution should represent the views of favored groups—and in particular the constituent groups of the Democratic Party—rather than be a place that encouraged deeper thought." Moreover, Piereson was increasingly disenchanted with the prospect of a career devoted to the quantitative analysis that was coming to dominate his field. "As a consequence, I began to lose interest in disciplinary research that did not address the broader challenges facing the university and the nation," he said.

When Bill Kristol heard that Joyce was looking to hire somebody to assist him at the John M. Olin Foundation, he immediately recommended his friend. Piereson traveled to New York and met with Joyce several times in the spring of 1981. "I was impressed by what they were trying to do, but it was a totally foreign world to me," said Piereson. Joyce persuaded him to take a chance. Piereson took a leave of absence from Penn and joined the foundation staff that fall. He never looked back.

As Joyce's understudy for four years, Piereson learned a great deal about philanthropy in general and the John M. Olin Foundation in particular. One of the most valuable lessons involved dealing with Bill Simon, whose fiery temperament could make him a difficult boss. It took a special kind of person to work with Simon, and an ability to work with Simon was in some ways the most important job qualification for anyone who served as the foundation's executive director. The relationship between Simon and Joyce had been successful, and it probably would have continued but for the Bradley Foundation's offering Joyce a remarkable opportunity to build a mighty philanthropic institution almost from scratch. Yet the two men occasionally clashed, and these clashes were a source of much frustration to Joyce. He would have been drawn to the job in Milwaukee under virtually any set of circumstances, but he also knew that in departing the John M. Olin Foundation, he was leaving behind Simon's volatility—and this was a relief.

If getting along with Simon was a prerequisite for working as the foundation's day-to-day manager, then Piereson was supremely qualified to become Joyce's successor. It would be inaccurate to say that Simon never raised his voice at Piereson—everybody who came into regular contact with Simon heard him holler. Yet Piereson navigated the shoals of Simon's temper with unusual skill. "Jim has a totally secure ego," said Kim Dennis, who worked at the foundation in the 1980s. "He has no trouble letting others take credit for things." This was a perfect formula for not just getting along with the chairman, but thriving alongside him.

Equally important was Piereson's personal knowledge of higher education, which was becoming a central focus of the foundation. Joyce was comfortable in the world of ideas, but he was a natural intellectual rather than a trained one. Piereson, by contrast, had attended graduate school, earned his Ph.D., and worked as a professor at three universities. This experience helped him develop an intuitive understanding of how the academy worked, from what motivated faculty hiring decisions to how professors succeeded in their fields. One of the main reasons Joyce had hired Piereson, in fact, was to take advantage of these insights.

Piereson would lead the foundation for the next two decades, joining its board of trustees in 1987. Along the way, he was aided by a group of key staffers. The first among several equals was probably Caroline McMullen Hemphill, who worked for Bill Simon as a secretary before shifting over to the foundation in 1979, handling programs as well as Simon's correspondence. A quick learner, she became increasingly involved in the foundation's grantmaking, especially in law and economics. Hemphill left for other jobs twice, but she returned for good in 1988 and served as Piereson's right hand—or, as Piereson once joked, the person "who quietly ran the foundation for all these years."

Another top staffer was Janice Bergmann Riddell, whom Joyce had hired at the Goldseker Foundation in Baltimore and then brought to New York. She married in 1981 and moved to Canada, where she pursued graduate studies under Clifford Orwin and Thomas Pangle at the University of Toronto. Her departure opened the position that Piereson filled. When Riddell moved back to New York several years later, Piereson welcomed her back to the foundation. She remained there until 2003, handling many of its projects involving elementary and secondary education. Kim Ohnemus Dennis started out as a receptionist, but her talents were obvious and she worked her way into a job as a program officer. Her libertarian leanings drew her toward much of the foundation's grantmaking in economics. In 1988, she left the John M. Olin Foundation, eventually becoming executive director of the Philanthropy Roundtable and later of the D&D Foundation. Her replacement, William Voegeli, was a Chicago native with a Ph.D. from Loyola and a strong interest in American politics. He handled many of the programs in books and higher education. Other important figures at the foundation included Bill Simon's close aide Mary Pat

McSherry Fortier, as well as Glenn Ellmers, Kelly McCarthy, Mary Schwarz, Betty Sturdy, Carmela Tolento, Damon Vangelis, Jill Viola, and Peter Welsh.

If these staffers shared a single trait, from Piereson on down, it was their ability to function as generalists. Although the John M. Olin Foundation hewed to a set of core principles, it also tried to apply them to a broad group of fields. A program officer would have to possess a basic understanding of how ideas influence culture and policy, plus specific knowledge of figures and institutions associated with everything from the law and economics movement to *The New Criterion*. It was an ideal job for curious and wide-ranging minds that combined the intellectual skills of scholars with the passionate commitments of activists. Notably, the program officers maintained close ties to the foundation and routinely stayed in their jobs for extended stretches. "They were all happy to go about their work and let the grant recipients take the credit for their accomplishments," said Piereson.

When Piereson took over from Joyce, he was well positioned to preserve the emphasis on higher education, which John M. Olin himself had made a dominant feature of his giving and which, after the 1960s, involved saving the universities rather than merely supporting them. Although the reformed hippie would become something of a cliché in American culture—idealistic radicals who went on to become conventional yuppies—many student protestors never did reform. They never even left school. Instead, they stayed on as graduate students, earned their Ph.D.s, and assumed positions inside the academy. On their long march to tenure, they developed a left-wing interpretation of Western history. Rather than seeing a story of freedom and prosperity, they invented a narrative of exploitation and injustice. The story of "a nation of immigrants" was supplanted by the story of "a nation of victims." During the 1970s and 1980s, as Piereson was earning his doctorate and taking over at the foundation, their ideas began to alter traditional curricula. The leading lights of Western civilization were summarily dismissed as "dead white males" and increasingly replaced by marginal figures who were said to represent the interests and perspectives of the oppressed masses. As the Stanford faculty debated eliminating a required course for freshmen on Western culture— a step it ultimately took—Jesse Jackson led a group in chanting a phrase that captured the prevailing spirit: "Hey, hey, ho, ho, Western culture's got to go!" Those who opposed these changes often faced cruel charges of racism, sexism, and homophobia. By 1990, even the *New York Times* was forced to recognize the "political correctness" phenomenon: "There is a large body of belief in academia and elsewhere that a cluster of opinions about race, ecology, feminism, culture, and foreign policy defines a kind of 'correct' attitude toward the problems of the world, a sort of unofficial ideology of the university."

Bill Simon had a favorite way of describing the transformation of American universities: "The inmates have taken over the institution." One of the ways he and the John M. Olin Foundation tried to wage a counteroffensive was through the Institute for Educational Affairs, where Philip N. Marcus had succeeded Mike Joyce as director. Although the IEA never achieved its main goal of encouraging corporations to practice better philanthropy, it did help provide the seed money for the Federalist Society in 1982. Another success was starting the Collegiate Network, a consortium of conservative and libertarian student newspapers on America's college and university campuses, which ultimately would become one of the John M. Olin Foundation's most important projects. Piereson said as much at the network's 25th anniversary dinner in 2004: "If everything we have done since 1979 was stripped away, leaving only the Collegiate Network as our legacy, we would still proudly say that our work yielded enormous success."

As long as there have been conservative students, of course, there have been conservative student publications. Yet few of them made much of an impact in the 1960s and 1970s, with one spectacular exception: *The Alternative.* Its editor, R. Emmett Tyrrell Jr., had come to Indiana University for the swim team, graduated in 1965, and remained in the area to begin publishing what he called "an unofficial anti–New Left magazine." It was a fast success, first as a campus magazine serving students in Bloomington, then as a regional publication distributed throughout the Midwest, and finally as a national soap box for Tyrrell and his circle of young writers, many of them students at Berkeley, Chicago, and Harvard. Money was always tight, but *The Alternative* became popular on the political Right and survived on donations from the Lilly pharmaceutical fortune as well as Richard Mellon Scaife. Piereson was an assistant professor at Indiana University in those days and beginning his conversion to conservatism. "He came out to the dilapidated farmhouse where we published," said Tyrrell. "He was always an independent-minded guy, always friendly and interested in ideas. But he wasn't really a part of our crowd."

That would change in the years ahead, as *The Alternative* grew more prominent and Piereson eventually came to write for it. By the middle 1970s, Tyrrell's magazine was becoming a favorite of neoconservatives. Contributors included Elliott Abrams, Harvey Mansfield, Michael Novak, and James Q. Wilson. Some of columnist George F. Will's early writings appeared on its pages as well. In 1974, Tyrrell became convinced that the magazine's name smacked of the 1960s liberalism he was fighting, and so he changed it to *The American Spectator*. The John M. Olin Foundation's support of the magazine began around this time—a $10,000 grant in 1975, with gifts following on a more or less annual basis for the next two decades. In 1985, Tyrrell moved operations to Arlington, Virginia, where the *Spectator* continued to publish through cycles of boom and bust. Simon eventually became a member of the board. "He was one of our strongest supporters," said Tyrrell. "He stuck with us through some of our most challenging periods." In total, the John M. Olin Foundation gave the *Spectator* nearly two dozen grants worth $760,000.

Despite the conspicuous success of *The American Spectator*, conservative student publications were a rarity in the 1970s. But at the dawn of the Reagan era, new opportunities began to present themselves. Once again, the story starts at the University of Chicago.

In the fall of 1978, a Chicago freshman joined the school paper and started writing movie reviews. But John Podhoretz did not last long at the *Chicago Maroon* because his film critiques failed to contain the proper kind of political content. "The second or third piece I wrote was on *The Deer Hunter* and I said the movie was not anti-Vietnam," said Podhoretz. "When the editor spiked it, I knew it would be impossible for me to continue writing there." Soon after, Podhoretz complained about the situation to Tod Lindberg, another freshman, who lived across the dormitory hallway. Lindberg described how he and some friends had started a literary magazine in high school. This became their inspiration. "We priced it out and sold some ads to raise money," said Podhoretz. The first issue came out in the spring of 1979. It was called *Midway*—a dual reference to a commons area on campus and to what Lindberg and Podhoretz regarded as the publication's middle-of-the-road politics. The lead article was an interview with the novelist Saul Bellow, who was teaching at Chicago at the time.

Podhoretz sent a copy of *Midway* to Irving Kristol, whom he knew from childhood. Podhoretz's father, Norman, was the editor of *Commentary* magazine, a flagship publication for neoconservatives like Kristol. "Irving and I weren't intimates, but we had met before," said Podhoretz. At the time, Kristol was becoming deeply involved with the John M. Olin Foundation and the Institute for Educational Affairs. He called Podhoretz and said he was impressed by *Midway*. He also offered a grant to support the publication. "I told him we didn't need the money," said Podhoretz. "We were self-supporting."

But then the support dried up. The problem was an article appearing in an issue the following school year, after Lindberg and Podhoretz had changed *Midway*'s name to *Counterpoint*. As fate would have it, a movie review sparked a controversy. The author was not Podhoretz but Roger Kaplan, a Chicago alumnus who was beginning to contribute to *The American Spectator* and *Commentary*. The film was *Cruising*, which starred Al Pacino as an undercover detective seeking to stop a serial killer who picked up his victims in gay bars. When the movie came out, gay activists strongly criticized its depiction of homosexuality and encouraged people to boycott it. Energized by the hullabaloo, a gay-rights group in Illinois objected to Kaplan's review—and contacted the businesses whose ads appeared in *Counterpoint*. "They all quit," said Podhoretz. "So I called Irving."

In March, Lindberg and Podhoretz formally requested a grant of $5,000 from the Institute for Educational Affairs. On March 28, 1980, the IEA board approved the grant. "Your magazine is lifting a lot of spirits in Hyde Park, I gather, and we look forward to its continued success," wrote Philip Marcus to Podhoretz. The funds were paid to *Counterpoint* through the campus administration. "At a University replete with 'little magazines' that live short and unhappy lives, *Counterpoint,* from the first issue, has had a quality and a vigor that augured well," wrote dean of students Charles D. O'Connell Jr. in a note to IEA. "The editors have great talent, but to their talent they added a willingness to work hard at the more mundane aspects of publishing—advertising, careful editing, and publicity." O'Connell applauded the institute's efforts to keep *Counterpoint* afloat.

Yet *Counterpoint* continued to face hostility on campus. Copies of the October 1980 issue vanished. "We discovered, a few hours after we distributed the magazine, that there were few left," wrote Podhoretz in a memo to the IEA. "We tempered our joy long enough to discover that the magazine had been placed in garbage cans all over campus." The staff managed to salvage many of the issues, but the experience was enormously frustrating. Podhoretz puzzled over the problem. Why would anybody want to destroy a magazine? Despite the flap over Kaplan's article, *Counterpoint* did not go out of its way to be controversial. "We wanted an intellectual magazine, like *Commentary* or *Harper's,*" said Podhoretz. One typical issue printed a speech by physicist I. I. Rabi and carried articles on Henry Kissinger, F. R. Leavis, and Dmitri Shostakovich.

Besides generating the money necessary for publication in the first place, the destruction of issues would become the most serious problem that the rising generation of conservative publications faced. IEA continued to alleviate *Counterpoint's* financial pressures, with a grant of $5,000 in 1981 and another for $3,000 the next year. But there was little anyone could do to prevent left-wing students from stealing issues that were free-dropped around campus.

The investments in *Counterpoint* were worthwhile if only for giving IEA an important idea: the notion that it might fund right-leaning student publications on campuses all around the country and provide a counterbalance to the mainstream student publications that were infected with the same left-wing extremism that was taking over the faculties. Within a couple of years, IEA was giving small grants to magazines and newspapers at schools such as Harvard, Northwestern, Princeton, and Yale. "I view this whole business as a war of ideas," Simon told *Time* magazine, which was one of many national publications that wrote stories on a new generation of "conservative rebels" who led a movement that was "just as embattled and indignant as its liberal forebears who condemned the war in Vietnam."

These IEA-supported publications came to be known as the Collegiate Network, and the John M. Olin Foundation helped create them and supported them over the years with more than $2 million. Having these monies pass through IEA (and different groups later on) made sense for the foundation, which lacked the manpower to handle scores of small grants to a large number of constantly evolving publications. There was also the problem of tax exemptions. Some of the CN newspapers were registered with the Internal Revenue Service as nonprofit organizations, but those without this status—typical among fledgling publications put out by amateurs in their dorm rooms—were not eligible to receive the foundation's funding.

For better or worse, the Collegiate Network came to be defined in the 1980s largely by the experience of one member in particular: the *Dartmouth Review*, at Dartmouth College in New Hampshire. No other student publication received more support from IEA—and none went on to achieve the same level of notoriety. Indeed, the *Dartmouth Review* probably became the most famous student publication in the country. The newspaper got its start in 1980, when Gregory Fossedal resigned from the college's daily newspaper and organized several of his conservative friends. They wanted to start a publication that would reflect their own views, and they decided to name it after William F. Buckley Jr.'s *National Review*. "I look at us as being the first real example of *God and Man at Yale* in practice," said Fossedal, referring to the book that had sparked Buckley's career as a public intellectual. The *Dartmouth Review*'s connection to *National Review* was more than merely inspirational: One of its faculty advisors was Jeffrey Hart, an English professor who was also a senior editor for *National Review*.

The *Dartmouth Review* dared to broach subjects that others ignored or were too frightened to address, such as the school's decision to change the name of its sports teams from "Indians" to "the Big Green"—a move opposed by many alumni but also felt necessary by liberal administrators. Other articles expounded conservative ideas more generally. In 1981, the *New York Times* said that the *Dartmouth Review* "has become must reading on campus." But it was also becoming fiercely controversial. The newspaper was a frequent target of vandalism, from stolen issues to office windows that were never completely safe from flying bricks. On one occasion, a delivery truck's tires were slashed. In another instance, an official with the college alumni fund physically assaulted a *Review* staffer.

The *Review*'s worst offense was an aggressive conservatism that challenged the Left's dominance on campus. To be sure, there were times when its sophomoric humor tested the bounds of decency: One article intending to satirize racial preferences was written in a style meant to approximate black dialect—but it was illiterate and vulgar, and many saw it as deliberate denigration. The reaction on campus was one of overwrought outrage, as the student council condemned the *Review* for racism and sexism and the faculty voted to censure it. Every year or two, it seemed, the antics of the *Dartmouth Review* made national news.

From time to time, the John M. Olin Foundation assisted the *Review* directly with small grants, and it helped in other ways as well. After a 1990 incident in which saboteurs inserted a statement from *Mein Kampf* into the pages of the *Review* shortly before it went to press, Simon rose to the defense of its young editors and writers with a column in the *New York Times*. He condemned Dartmouth's president, James O. Freedman, for trying to shut down the publication. "The issue is not whether we agree with all of the *Review*'s content. I certainly don't," he wrote. "But the administration should not be allowed to silence Dartmouth's only independent source of news and of dissent." In words that could have applied to just about any paper in the Collegiate

Network, Simon praised the *Review* for its efforts "to question, challenge, and even deride the dominant liberal orthodoxy on campus."

The *Dartmouth Review* helped inspire other young journalists on other campuses. In 1982, IEA sponsored its first national conference of student editors and writers. By 1983, it was giving away $180,000 to some thirty publications. Many of these did not survive for long. High rates of failure are almost inevitable, given that the students who volunteer to produce them still have to deal with all the normal stresses of college life, to say nothing of the unique pressures of printing material that consciously challenges reigning orthodoxies on campus. There were also endless transition problems, with students coming and going. (*Counterpoint* was typical in this respect: It folded within a couple of years of Lindberg and Podhoretz's graduation.)

For every step backward, however, the Collegiate Network seemed to take two steps forward: The movement of conservative student journalists did nothing but grow. By the end of the 1980s, the CN boasted papers on fifty-one campuses. "Over one thousand students now publish, edit, or write for the papers and magazines in the Network and over 500,000 read them," said a CN report on the 1989–90 school year. As the campus wars over political correctness intensified, CN staffers boasted of increased mainstream acceptance: "Instead of being treated in the press as right-wing intruders, foisted on American campuses by a cabal of rich businessmen and narrow-minded politicians, the papers are now portrayed as presenting a legitimate—if still controversial—viewpoint on important issues in higher education."

The Institute for Educational Affairs always intended to help the CN papers get on their feet and then pay their own way through advertising and subscriptions. But this hope proved illusory, as publications struggled with staff turnover and ad boycotts. Only the *Dartmouth Review* and the *Stanford Review* were able to support themselves for long spans of time, largely because of alumni who mobilized on their behalf following nationally publicized controversies.

Another unrealized goal of the Collegiate Network was to create papers that would function as gateways to the mainstream media. Its founders had hoped that a set of alternative publications would give conservative students the journalism experience they needed to gain jobs at the country's most influential newspapers and on the television networks. Although there were several cases of this actually happening—Jonathan Karl of the *Vassar Spectator*, for example, worked as a correspondent for CNN and ABC News—it certainly did not become a trend. One problem was that elite news organizations refused to hire conservatives, no matter what their potential. Top graduates of the program were more likely to find homes on conservative editorial pages or at explicitly conservative publications. Lindberg, for instance, served as editorial-page editor of the *Washington Times* and then as editor of *Policy Review*. Podhoretz worked at the *Weekly Standard* as well as on the editorial page of the *New York Post*. Richard Lowry of the *Virginia Advocate* joined the staff of *National Review* and eventually became its editor. Ramesh Ponnuru, also of *National Review*, cut his teeth at the *Princeton Sentinel*. Laura Ingraham of the *Dartmouth Review* became a popular political commentator with her own radio show. Ann Coulter of the *Cornell Review* became a bestselling author and columnist, as did Michelle Malkin of the *Oberlin Forum*. The *Yale Political Monthly* produced writers Maggie Gallagher and Fareed Zakaria.

Yet many of the students who joined CN papers had little interest in media careers. The publications attracted them as undergraduates in large part because conservative ideas interested them and the papers served as mechanisms for meeting like-minded students. In this sense, they were like social clubs or fraternities. As a result, the CN became a talent pool for the entire conservative movement. Graduates took jobs at think tanks, on Capitol Hill, and in the White House. A few even went on to graduate school and became professors.

FOR ALL ITS INTEREST IN THE COLLEGIATE NETWORK, the John M. Olin Foundation believed that student newspapers represented only a single front in the war over higher education. As its experience with the law and economics movement shows, the foundation was especially committed to working with an existing generation of responsible scholars. It wished to extend their influence both within the ivory towers and upon American society. And so the foundation's staffers were on a constant lookout for allies within the academy. On one occasion in particular, they made a momentous discovery.

At a John M. Olin Foundation board meeting on November 25, 1981, Michael Joyce—still in his heyday as executive director—proposed spending $50,000 on a scholar nobody else in the room knew much about. The basic idea was to make it financially possible for a number of the professor's former students from several institutions to connect with his current ones at the University of Chicago.

Allan Bloom, at that time, was renowned inside a small circle of academics for his translations of Plato's *Republic* and Rousseau's *Émile.* He was a disciple of Leo Strauss, and as such he believed that the slow and patient study of the classics formed the backbone of a proper education in the Western tradition. Furthermore, the Straussians—sometimes called "Leo-cons"—thought it was necessary to understand ancient authors as they had understood themselves, rather than in the way history has chosen to interpret them. They believed that obtaining an intimate appreciation of these old books and writers allowed readers to participate in humankind's greatest dialogues. One typical concern of Straussians was the fear that modern liberalism had a tendency to veer into relativism and even nihilism. If a single characteristic marked Straussian thought—and it was certainly a prominent feature of Bloom's—it was perhaps a forthright refusal to suspend moral judgment.

Many considered Bloom to be Strauss's greatest student. Outside a small community of academics, however, he was virtually unknown—and Joyce's superiors at the foundation balked at the suggestion of devoting so much money to one person, especially when they had not heard of him before. Wasn't $50,000 an unduly large grant, wondered Bill Simon and George Gillespie? Perhaps half that amount would be more appropriate. But Joyce insisted: Bloom was worth the investment, and if the John M. Olin Foundation made a clear statement with a sizable grant, Bloom would find it easier to raise additional funds from other sources. He would also gain some extra time to do a little writing.

Joyce made his case well enough to win over Simon and Gillespie. The full grant was approved, and it would turn out to be one of the most significant expenditures in the John M. Olin Foundation's history. Although the foundation had already spent millions on college and university programs, this gift marked its formal entry into the coming wars over the very purpose of liberal education—even though Joyce and the others had little idea of what lay ahead, or how the foundation's $50,000 would shape an important debate a few years hence. The grant to Bloom also demonstrated one of the things that the foundation did extraordinarily well during its life: identify promising intellectuals and give them the means to spend their time as they saw fit. "Talented people do talented stuff," said Joyce. "If you have to tell them what to do, then you've failed."

Nobody told Bloom to write an essay for *National Review*, but that was one of the ways he spent his time after receiving the grant. Spread across seven pages, it appeared in the issue dated December 10, 1982. Its title, "Our Listless Universities," would not have come as a surprise to the magazine's readers, who were well acquainted with criticisms of higher education. For most of them, however, Bloom was a fresh voice. Like so many professors, the Chicago man had spent his entire adult life around universities. At the age of fifty-two, he was ready to issue some judgments—and to pose a serious challenge to academia with the engaging erudition that was his trademark.

The opening words of his *National Review* article were gripping:

> I begin with my conclusion: students in our best universities do not believe in anything, and those universities are doing nothing about it, nor can they. An easygoing American kind of nihilism has descended upon us, a nihilism without terror of the abyss. The great questions—God, freedom, and immortality, according to Kant—hardly touch the young. And the universities, which should encourage the quest for the clarification of such questions, are the very source of the doctrine which makes that quest appear futile.

He then launched a full-scale attack on cultural relativism and the "equality of values," blaming much of higher education's plight on "the routinization of the passions of the Sixties." The fundamental problem was a stubborn refusal, by students and those who taught them, to recognize the difference between right and wrong:

> Schools once produced citizens, or gentlemen, or believers; now they produce the unprejudiced. A university professor confronting entering freshmen can be almost certain that most of them will know that there are no absolutes and that one cannot say that one culture is superior to another. They can scarcely believe that someone might seriously argue the contrary; the attempt to do so meets either self-satisfied smiles at something so old-fashioned or outbursts of anger at a threat to decent respect for other human beings.

Bloom complained that students did not read books (which form "a part of the soul's furniture"), listened to too much rock music (whose very beats and rhythms were corrosive), and engaged in too much meaningless sex (thanks to a sexual revolution that had robbed sex "of seriousness as well as charm" and a feminist ideology that sought to obscure real differences between men and women). "All the doubts which tradition should inspire in us in order to liberate us from the prejudices of our time are in principle closed to us," wrote Bloom in the essay's conclusion. "I do not say that the situation is impossible or worse than it ever was. The human condition is always beset by problems. But these are *our* problems, and we must face them clearly. They constitute a crisis for humane learning but also reaffirm the need for it."

Although Bloom based the bulk of his essay for *National Review* on his personal observations and experiences, he did not include much autobiographical material in it. Yet his story was both interesting and relevant. He was raised in Indianapolis as the child of Jewish immigrants. A precocious boy, he entered the University of Chicago at the age of fifteen, when he was accepted to an early-admissions program for gifted students. He ultimately earned his doctorate there, taught in Europe, and then came back to the United States for a series of teaching posts.

As a professor at Cornell in the 1960s, he was a popular and charismatic teacher who earned a reputation for chain-smoking during his lectures. Bloom possessed a lively mind that often ran faster than his mouth; he was notorious for starting a new sentence before finishing the one he was on. He made a powerful impression on people such as Alison Lurie, who taught in Cornell's English department and became an acclaimed novelist. (Bloom was probably the model for C. Donald Dibble, one of the characters in her 1974 book *The War Between the Tates*.) He certainly attracted some of the school's finest students. One of these was Francis Fukuyama, who would become a leading foreign-policy intellectual. Another was Paul Wolfowitz, who would go on to serve in a variety of government posts, including deputy secretary of defense in the second Bush administration and then president of the World Bank. Bloom, in fact, was instrumental in convincing the young Wolfowitz to pursue a graduate degree in political science, against the wishes of Wolfowitz's father, a mathematics professor at Cornell.

Bloom was still at Cornell in 1969, when a group of gun-toting black students seized control of the student union. He was appalled by the incident, and especially by the administration's failure to provide protection to professors whose lives had been threatened. The administration also angered him with its eagerness to appease the militants and indulge their demands regarding admission standards. As one Cornell professor said of Bloom and his colleagues, "These men were morally committed to treating blacks with the same respect they'd give any other students. What they would not do is treat them *more* equally." For Bloom, there was personal bitterness as well. One of the leaders of the student radicals was Edward Whitfield, who had been a student of his and had said that he dreamed of becoming a "black Plato." Bloom took it hard that a young man who encountered great books under his own tutelage should rebel against him in such a flamboyant and destructive way.

Those tempestuous days at Cornell became a touchstone in Bloom's life. Although he could not have known it at the time, they helped create the conditions for the John M. Olin Foundation to support his work in the 1980s and 1990s, because they also pressed on the mind of Olin himself just as he was turning his attention away from business and toward philanthropy. More immediately, the student takeover convinced Bloom that Cornell's administration operated without integrity. "The president [of Cornell] appeared to be interested only in protecting himself and avoiding having to confront the black student association or any other radical group," wrote Bloom some years later. "He was of the moral stamp of those who were angry with Poland for resisting Hitler because this precipitated the war." Although he had become comfortable at Cornell and might have spent his remaining years as a professor there, Bloom resolved to leave in 1970.

But he did not forget. "Everything that has happened in American universities since then has its roots in that period," he told the *Sunday Telegraph* of London in 1991. "That was when they decided that much more important than truth seeking was 'sensitivity'—which means following other people's opinions." Bloom continued to pursue his scholarly interests, but he also began to think deeply about a crisis in higher education.

After Cornell, Bloom had trouble finding a job. There were simply no takers in the United States, and so he wound up at the University of Toronto. By 1977, however, he was back where he started, at the University of Chicago, which already had strong counterestablishment credentials because of the scholars in its economics department and law school. Bloom formed many friendships at Chicago, and one of the most important was with the novelist and Nobel laureate Saul Bellow. (In 2000, Bellow published *Ravelstein,* a roman à clef based on Bloom.)

Bellow encouraged Bloom to expand his *National Review* essay into a book and persuaded his own literary agent to represent this little-known academic. Meanwhile, the John M. Olin Foundation was rapidly increasing its support of Bloom. In the summer of 1982, it sponsored a pilot program, run by Bloom, that sought to connect policymakers with political theory. This was deemed a success, and the "Fatter Memo" written by Joyce and Piereson a few months later recommended spending between $100,000 and $200,000 per year on such a project. These figures turned out to be low. In 1983, the foundation underwrote

the John M. Olin Center for Inquiry into the Theory and Practice of Democracy with a three-year grant worth $1.1 million.
Bloom served as co-director along with Nathan Tarcov, a political scientist. The center immediately began a vigorous program
of lectures, conferences, and fellowships—and also allowed
Bloom the time to write his book. It was eventually signed by
Simon & Schuster, which figured that Bloom's volume would do
well if it sold a few thousand copies.

*The Closing of the American Mind* appeared in the spring of
1987, carrying a provocative subtitle: "How Higher Education
Has Failed Democracy and Impoverished the Souls of Today's
Students." Its themes were familiar to readers who remembered
the *National Review* essay, but Bloom was no longer limited by
the number of lines his magazine editors doled out to him.
"There is one thing a professor can be absolutely certain of:
almost every student entering the university believes, or says he
believes, that truth is relative," wrote Bloom. "Relativism is necessary to openness; and this is the virtue, the only virtue, which
all primary education for more than fifty years has dedicated
itself to inculcating." He did not approve of this trend, of course:
"What is advertised as a great opening is a great closing," he
wrote. "No longer is there a hope that there are great wise men
in other places and times who can reveal the truth about life."
His observations and arguments spanned nearly four hundred
pages, and it became impossible for an educated person to ignore
them.

The book's first reviews ensured as much, because they
seemed to compete with each other over which one could heap
the highest praise on the Chicago don. Even many liberals liked
it, and though they may have disagreed with certain elements of
Bloom's argument, they felt a need to respond with the same
honesty and fervor that had led Bloom to write it in the first
place. A *New York Times* daily reviewer, Christopher Lehmann-
Haupt, remarked that the book "hits with the approximate force
and effect of what electric-shock therapy must feel like." And for
Lehmann-Haupt, this was a welcome sensation: "By turns passionate and witty, sweetly reasoned and outraged, it commands
one's attention and concentrates one's mind more effectively

than any other book I can think of in the past five years." Soon after, in the *New York Times Book Review*, Roger Kimball gave Bloom's opus the kind of copy that publicists crave, so that they may decorate the paperback edition with words of commendation: "*The Closing of the American Mind* is essential reading for anyone concerned with the state of liberal education in this society." Kimball (who would later join the staff of *The New Criterion*) also declared it "that rarest of documents, a genuinely profound book, born of a long and patient meditation on questions that may be said to determine who we are, both as individuals and as a society."

Not all of the reviews were so laudatory. Many critics latched on to Bloom's colorful denunciations of rock music, which he deemed responsible for turning life into "a nonstop, commercially prepackaged masturbational fantasy." (The index includes an entry for Hitler, followed by this subentry: "rock videos and.") Yet Bloom's foes soon realized that they could neither belittle nor ignore what he was saying. "This book will find many enemies," prophesied Kimball in his original critique. If nothing else, he was right about that. "How good a philosopher, then, is Allan Bloom?" asked Martha Nussbaum in the *New York Review of Books*. "The answer is, we cannot say, and we are given no reason to think him one at all." David Rieff was so flustered by *The Closing of the American Mind* that he characterized it as a book "decent people would be ashamed of having written."

Judging from its commercial success, however, plenty of people did not feel ashamed about buying it. The public appreciated Bloom's popularization of Straussian ideas, even though few of them knew anything about Leo Strauss. Within a few months of its release, hundreds of thousands of copies of *The Closing of the American Mind* had flown off bookstore shelves. It spent ten weeks as the No. 1 *New York Times* bestseller and eventually sold more than a million copies. This accomplishment would have delighted Stephen King—and it was an especially notable achievement for a book whose chapters have titles such as "From Socrates' *Apology* to Heidegger's *Rektoratsrede*." (Bloom later joked about writing a sequel called *How to Make a Fortune by Reading Old Books*.)

Bloom's stunning success significantly raised the John M. Olin Foundation's visibility. Every reporter who covered the Bloom phenomenon noted that he received philanthropic backing. "*The Closing of the American Mind* may well have been our first 'blockbuster' success," said Piereson. At the very least, it marked the foundation as an intellectual force and brought considerable public attention to the idea of private foundations paying for the production and promotion of scholarly ideas.

Meanwhile, the John M. Olin Center for Inquiry into the Theory and Practice of Democracy flourished. The John M. Olin Foundation's level of support varied from grant to grant, but it was always high: $1.1 million in 1983, $1.85 million in 1985, $1.8 million in 1988, and so on. After the foundation awarded its final gift in 2001, it had committed more than $9 million to Bloom's center.

The center described its mission as creating "a new generation of thoughtful scholars aware of the complexities and responsibilities of practical life" and "reflective participants in public life open to the questions of theory." To this end, it sponsored conferences, lectures, and seminars on a broad range of topics. During the 1986–87 school year, for instance, the center focused on "The Problem of Evil in Twentieth-Century Politics." Speakers included Robert Conquest on Stalinism, Leonard Garment on Watergate, and James Q. Wilson on crime. Other themes included the legacy of Leo Strauss, the character of American democracy, and the role of religion in the United States. The center's programs became forums for big ideas. In a 1991 grant proposal to the John M. Olin Foundation, Bloom and Tarcov had every right to boast: "You must remember that, among America's front-line universities, the University of Chicago is the salient bastion of a true diversity of *intellectual* alternatives." Walter Berns (who occupied a John M. Olin Chair in Constitutional and Legal Studies at the American Enterprise Institute) assessed the center's proposal that year, at the request of the foundation's staff. "My judgment," he wrote, "is that Bloom and Tarcov have built the finest educational program of its kind to be found anywhere, a program which the Olin Foundation should be proud to support."

An important part of the Olin Center's programs was its people—and not just Allan Bloom. It offered fellowships for both graduate and undergraduate students, producing scholars who would teach at schools such as Bowdoin College, Emory University, Boston College, Boston University, Colgate University, Georgetown University, the University of Kentucky, Michigan State University, the U.S. Air Force Academy and others. These placements were less impressive than those associated with the foundation's law and economics programs, in large measure because law and economics was a growing academic field and political philosophy was not. Moreover, the Straussian approach to political philosophy was out of step with many of the current trends in higher education. At some level, it was a challenge for these students to find jobs anywhere, to say nothing of the Ivy League. Many of the Olin Center's graduates did not bother with the academy at all, such as Kenneth Weinstein of the Hudson Institute and Adam Wolfson of *The Public Interest* and *Commentary*.

The professors who mentored these students produced their own scholarship, which included everything from translations of Machiavelli to commentary on Shakespeare. Besides Bloom, the best-known figure associated with the Olin Center probably was Leon Kass, an associate director who later entered the public spotlight as head of the President's Council on Bioethics, which led national debates on human cloning and stem-cell research. "Perhaps only among our Associate Directors could a scholar be found who both teaches Genesis and Aristotle's *Ethics* every other year and clarifies complex technical and philosophical dilemmas for the nation's highest elected officials," wrote Tarcov in a 2001 grant request.

After Bloom's death in 1992, the John M. Olin Foundation solicited comments about its ongoing support of the center. The response was enthusiastic. Donald Kagan of Yale wrote that although there was no replacing Bloom, his personal experience with the center told him "the faculty and students in the program were of the highest quality" and the center appeared well positioned for the future. Irving Kristol was equally encouraging: "If only all such requests for funding were so meritorious." So the grants kept on coming: $750,000 in 1994, $810,000 in

1996, and nearly $1.4 million in 1998. As Tarcov wrote in 2001, "The Olin Center has helped to keep the University of Chicago a place where independent thought and genuine education can take place free of faddish distractions and ideological partisanship, where responsible and thoughtful inquiry into the theory and practice of democracy can truly flourish." In a grant evaluation that same year, the foundation called the center one of its "flagship programs."

A similar program—described as "one of the foundation's finest and most effective" in a staff write-up—supported Harvey Mansfield's Program on Constitutional Government at Harvard. It began as a lecture series sponsored by the foundation in 1983, and grew to include seminars, fellowships, and research support. The central goal, as described in a 2004 grant proposal, was to "raise constitutional government out of its recent obscurity and to bring it back to the attention of scholars and students at our universities." A teacher in the Straussian tradition, Mansfield said his program could "provide an alternative to the foes of constitutionalism here at home—the relativists who sing weary post-constitutional blues and the zealots who want to use the Constitution as their private, partisan instrument." He also understood his program's subversive element: "Our rule has been to invite those who are deserving of a Harvard audience and who would otherwise not be invited because of Harvard's indifference or hostility." Across two decades, the John M. Olin Foundation donated $3.3 million to its activities.

Although the Harvard center did produce significant scholarship, none of it approached the popular success of *The Closing of the American Mind*. In 1993, Richard Bernstein of the *New York Times* described Bloom's book as "the surprise best seller that in many ways was the opening conservative salvo in the ongoing culture wars." Many more salvos followed, often in book form. Bloom was by no means the first person to criticize higher education, but *The Closing of the American Mind* gave birth to a whole genre of books that disapproved of the Left's domination of the universities. One of the best in this class was *Tenured Radicals*, by Roger Kimball, the man whose *New York Times* review helped launch Bloom's success. Charles Sykes reached a wide audience

with two books, *Profscam* and *The Hollow Men.* William Bennett
and Lynne Cheney also bemoaned the state of higher education
from the bully pulpit of the National Endowment for the Humanities. (One critic of these newly energized conservatives dubbed
them the "Killer B's," in reference to Bloom, Bennett, and
Bellow.)

Yet the most important successor to Bloom was probably
Dinesh D'Souza. He was half Bloom's age when he burst onto
the national scene in 1991 with his book *Illiberal Education,* a
muckraking account of how politics had overrun colleges and
universities. Whereas Bloom was a Jewish professor from the
Midwest, D'Souza was a Catholic immigrant from Bombay. He
had attended high school in India, but finished as an exchange
student in an Arizona border town. Although his parents expected
him to return to Bombay, he decided to remain in the United
States and attend Dartmouth, where he was one of the founders
of the *Dartmouth Review.* He eventually landed in Washington
and worked at the Heritage Foundation and then in the Reagan
White House. Following these stints, he joined the American
Enterprise Institute and became a John M. Olin Fellow.

D'Souza possessed a genius for polemics and his book com-
pellingly documented the problem of political correctness. If
Bloom had probed its root causes, D'Souza described its grim
manifestations. *Illiberal Education* was an instant success. An
excerpt in the liberal *Atlantic Monthly* helped give the author
mainstream credibility and avoid the label of right-wing crank.
D'Souza also was able to find common cause with certain liberals who opposed speech codes—policies that university administrations were deploying upon their students in earnest attempts
to crack down on so-called hate speech, but which often had the
effect of chilling free speech. Moreover, he was a skillful and
entertaining debater, on television and in person. His relative
youth was an asset, and so was his ethnic background. "I'm discussing topics that are definitely taboo," he said. "If I were white,
it would be virtually impossible for me to be as candid."

D'Souza's most noteworthy accomplishment probably was
popularizing the term "political correctness." Its entrance into
the American lexicon owes more to D'Souza than to any other

person, and it immediately gave conservatives a shorthand way to describe the problem of left-wing dominance at colleges and universities. Before long, everybody was using it—even President George H. W. Bush. "The notion of political correctness has ignited controversy across the land," he said at a University of Michigan commencement address. "And although the movement arises from the laudable desire to sweep away the debris of racism and sexism and hatred, it replaces old prejudice with new ones. It declares certain topics off-limits, certain expressions off-limits, even certain gestures off-limits."

D'Souza's achievement might not have been possible without the John M. Olin Foundation's support—and that included the foundation's hands-off approach to dealing with the scholars whose work it underwrote. When D'Souza first became an Olin Fellow, for instance, it was not even clear what topics he would write about. He had several projects in mind, including one on colleges and universities that ultimately became his book. "We felt Dinesh was an important young talent and decided to invest in him, rather than in a particular cause," said Piereson. The relationship with Olin lasted more than a decade and helped produce several other books, including *The End of Racism* and *Ronald Reagan: How an Ordinary Man Became an Extraordinary Leader.* "The wonderful thing about Olin is that they don't try to choreograph the work they fund," said D'Souza. "They pick good people and support what they do."

The foundation took this approach repeatedly, and did so most directly with its John M. Olin Faculty Fellowships program. It intended to help promising young scholars achieve tenure by giving them the financial means to take a year off teaching to write a book or journal articles—vital credentials in the "publish or perish" world of higher education. The fellowships began in 1985 and assisted more than a hundred scholars. The typical recipient was an assistant professor who had accumulated some experience but still had a couple of years to go before tenure review. Most of the fellowships went to political scientists, historians, legal scholars, and philosophers. They were usually identified by a group of about seventy-five scholars whom the foundation staff knew and trusted. Recipients included Peter

Berkowitz of George Mason University, John DiIulio of Penn, Aaron Friedberg of Princeton, Carolyn Hoxby of Harvard, Frederick Kagan of West Point, Jennifer Roback Morse of the Hoover Institution, Jeremy Rabkin of Cornell, Paul Rahe of the University of Tulsa, C. Bradley Thompson of Ashland University, Eugene Volokh of UCLA, and John Yoo of Berkeley. Several of the faculty fellows made an imprint outside the academy, such as Mark McClellan, who served as commissioner of the Food and Drug Administration before becoming the chief administrator of Medicare and Medicaid. By the time the program was discontinued in 2003, the John M. Olin Foundation had spent more than $8 million on it.

THE FOUNDATION'S SUPPORT OF BLOOM, D'Souza, and the John M. Olin Faculty Fellows was a classic example of nurturing the counterintelligentsia, as Bill Simon had described it in *A Time for Truth*. Yet the foundation also recognized that the counterintelligentsia needed a set of counterinstitutions. During the 1980s and 1990s, it became depressingly obvious that scholarly groups such as the American Historical Association and the Modern Language Association were controlled by the same forces that Bloom and D'Souza exposed and critiqued. This was inevitable, given that membership organizations are run by their members— and a radical generation of scholars was tightening its grip on the academy every time an old professor retired from the faculty.

The most important institution in fighting this trend was the National Association of Scholars. It was an outgrowth of the Campus Coalition for Democracy, an informal group of New York City professors who were worried about the same trends in higher education that animated Bloom and D'Souza. Their ringleader was Stephen Balch, a professor at John Jay College and a skillful networker. In 1987, Balch and his friends opened an office, started referring to themselves as the NAS, and began approaching foundations for support. Their plan was to recruit faculty members, trustees, and graduate students around the country and rally them in support of traditional liberal education. The Smith Richardson Foundation became the first major contributor to the NAS. The John M. Olin Foundation followed shortly thereafter with a grant of $50,000, which increased to $85,000 in 1988. In succeeding years, the NAS never received less than $100,000 from the foundation—more than $2 million overall.

In its first fifteen years, the National Association of Scholars experienced steady growth and eventually was able to boast more than four thousand members. They became a cadre of critics and whistleblowers who spoke to each other at annual conferences, through newsletters, and on the pages of a quarterly journal called *Academic Questions*. The NAS established affiliates in just about every state. Some were more active than others, and one in particular—the California Association of Scholars—waged what was perhaps the country's most effective insurgency against racial preferences. Two of its leaders, Glynn Custred and Thomas Wood, authored a ballot measure to ban racial preferences in the operation of state government (which included university admissions and hiring). Their initiative eventually became known as Proposition 209, and voters approved it in 1996. Most outsiders associated its success with Ward Connerly, who led the political campaign. Yet it is hard to believe that Proposition 209 would have become a reality without the National Association of Scholars.

In 2003, the foundation's staff prepared an evaluation of the NAS that described the group as "one of the best organizations we support." Part of its effectiveness came from the ability to spin off separate organizations that focused on particular aspects of higher education's plight. In 1991, the American Academy for Liberal Education was founded to counter harmful trends among the accrediting agencies that are responsible for certifying colleges and universities to receive federal government financing, including student loans and research grants. These accrediting agencies seemed to be less concerned with academic content and performance than with the racial and ethnic makeup of student and faculty populations. In 1990, for instance, the Middle States Association of Colleges and Universities refused to accredit Baruch College in New York because its minority retention rate failed to meet an arbitrary standard. The AALE, by contrast, decided to base its accrediting process on curricular standards—providing an alternate route to accreditation for schools that might otherwise find themselves becoming the victims of politically correct accreditors. The John M. Olin Foundation supported the AALE from its inception, with grants totaling more than $1 million. The foundation also helped the American Council of Trustees and Alumni, another NAS outgrowth, with grants worth nearly $1 million. Whereas the NAS sought to influence schools through their faculties, the ACTA tried to tap the people who control the purse strings—the alumni who write checks to their alma maters and the trustees who approve budgets. With Lynne Cheney serving as its national chairman until her husband was sworn in as vice president in 2001, the ACTA developed a special knack for publicizing the problems afflicting higher education. The NAS also was instrumental in founding several new scholarly organizations meant to serve as alternatives to those dominated by tenured radicals. The two most prominent were the Historical Society, formed in protest to the politicization of both the American Historical Society and the Organization of American Historians, and the Association of Literary Scholars and Critics, a reaction to the left-wing drift of the Modern Language Association.

The Center for the Study of Popular Culture, headed by David Horowitz in Los Angeles, received some $2 million for its campus activism. Its most noteworthy initiative focused on higher education was an "Academic Bill of Rights," which aimed to bring more intellectual diversity to colleges and universities. Another favorite recipient of the foundation's grants was the Center for Equal Opportunity, which under the leadership of Linda Chavez produced a series of detailed reports on racial preferences in college admissions. Before founding the center, Chavez had been a John M. Olin Fellow at the Manhattan Institute, where she wrote *Out of the Barrio,* her book on Hispanic assimilation.

In 2000, at a time when the foundation was turning down virtually every new proposal that came its way, it decided to provide $525,000 in startup money for the James Madison Program in American Ideals and Institutions at Princeton University. Headed by Robert P. George, a professor of politics, it aimed to teach constitutional principles to a generation of students who were not receiving much instruction in them, as well as promote scholarship in economic liberty, religious freedom, and political thought. Just as the foundation had taken advantage of a controversy over Critical Legal Studies at Harvard Law School to set up a law and economics center there, the Madison Program benefited from a debate surrounding Princeton's decision to hire Peter Singer, a left-wing advocate of eugenics, to lead what was supposedly a center for bioethics. In a 2002 staff evaluation, the foundation praised George for creating "a beachhead for scholarship on the founding principles of American government."

As the John M. Olin Foundation prepared to close in the early months of 2005, Piereson reflected upon all the resources it had devoted specifically to improving the climate for higher education. "The campuses were a main focus of our activities," he said, "though I'm not sure we were able to change them much." In one sense he was correct: In the quarter-century that the foundation was most active in this arena, the Left did not loosen its chokehold on higher education even slightly. The problems that Allan Bloom had identified in the 1980s were just as pervasive and troubling in the first decade of the twenty-first century. Yet the John M. Olin Foundation in fact had accomplished one of the main goals that Bill Simon set for it many years earlier: It had supported a counterintelligentsia for an entire generation, helped it build a set of academic counterinstitutions, and made its numbers greater and its influence broader than it would have been in the foundation's absence. The foundation perhaps did not transform higher education for the better, but it kept alive the possibility of improvement—and allowed improvement to be a hope rather than a fantasy.

# CHAPTER EIGHT

# HISTORY CLASH

F RANCIS FUKUYAMA WAS NERVOUS when he walked into the Social Science Lecture Hall at the University of Chicago on the afternoon of February 8, 1989. He had good reason to be, as he was about to propose a startling concept to a room filled with brilliant thinkers. Moreover, he was part of a speaker series that included titans such as Saul Bellow, Walter Berns, and Middle East expert Bernard Lewis. And at the age of thirty-six, he was relatively young and virtually unknown.

Yet he was a man of enormous ambition, or at least a man who had enormous ambitions for a provocative idea. Fukuyama intended to discuss "the end of history." His talk actually marked the end of nothing, but rather the start of a great debate — certainly the greatest debate to engage foreign-policy intellectuals in the final years of the twentieth century. It might even be said that Fukuyama's Chicago lecture launched the most talked-about thesis on global affairs since George Kennan, writing anonymously as "X," published his famous article on containing Soviet aspirations more than forty years earlier. Kennan, of course, was trying to frame American policy choices at a time of complicated transition, as the United States and the world hunkered down to fight the Cold War. For his part, Fukuyama meant to explain international relations at a similar moment of flux, with the Cold War concluding and a new age of uncertainty beginning to present itself.

Fukuyama had come to Chicago at the invitation of the John M. Olin Center for Inquiry into the Theory and Practice

of Democracy, the organization that the John M. Olin Foundation had assisted Allan Bloom and Nathan Tarcov in creating a
few years earlier. Bloom's bleak assessment of American culture
in general and higher education in particular, offered on the
pages of *The Closing of the American Mind,* stood in stark contrast
to the sense of triumph that many conservatives felt as the Soviet
Union teetered on the brink of collapse. The lecture series in
which Fukuyama participated was entitled "The Decline of the
West?" The question mark was essential. Many prominent thinkers
of the 1980s, such as Paul Kennedy, the author of a bestselling
book called *The Rise and Fall of the Great Powers,* believed that the
West's decline would inevitably result from imperial overstretch.
Bloom and Tarcov harbored different doubts that reflected their
Straussian tendencies: They worried that liberal democracies
were vulnerable to their own naïveté and softness. Compared
with these schools of thought, Fukuyama was an outright optimist.

The story of Fukuyama's end-of-history thesis is a case study
in how the John M. Olin Foundation went about its business,
and highlights the fact that so many of its accomplishments were
essentially unplanned. Fukuyama deserves full credit for his own
ideas, of course, yet the foundation helped create the conditions
for them to take flight. Not only was his initial lecture given under
the auspices of Chicago's Olin Center, but the article that flowed
from it and was responsible for his subsequent recognition
appeared on the pages of *The National Interest,* a journal heavily
supported by the foundation. Finally, many of the critics of
Fukuyama's thesis, such as Samuel P. Huntington, were also beneficiaries of the foundation. It was almost as if the John M. Olin
Foundation had created a debating club and funded all points
of view. The result is not in dispute: the most fascinating discussion about the state of the world in a generation, and one that
continues to resonate into the twenty-first century. It is perhaps
noteworthy that the debate was not waged between Left and
Right, but almost entirely among people who may reasonably be
described as conservatives.

The end of history began at Cornell, where Fukuyama
matriculated as a freshman in the fall of 1970. The school had
suffered its worst difficulties with student radicalism a year and

a half earlier, and it was continuing to endure the fallout. Allan Bloom, for instance, was in the process of leaving campus. Yet he had not gone entirely. Even after taking a job at the University of Toronto, he commuted back to Ithaca to fulfill his final teaching obligations. "I caught him at the tail end of his Cornell period," said Fukuyama. "He had a great influence on me, and he was the reason why I majored in classics, read Hegel, and studied political theory."

After graduating from Cornell, Fukuyama knew he wanted to pursue an advanced degree. He traveled to Paris and studied with the literary theorist Jacques Derrida for six months, and then came back to the United States for a year of comparative literature at Yale. Ultimately he wound up at Harvard, where he assumed that he would study political theory with Harvey Mansfield. Although he took a course with Mansfield and Tarcov, who was then teaching at Harvard as well, his interests pushed him in a more practical direction. He became an expert on Soviet politics, with an emphasis on Soviet foreign policy in the Middle East. After earning his Ph.D., he worked for ten years at the Rand Corporation, a think tank in California, except for a brief interlude as a member of the policy planning staff at the Department of State. One of Fukuyama's colleagues at Foggy Bottom was Tarcov, and their boss was Paul Wolfowitz, yet another student of Bloom's from Cornell.

Because of all these ties, Fukuyama probably would never have slipped out of Bloom's sight entirely. Yet the two men also were able to reconnect in a personal way in the early 1980s, when Fukuyama's father, Yoshio, a minister in the Congregational Church, became a professor at the Chicago Theological Seminary and moved into a home across the street from Bloom. "I would see Allan when I was visiting my parents," said Fukuyama. Although Fukuyama spent most of his time writing detailed appraisals of Soviet foreign policy—papers that Bloom almost certainly did not read—he remained well within the orbit of his mentor.

In the spring of 1988, as Bloom and Tarcov were preparing the Olin Center's program for the next academic year, they thought of Fukuyama. "Our goal was always to mix theory and

practice," said Tarcov. "We knew Frank was smart and thoughtful. Besides, how many classics majors and comp-lit students were
also experts in national security?" Independently, Fukuyama was
formulating the ideas that would make him famous. The Olin
Center extended an offer to speak and Fukuyama accepted. He
spent several months organizing his sprawling thoughts into a
coherent speech.

More than a hundred people attended Fukuyama's address.
Few of them knew much about Fukuyama or what he was going
to say. They were there in large part because they made a point
of being at events sponsored by the Olin Center, whose lecture
series had established a solid reputation on campus for lively discussion. When it was over, Fukuyama was unsure about his performance. "I thought I hadn't done a very good job of presenting
my ideas," he said.

What were those ideas? Put simply, Fukuyama proposed that
civilization had reached a developmental endpoint and that political and economic liberalism had prevailed. He was not speaking merely in terms of the Cold War, in which the democracies
of the West defeated the Soviet Communists. Instead, he meant
that in the long sweep of history, the combination of democratic
governance and market capitalism had proven itself as the very
best form of social organization and that no rival would emerge
to challenge or displace it. Fukuyama did not say—as many would
misinterpret him as having said—that the future would be free
of conflict. But he did suggest that mankind's ideological evolution had crossed a finish line and come to a halt. In this sense,
history really had ended.

Fukuyama may have been nervous that afternoon, and he
may have felt his performance was not as strong as possible, but
in reality he had not let anybody down, either during his speech
or during the more intimate roundtable discussion he held with
the Olin Center's fellows that evening. "It was one of the most
electrifying sessions I remember the Olin Center putting on,"
said Adam Wolfson, who attended both gatherings as a graduate student. Bloom himself "was clearly excited by the talk," said
John J. Mearsheimer, a political science professor at Chicago.
"But he wasn't convinced that Frank was right. He certainly

wanted Frank to be right, but for a cynic like Allan it all sounded too good to be true."

What happened next really was too good to be true, not only from the perspective of Fukuyama and the Olin Center, but from the standpoint of anybody interested in ideas. Fukuyama's speech might easily have vanished the way so many speeches do. Yet it did not, and the John M. Olin Foundation played a crucial role in helping Fukuyama gain access to an audience far beyond the walls of the Social Science Lecture Hall in Chicago.

Fukuyama's talk as part of the Olin Center's lecture series was by no means the foundation's first foray into foreign policy. Although the trustees had not concentrated on the subject during the 1970s, the board and staff began to broaden the foundation's mission in the wake of Olin's death. "The Foundation has come to see that the preservation of American institutions requires that attention be given to national security issues and the interests of the United States in the international arena," wrote Joyce and Piereson in the "Fatter Memo" of 1982. They believed that devoting a portion of the foundation's resources to international issues would help advance their overall goals. Consequently, the foundation began supporting democratic movements in Eastern Europe with small grants. It contributed $35,000, for instance, to "the publication of a series of books on international affairs and public policy issues, for distribution by underground publishing houses in Poland." The foundation's interest in the Cold War remained strong, even after that episode had ended. It helped subsidize Sam Tanenhaus as he wrote his acclaimed biography of Whittaker Chambers and also supported Anne Applebaum as she worked on her Pulitzer Prize-winning book, *Gulag: A History*.

For all of these accomplishments, the Fatter Memo pointed out a fundamental weakness in the conservative movement: "The lack of a coherent, thoughtful, and forceful conservative voice in foreign policy and security discussion is in striking contrast to the situation in the domestic policy debate." Groups such as the Heritage Foundation were enjoying a great deal of influence. What conservatives needed were foreign-policy counterparts that would present viewpoints on arms control, détente, the projection of military power, development aid, and the role of international organizations.

In the early 1980s, Herman Kahn, a nuclear strategist who had helped establish the Hudson Institute in 1961, was promoting the concept of a Washington-based think tank that would allow conservatives to focus on diplomatic and security issues. He was joined in this effort by Irving Kristol as well as Alexander Haig, the retired Army general who had worked as Nixon's chief of staff and Reagan's secretary of state. The three believed that despite the steady enlargement and increasing influence of conservative think tanks, vital work was being left undone. "Although this growth had resulted in some important research, it had also been largely *ad hoc* and diffuse, often guided by the availability of funds and passing policy concerns rather than careful consideration of the United States' long term policy concerns," said a report by the John M. Olin Foundation staff in the fall of 1983. It continued:

> The result in general was, [Kahn, Kristol and Haig] concluded, unwieldy and incoherent programs staffed by a mixture of high-quality people and second-raters. More importantly, these programs had failed to produce what was decidedly necessary—a conservative voice in the national security and foreign policy discussion which would be thoughtful and solidly grounded but at the same time forceful and coherent. They further concluded that this was the result of the lack of a truly productive organizational setting rather than a shortage of high-quality conservative experts.

When Kahn founded the Hudson Institute, he had promised that it would focus on "important issues, not just urgent ones." He also had hoped that opening a Washington office of his own think tank, which was then headquartered in New York, would address the problem that worried him and his colleagues. Yet his own sudden death from a stroke in 1983 threw the Hudson Institute into a leadership crisis, and several of its best people departed.

Kristol and Haig responded to Kahn's passing by proposing a completely new institution, which they would head jointly. They approached the John M. Olin Foundation with a plan to create a John M. Olin Center for Foreign Policy and Defense Studies in Washington. They sought an immediate commitment of $1.2 million, as well as a pledge for similar levels of support over the next three to five years if the group met the foundation's expectations. They also mentioned several individuals they would approach about joining the center, such as the strategist Edward Luttwak and several current and former government officials, including Charles Fairbanks, Michael Ledeen, Carnes Lord, and Steven Rosen.

The foundation's steering committee reviewed the proposal and generally approved of it, but asked the full board of trustees to give it a careful appraisal before moving ahead. The board complied—and in doing so, raised several concerns about the application. Haig was a major stumbling block, as the steering committee noted in a memo to the trustees: "While no question was raised regarding the merits of Mr. Kristol's participation and indeed, enthusiasm was expressed, the case was somewhat different with General Haig due to the mixed impressions his public career has given rise to and which perhaps naturally attach themselves to anyone in public life." The question was especially sensitive "in view of the fact that this center would bear John Olin's name."

The previous year, Haig had concluded a stormy, eighteen-month tenure as secretary of state. During that time, he became the target of intense criticism—as well as the butt of numerous jokes—for what he had said after Ronald Reagan was wounded in an assassination attempt: "As of now, I am in control here in the White House." Although Simon retained a good impression of Haig from their days in the Nixon administration and seemed inclined to support the Kristol-Haig project, he did not push the matter with the full force of his personality. Meanwhile, trustee John J. McCloy announced his strong opposition. This sounded a death knell for the proposal, because the board of trustees always aimed to operate by consensus. There was considerable reluctance to take votes, as this risked splitting the board into factions. If a single trustee objected to something with a certain level of intensity—as McCloy was doing in this instance—then it was enough for everybody else. And McCloy, a past president of the World Bank, was no ordinary member of the board when it came to foreign affairs. His opinion would have mattered a great deal even if the board had not given each of its members something akin to veto power. The proposal for a foreign-policy think tank was set aside.

The failure to create a new John M. Olin Center, of course, did nothing to address the concern that conservatives needed a fresh platform for serious thinking on foreign policy and national security. As Kristol saw it, liberals were able to dominate so many discussions because they controlled so much of what appeared on the pages of *Foreign Affairs* and *Foreign Policy,* the country's two most prestigious journals on these topics. The problem was not that conservatives had no voice at all: *Commentary* magazine was a tremendous asset, and Jeane J. Kirkpatrick's article there on the differences between authoritarian and totalitarian regimes had led directly to her appointment as Reagan's first ambassador to the United Nations. Yet *Commentary* did not focus exclusively on foreign policy—it covered everything from welfare policy to the arts—and so it did not fit Kristol's bill.

Kristol certainly knew something about how to take an idea, present it to an elite audience, and use it to shape public perceptions. In 1965, he and Daniel Bell had founded *The Public Interest,* a quarterly journal that examined social policy in articles by James Coleman, Daniel Patrick Moynihan, and James Q. Wilson. (Nathan Glazer eventually replaced Bell as co-editor.) Over the years, it evolved into one of the house organs of the neoconservative movement. Its circulation was low—never more than ten thousand subscribers—but its influence was high. Until its final issue was published in 2005, *The Public Interest* was required reading for opinion leaders. Its ideas often trickled down into scholarly books, popular journalism, and political debates. A good case could be made that in the second half of the twentieth century, no small magazine mattered more than *The Public Interest.*

The John M. Olin Foundation never provided much direct support to *The Public Interest,* giving it only $92,000 over the years, in part because it was underwriting Kristol's positions at New York University and the American Enterprise Institute. Yet the foundation would become an indispensable contributor to the establishment of *The National Interest,* a quarterly journal that aimed to scrutinize international relations with the same intelligence and rigor that Kristol and his colleagues were bringing to domestic affairs on the pages of *The Public Interest.* In 1984, the John M. Olin Foundation supplied Kristol with a grant of $750,000 to launch the sister publication.

One of Kristol's first tasks was to find someone who could manage the day-to-day problems of soliciting articles, editing them, and placing them into production. He had a particular person in mind: Owen Harries, a Welshman living in Australia. Harries came from a gritty mining town in Wales, earned an education at the University of Wales and Oxford, and then migrated to academic posts in Australia. He eventually found himself editing *Quadrant,* a magazine modeled on Kristol's *Encounter,* which Harries had read with enthusiasm in the 1950s. The two men met in 1968, when Harries used a sabbatical to make his first visit to the United States. Back in Sydney, he entered the political arena, advising the government of Prime Minister Malcolm Fraser in the late 1970s and becoming Australia's representative to the United Nations Educational, Scientific and Cultural Organization (UNESCO) in Paris. In the spring of 1983, a change in Canberra's government forced him to resign his post. That left him in need of a job.

Like Kristol and so many American neoconservatives, Harries had gone through his own left-to-right political transition. He did not want to return to academic life in Australia, which he considered inhospitable, so he looked around for other opportunities. At a conference in Berlin, he saw Kristol again and met Michael Joyce for the first time. Kristol thought Harries would be ideal for a magazine in the United States, both because he was a foreign-policy intellectual with real-world experience and also because, as a foreigner, he would not have built a reputation in Washington as belonging to a particular clique.

When Joyce returned to New York, he decided to try to create a fellowship for Harries that would get him to the United States, while Kristol continued planning for a foreign-policy magazine. Joyce's first call went to the American Enterprise Institute.

He offered to underwrite all the expenses associated with Harries, but AEI was not interested. ("I never really understood why," said Joyce.) But Joyce did not give up. He contacted the Heritage Foundation, where Ed Feulner immediately cooperated, and Harries became the John M. Olin Fellow there. With no magazine to edit, he took on the separate task of convincing the United States to quit UNESCO, which he had come to consider insurmountably corrupt as well as relentlessly hostile to capitalism and the United States. In op-eds for major newspapers, an article for *Reader's Digest,* and policy papers for the Heritage Foundation, Harries made a powerful case against the organization. Remarkably, the Reagan administration took his advice and pulled out of UNESCO in 1984. "It was a huge accomplishment," said Joyce. "And it was one of the first really measurable examples of the Heritage Foundation making a big difference."

By this time, *The National Interest* had secured its startup grant from the John M. Olin Foundation and had risen from the ashes of the Kristol-Haig proposal. The magazine succeeded with the trustees in part because Haig was not involved (and despite some resistance from Simon, who wondered aloud at a board meeting about the effectiveness of magazines). Harries signed on as co-editor, along with Robert Tucker, a professor at Johns Hopkins who lent substantial ballast to *The National Interest* and contributed to its pages. For all practical purposes, however, the magazine belonged to Harries, who would remain in charge until 2001. From his perch as publisher, Kristol insisted that they produce a "magazine" rather than a "journal." By this he meant that *The National Interest* would print articles for intelligent lay readers, rather than specialists. The focus would be on smart ideas and persuasive arguments, rather than policy minutiae and exhaustive footnotes. Above all, the magazine would be well written.

The title of the magazine actually came from Harries. "I thought it would balance *The Public Interest* nicely," he said. "Irving was an ideology man, but he reluctantly agreed." Kristol and Harries both contributed to the inaugural issue, which came out in the fall of 1985, and they found themselves debating the meaning of Harries' term. Like bookends, their essays appeared first and last in the magazine. Kristol argued for an American foreign policy based on something other than "national interest" as it was typically understood. "Those who make American foreign policy," he wrote, "will discover that any viable conception of the United States's 'national interest' cannot help but be organically related to that public philosophy—ideology, if you wish—which is the basis of what we have come to call 'the American way of life.'" Harries disagreed, saying there need be no contradiction between traditional conservative statecraft and a foreign policy based on American ideals.

From the start, it was clear that *The National Interest* would devote itself to lively disputation. After providing the seed money, the John M. Olin Foundation remained an important donor. The large initial grant was followed by $100,000 in 1986. In all, the foundation provided nearly $2 million. (The Bradley Foundation, under Joyce's leadership, eventually became a more important source of funding.) Over the years, *The National Interest* became the primary forum for conservatives to present and discuss foreign-policy ideas. It even compelled *Foreign Affairs*, its liberal competitor, to adopt a more dynamic format and pay more attention to ideas from the political Right. By any reasonable account, *The National Interest* became everything its founders and donors could have hoped for.

The magazine's most significant accomplishment, however, grew out of a meeting over lunch between Harries and Fukuyama. Through a mutual friend, Harries had learned of Fukuyama's lecture at the Olin Center in Chicago. Fukuyama was working for Rand at the time, so Harries arranged a visit in Los Angeles on the return leg of a trip he had taken to Australia. "I usually paid $500 for a piece," said Harries. "But his ideas were so interesting that I offered him $1000." The article arrived a few weeks later. "I knew it was a winner," said Harries. He commissioned several people to write responses. The bulk of the summer 1989 issue was given over to Fukuyama and his critics.

The talk in Chicago had been called "Are We Approaching the End of History?" In *The National Interest*, Harries trimmed the first three words but kept the rest, including the question mark: "The End of History?" Fukuyama began by suggesting that great things were afoot: "It is hard to avoid the feeling that something very fundamental has happened in world history." He announced "the triumph of the West," which he described as "the total exhaustion of viable systematic alternatives to Western liberalism." Marxism, he noted acidly, may still retain a few true believers "in places like Managua, Pyongyang, or Cambridge, Massachusetts," but as "a living ideology of world historical significance" it was spent. Yet Fukuyama's fundamental claim involved far more than a simple obituary for a dead ideology: "What we may be witnessing is not just the end of the Cold War, or the passing of a particular period of post-war history, but the end of history as such: that is, the end point of mankind's ideological evolution and the universalization of Western liberal democracy as the final form of human government." He did not mean that nothing of significance would happen in the future, nor did he intend to suggest that the whole world was on the verge of accepting Western values. But he did believe that over time, they would prevail everywhere.

Fukuyama's analysis leaned heavily on the German philosopher Georg Wilhelm Friedrich Hegel (1770–1831), as well as the way in which Russian émigré Alexandre Kojeve (1902–1968) had interpreted Hegel in the 1930s. Most readers, however, focused on the practical implications of what Fukuyama was saying as he took readers on a tour of the world, as well as through twentieth-century history, to explain why Western liberalism had prevailed. Challengers such as fascism and communism were permanently vanquished, wrote Fukuyama, and Western liberalism also would drive off threats posed by nationalism and religion. Eventually it would take hold even in a place like China. The identifiable adversaries simply did not impress him. "In the contemporary world only Islam has offered a theocratic state as a political alternative to both liberalism and communism," he wrote. "But the doctrine has little appeal for non-Muslims, and it is hard to believe that the movement will take on any universal significance."

His argument was full of qualifications—starting with that question mark in the title. He refused "to rule out the sudden appearance of new ideologies or previously unrecognized

contradictions in liberal societies." Fukuyama also was careful
not to sound utopian: "This does not by any means imply the
end of international conflict per se." He pointed to frustrating
problems all over the world: "Palestinians and Kurds, Sikhs and
Tamils, Irish Catholics and Walloons, Armenians and Azeris, will
continue to have their unresolved grievances." Violent animos-
ity still had a future: "Terrorism and wars of national liberation
will continue to be an important item on the international
agenda." At the same time, however, he insisted that the human
race had turned a corner: "Large-scale conflict must involve large
states still caught in the grip of history, and they are what appear
to be passing from the scene."

The issue of *The National Interest* containing Fukuyama's
article also carried six responses from leading intellectuals. All
were in some fashion critical. Senator Daniel Patrick Moynihan,
for instance, declared himself "skeptical about any proposition
asserting there is now to be nothing new in human experience."
The historian Gertrude Himmelfarb (Irving Kristol's wife) added
her own doubts: "I myself have been too traumatized by communism and Nazism to have any confidence in the eternal real-
ities of history—except the reality of contingency and change,
of the imponderable and the unanticipated (and, as often as
not, the undesired and undesirable)." Yet most of the respon-
dents also praised Fukuyama. Bloom called the article "bold and
brilliant." He did not embrace the theory—"I would suggest fascism has a future," he wrote—but he was clearly intrigued by it.
Kristol called Fukuyama's ideas "quite persuasive"—but also
quipped, "I don't believe a word of it."

Even before the summer 1989 issue of *The National Interest*
appeared in print, Harries understood the potential for
Fukuyama's article to generate debate and controversy. That was
why he pursued the piece in the first place and then solicited
thoughtful responses. Yet he certainly did not envision "The End
of History?" becoming a popular sensation. "When the issue
appeared, there were a couple of quiet weeks," said Harries.
"Then it took off like a rocket. I still remember the proprietor
of a very busy news outlet on K Street telling me with wonder
that it was outselling the pornography." It became the great topic

of the day—a thesis on which everybody, or at least everybody in foreign-policy circles, needed to have an opinion. Fukuyama's article became the subject of intense debate on newspaper editorial pages, in the salons of Georgetown, and even at the highest level of government. In Great Britain, Prime Minister Margaret Thatcher felt compelled to offer her own assessment (which was not favorable).

Fukuyama certainly benefited from exquisite timing. "If my essay had been published a year earlier or a year later," he said, "nobody would have noticed." Although he was still on the staff of Rand when he delivered his Chicago lecture and wrote his article for *The National Interest*, Fukuyama since then had become deputy director for policy planning at the State Department. Onlookers who watched Foggy Bottom the way Kremlinologists studied Moscow vainly wondered if Fukuyama was providing a glimpse of how the new president, George H. W. Bush, planned to approach the world. More important, however, was the fact that 1989 was a year of great international turmoil, as Communist regimes in Europe collapsed like a row of dominoes. The rumblings began to be heard in the months before Fukuyama's article appeared, as Soviet troops evacuated Afghanistan and Mikhail Gorbachev continued his policy of *glasnost*. In the months immediately following, Poland acquired the Warsaw Pact's first non-Communist prime minister since the end of the Second World War and Hungary opened its borders. Then, in November, the Berlin Wall fell. At a time of confusing change, Fukuyama offered a compelling interpretation of current events.

The most formidable response to Fukuyama came in the fall issue of *The National Interest*, which devoted even more space to the subject. Its author was Samuel P. Huntington, one of the best-known political scientists in the country and a member of the National Security Council during the Carter administration. "If American political science leaves any lasting intellectual monument," wrote Robert D. Kaplan in the *Atlantic Monthly*, "the work of Samuel Huntington will be one of its pillars." Although Huntington's pillar stood in Cambridge, Fukuyama had not taken any classes with him at Harvard because Huntington was serving in Washington when Fukuyama was doing his graduate coursework. Yet the two men knew and respected each other, especially from summertime gatherings of professors and students who had studied security issues at Harvard.

Like Bloom and Kristol before him, Huntington hailed Fukuyama's essay as "brilliant." Then he proceeded to dismantle it. "The record of past predictions by social scientists is not a happy one," he wrote. He accused Fukuyama of overemphasizing "the predictability of history and the permanence of the moment." He allowed for the possibility of communism's revival and deadpanned that "a billion Chinese engaged in imperial expansion are likely to impose a lot of history on the rest of the world." The one thing that he was convinced would not change was "the weakness and irrationality of human nature." Fukuyama's thesis, he believed, cried out for rejection: "To hope for the benign end of history is human. To expect it to happen is unrealistic. To plan on it happening is disastrous."

As director of the John M. Olin Institute for Strategic Studies at Harvard University, Huntington enjoyed a much closer connection to the John M. Olin Foundation than Fukuyama ever did. About a decade before the end-of-history debate, Huntington had begun acquiring the seed money for what eventually became the Olin Institute. It was originally called the Center for International Affairs, and the Smith Richardson Foundation supplied much of the funding. "Sam was a strong Democrat," recalled Leslie Lenkowsky of Smith Richardson. "Some of the conservative foundations were nervous about supporting him because he had worked for Carter. But I explained how left-wing students had vilified Sam for his support of the Vietnam War, and I knew his program was a good investment." The John M. Olin Foundation chipped in $55,000 for fellowships in 1981 and 1982. It soon passed Smith Richardson as Huntington's major sponsor, with annual donations averaging just under $100,000 between 1983 and 1986. Most of the money supported a small number of fellowships for graduate students and postdoctoral researchers in the field of national security.

In the mid-1980s, the John M. Olin Foundation was actively searching for new grant recipients. It was giving away more money every year, but a strong stock market was causing the value of its

assets to increase at the same. "We weren't spending enough
money," said executive director Jim Pierson. "We needed to find
ways to spend more." Huntington was a natural choice. Not only
was the foundation both familiar and comfortable with him from
its previous giving, but Harvard was exactly the kind of elite institution that the foundation was trying to target and Huntington
was teaching his students from a perspective the foundation
could embrace. Pierson also admired several of Huntington's
former students, such as Eliot Cohen, whom he came to know
through Bill Kristol during their days at Penn.

In 1986, the foundation began expanding its support of
Huntington with a grant of $618,000 to underwrite Soviet stud-
ies and a conference of young scholars. This donation was supposed to last for three years, but in 1987 the foundation
committed an additional $1.4 million—and in so doing, gave
birth to the Olin Institute. Overall, the foundation spent $8.4
million on the program.

The foundation was especially enthusiastic for Huntington's
project because it remained immune to some of the worst trends
in higher education. "American universities maintain an uneasy
relationship with the study of war," said the Olin Institute in a
2002 grant application. "Though it is a generation after the years
of greatest anti-war sentiment, the dominant tendencies of political science and history departments are determined by hiring
decisions made long ago." That was a diplomatic way of saying
that the Left controlled much of the academy and that it was
relentlessly hostile to American power. "The Olin Institute has
been successfully helping to restore balance in American universities by giving support and a high profile to the best young
scholars studying national security," said the institute's application.

One of the central goals of the Olin Institute was to train a
new generation of scholars for public service and university
appointments. Between 1990 and 2001, eighty-eight Olin Fellows went through the Harvard program, and fifty-six of them
went on to tenured or tenure-track positions at Harvard, Columbia, Dartmouth, Chicago, Cornell, Georgetown, MIT, Penn, and
Yale. Those who did not become professors served in the State
Department, at think tanks, and in the media. "For various

historical and ideological reasons, the study of national security issues has not been widely popular in academia since the 1970s. The Olin Institute has provided support and haven for those interested in these critically important issues," said MIT political scientist Thomas Christensen, a China expert who was an Olin Fellow from 1991 to 1993. "There is an Olin network out there and I feel greatly privileged and honored to be part of it." Some of the most prominent members of the Olin network included Daniel Drezner, a University of Chicago professor who started a popular website on economics, politics, and globalization; John J. Mearsheimer, another Chicago professor; Kenneth Pollack, a bestselling author who became one of the country's most potent advocates for the invasion of Iraq; and Fareed Zakaria, another bestselling author who went on to edit *Foreign Affairs* and then took over *Newsweek*'s international edition. (If Francis Fukuyama had been a generation younger, he almost certainly would have been one of Huntington's Olin Fellows as well.)

In addition to supporting a new generation of scholars, the Olin Institute served as a base for Huntington to pursue his own work. Although it is difficult to identify the most significant book in Huntington's long career—*The Soldier and the State* (1957) and *Political Order in Changing Societies* (1968) are modern classics— one candidate surely would be *The Clash of Civilizations and the Remaking of World Order,* which Huntington wrote during the Olin Institute's heyday. As with Fukuyama, the book was first a speech: a Bradley Lecture, sponsored by Joyce's Bradley Foundation, at the American Enterprise Institute on October 19, 1992. Then Huntington turned it into a paper for an Olin Center series, followed by an article for *Foreign Affairs* in the summer of 1993. "That article, according to the *Foreign Affairs* editors, stirred up more discussion in three years than any other article they had published since the 1940s. It certainly stirred up more debate in three years than anything else I have written," wrote Huntington in the preface to the book that ultimately emerged in 1996. "Whatever else it did, the article struck a nerve in people of every civilization."

Huntington's clash-of-civilizations hypothesis was occasionally described as a response to Fukuyama, which it was not—

though it did confront similar issues while offering an entirely
different way of thinking about foreign relations. With the Cold
War struggle between freedom and communism finally over,
Huntington said, the world would shift away from ideological
showdowns: "The great divisions among humankind and the
dominating source of conflict will be cultural. Nation states will
remain the most powerful actors in world affairs, but the principal conflicts of global politics will occur between nations and
groups of different civilizations." One of his most prescient warn-
ings made him sound like a pre-9/11 Cassandra: "Somewhere
in the Middle East a half-dozen young men could well be dressed
in jeans, drinking Coke, listening to rap, and, between their bows
to Mecca, putting together a bomb to blow up an American air-
liner." A modernizing world, he wrote, is not necessarily a West-
ernizing world. He worried that modernization might actually
weaken the relative power and influence of the West and urged
the United States to maintain technological superiority, prevent
China and the Islamic world from developing military might,
and pick its allies with care: "In the clash of civilizations, Europe
and America will hang together or hang separately." He called
these post–Cold War quarrels "the latest phase of the evolution
of conflict in the modern world."

This stood in stark contrast to Fukuyama's thesis, which
Huntington described as a paradigm signaling "the end of significant conflict in global politics and the emergence of one relatively harmonious world." Huntington remained completely
unconvinced. He pointed out that the First World War was once
called the "war to end wars." He also cited Franklin D. Roosevelt's
prediction in the final year of the Second World War that international relations would occur within a "permanent structure of
peace." These were seductive but brutal chimeras, and Huntington warned against the temptation of succumbing to similar ones
in the 1990s:

> The illusion of harmony at the end of that Cold War was soon dissipated
> by the multiplication of ethnic conflicts and "ethnic cleansing," the break-
> down of law and order, the emergence of new patterns of alliance and
> conflict among states, the resurgence of neo-communist and neo-fascist
> movements, intensification of religious fundamentalism, the end of the

"diplomacy of smiles" and "policy of yes" in Russia's relations with the West, the inability of the United Nations and the United States to suppress bloody local conflicts, and the increasing assertiveness of a rising China. In the five years after the Berlin wall came down, the word "genocide" was heard far more often than in any five years of the Cold War.

At bottom, Huntington considered it fanciful to proclaim the end of history. He called Fukuyama's paradigm "far too divorced from reality to be a useful guide to the post–Cold War world."

AS TIME PASSED, THE DEBATE between Fukuyama's "end of history" and Huntington's "clash of civilizations" refused to fade away. Like Huntington, Fukuyama turned what began as a speech into a book, *The End of History and the Last Man*. The furor over his article in *The National Interest* was so strong that Fukuyama had to leave the State Department in order to expand upon his ideas and defend them, which he now did at great length in the book. He also offered his own appraisal of Huntington and his "unduly pessimistic view of world politics" in the *Wall Street Journal*. The world was not a battleground between warring civilizations, said Fukuyama, but rather a place where "sects within weak nation-states" fought skirmishes. He also took issue with Huntington's belief that modernization and Westernization are separate phenomena.

The ideas of Fukuyama and Huntington mattered not because they gave academics something to dispute, but because they provided high-level guidance to policymakers on a series of vital questions, such as confronting the menace of terrorism, assessing the value of regime change, and analyzing the potential for liberalization in the Middle East. The fact that neither Fukuyama nor Huntington would have predicted that these particular concerns would come to the forefront of American life in the early twenty-first century—but that their paradigms nevertheless have much to say about them—speaks directly to the value of their ideas. In the wake of September 11, it is possible to view the foreign policy of President George W. Bush as a kind of fusionist view that accepts many of Huntington's premises but tempers them with a belief that Islamic culture may be open to democratic ideals.

Whatever the case, fifteen years after he first spoke at Chicago, Fukuyama was still addressing audiences about the end of history—only this time they were much larger, and Fukuyama's reputation preceded him. On March 15, 2004, he spoke to a large audience at Tel Aviv University in Israel. Two former prime ministers, Benjamin Netanyahu and Shimon Peres, sat on a panel with him. Fukuyama did not retreat from his original idea. "The original article 'The End of History?' had a question mark at the end of it and I was posing it as a general question," he said, "and I believe that as a hypothesis it remains open." With respect to the specific threat of Osama bin Laden, al-Qaeda, and radical Islamists generally, Fukuyama described the hard choice facing the West: "The real issue is whether ... what we are facing is a genuine Huntingtonian clash of civilizations or whether this represents in some sense a deviant or minority view within the broader tradition of Islam." He tended to think it was the latter.

Fifteen years after Fukuyama stood athwart history yelling it had stopped, the debate he started raged on.

# CHAPTER NINE

# "Perpetuity Is a Very Long Time"

THE FINAL PAGE OF THE "Fat Memo" that Frank O'Connell gave to John M. Olin in 1975 mentioned an idea that would come to define the John M. Olin Foundation almost as much as the content of its philanthropy: "This program should not aim at perpetuity, but rather at liquidation within a given period (perhaps 25 years)—or sooner, in the discretion of the Trustees, should events indicate that to be a necessary or desirable course, in order to avoid frustration of the basic purpose."

What Olin was planning, in collaboration with O'Connell and the members of his board, was the eventual demise of the John M. Olin Foundation. He worried that if it did not cease to exist at some point in the not-too-distant future, the enemies of free enterprise might seize control of the foundation's assets and turn them against their original objective. Moreover, Olin believed that later generations of Americans would be much better able to address the problems they faced than he would be able to anticipate them. Meanwhile, the intellectual defense of capitalism needed all the help it could get as soon as it could get it. All this led Olin to conclude that his foundation should spend its money on the present and let the future take care of itself.

This concept did not leap out of nowhere. Some of America's earliest philanthropists would have been surprised to learn that foundations had become perpetual. In 1867, the Massachusetts-born financier George Peabody (1795–1869) created the Peabody Fund to assist with the education of southerners in the wake of the Civil War. The Peabody Fund is sometimes called the first modern foundation because it leveraged capital by issuing challenge grants to communities. Less well known is the fact that Peabody gave it a fifty-year lifespan. Many of the major twentieth-century philanthropists were familiar with his example. The John D. Rockefeller Foundation has no intention of turning off the lights, but there is some evidence to suggest that its benefactor did not believe his creation would live forever. "As my grandfather once said, 'Perpetuity is a very long time,'" remarked John D. Rockefeller III in 1953.

Olin probably first learned of the concept of term-limited foundations from the case of Julius Rosenwald (1862–1932), the salesman who invented the ordering process that fueled the success of Sears, Roebuck in the first part of the twentieth century. As Rosenwald became a wealthy man, he increasingly thought about the practice of philanthropy. In 1909, he warned of charities that "outlived their usefulness." For the remainder of his life, he crusaded against perpetuities. "I am opposed to the permanent or what might be styled the never-ending endowment," he said in 1913. "Permanent endowments tend to lessen the amount available for immediate needs; and our immediate needs are too plain and too urgent to allow us to do the work of future generations." These future generations, he believed, would know how to take care of their own problems as they arose. Rosenwald summed up his beliefs in a pair of articles for the *Atlantic Monthly* in 1929 and 1930. "It is almost inevitable that as trustees and officers of perpetuities grow old they become more concerned to conserve the funds in their care than to wring from those funds the greatest possible usefulness," he wrote in the first of these articles. "Real endowments are not money, but ideas," he observed in the second. "Desirable and feasible ideas are of much more value than money, and when their usefulness has once been established they may be expected to receive ready support as long as they justify themselves. We may be confident that if a public need is clearly demonstrated, and a practicable way of meeting that need is shown, society will take care of it in the future." Rosenwald certainly practiced what he preached: The Julius Rosenwald Fund, established in 1917, was ordained to halt operations twenty-five years after its benefactor's death. As it happened, the fund spent its last dollar in 1948 and closed well ahead of schedule. When all was said and done, Rosenwald was responsible for giving away $63 million, much of it for the education of African Americans.

The historian Daniel J. Boorstin hailed Rosenwald's example. "The foundations which dominate the scene nowadays are extremely general in their purpose," he observed in *The Decline of Radicalism*. "The public dangers which arise from them come precisely from the fact that there is no prospect that they will ever become obsolete." He even hinted that perpetuity cut against basic American principles: "Spontaneity, drift, fluidity, and competition among American institutions have given our culture much of its vitality. Some of the dangers which come from the new large foundations spring from the very vagueness and generality of their purposes as well as from their sheer size," he wrote. "They show few signs of that self-liquidating tendency that Rosenwald rightly insisted to be a feature of a healthy foundation."

Despite such cautions, perpetuity became the rule for foundations in the United States. Favorable tax laws fueled their explosive growth in the twentieth century, and philanthropy became a key part of estate planning and even corporate strategy. All the while, Congress made fitful attempts to rein in foundation abuses. The possibility of restricting the lives of foundations occasionally entered the discussion. Amid debate surrounding the Tax Reform Act of 1969, the House of Representatives actually passed a bill that would have limited the lifespan of foundations to forty years. The Senate refused to act on this proposal, however, and the measure was dropped from the final bill—in large part because the foundations themselves waged an aggressive lobbying campaign against it. To them, it looked like an anti-jobs bill (confirming Rosenwald's suspicions about the sentiments of philanthropic caretakers). Yet Congress did require foundations to disburse a percentage of their assets every year. At first, the figure was set at 6 percent; in 1975, it was reduced to 5 percent. (Because administrative expenses can count in the equation, the real giving of many foundations equals less than 4 percent of their endowments.) In the years that followed—the years in which the John M. Olin Foundation was most active—Congress did not pay much attention to foundation law. As a consequence, the debate over perpetuity has shifted from what the government should compel to what donors ought to insist upon.

If Olin had any mixed feelings about ordering his foundation's end, they vanished in 1977 when Henry Ford II announced that he was quitting the board of the Ford Foundation, the country's biggest foundation, with an endowment then worth $2.3 billion. Ford had been a trustee since 1943, a few years after his father and grandfather created the foundation. His departure meant that for the first time, the Ford Foundation would not have a member of the Ford family on its board of trustees. Under the leadership of McGeorge Bundy, the foundation had become controversial for, among other things, supporting separatist black-power organizations. Despite these tendencies, Henry Ford II had often defended the foundation's activities from conservative critics, including Ford Motor Company shareholders. In the end, however, the foundation's commitment to left-wing politics compelled him to quit.

Ford explained his thinking in a remarkable four-page letter of resignation that made headlines around the country:

> The foundation exists and thrives on the fruits of our economic system. The dividends of competitive enterprise make it all possible. A significant portion of the abundance created by U.S. business enables the foundation and like institutions to carry on their work. In effect, the foundation is a creature of capitalism—a statement that, I'm sure would be shocking to many professional staff people in the field of philanthropy. It is hard to discern recognition of this fact in anything the foundation does. It is even more difficult to find an understanding of this in many of the institutions, particularly the universities, that are the beneficiaries of the foundation's grant programs.
>
> I am not playing the role of the hard-headed tycoon who thinks all philanthropoids are socialists and all university professors are Communists. I'm just suggesting to the trustees and the staff that the system that makes the foundation possible very probably is worth preserving. Perhaps it is time for the trustees and staff to examine the question of our obligations to our economic system and to consider how the foundation, as one of the system's most prominent offspring, might act most wisely to strengthen and improve its progenitor.

Ford's bitter resignation had a profound effect on Olin. The aging businessman had channeled most of his charity in the direction of preserving free enterprise—and he dreaded the notion that sometime after he was gone, the people running his foundation would turn against its first principles.

Bundy's cavalier response to Henry Ford II justified Olin's fears: "I don't think one letter from anyone is going to change the foundation's course." To Bundy, Ford was an inconvenient crank. The heads of other foundations were just as dismissive. David Rogers of the Robert Wood Johnson Foundation, which was then the nation's second largest philanthropy, said that Ford's comment on free enterprise "worried me." John H. Knowles of the Rockefeller Foundation suggested that organizations such as his own did not need to concern themselves with strengthening capitalism because corporations would do it on their own. An official at the Carnegie Endowment for International Peace was flabbergasted at Ford's letter: "Is that what the Ford Foundation is set up for, to promote free enterprise?" He considered the notion outrageous.

The episode shook Olin's faith in philanthropy. "It really distressed him," said O'Connell. To guarantee that his own foundation would not go the way of Ford, Olin made clear to everyone that he did not want it to exist in perpetuity. Just as he believed that the government's central planners lacked the wisdom and information necessary to secure economic prosperity, he thought the problems of tomorrow were best left to future generations. Moreover, he could see pressing problems all around—in particular, dire threats to free enterprise. Left unaddressed, these would erode capitalism further and make the plight of later generations even more troubled. It was like what his old chemistry professor at Cornell used to say: If you can define a problem, the solution suggests itself. By the 1970s, Olin figured that he and his close colleagues understood the problem well enough. The solution, to the extent that they might contribute to it, was to spend his fortune in philanthropy. Hoarding it in a bank vault would diminish its impact. Even worse, enemies might seize it.

And so Olin called for his foundation to spend its entire endowment—not necessarily within his own lifetime, but

certainly within the lifetimes of the younger people he was selecting to serve as trustees. In the late 1970s, in fact, the foundation's board was a mix of people roughly Olin's own age (Hanes
and McCloy) and those who were about a generation younger
(Gillespie and Simon). All were made to understand his desire
that one day the John M. Olin Foundation would run out of cash
and close its doors for good. Curiously, Olin was reluctant to
specify his wishes in writing. He simply stated his intention and
expected the trustees to abide by it.

They remained committed to this obligation. Simon believed
in Olin's vision so much, in fact, that he directed his own William
E. Simon Foundation to spend down its assets. The mission of
the Simon Foundation differed from that of the John M. Olin
Foundation: "The main purpose of my foundation is to help the
needy by providing the means by which they may help themselves—in essence, the philosophy expressed by Andrew Carnegie
in his essay, 'The Gospel of Wealth,'" wrote Simon in *A Time for
Reflection*. When it came to the question of perpetuity, however,
Simon wanted to follow Olin's example. "When I die," he wrote,
"various trusts will continue to fund the foundation, but it will
not last beyond the lifetimes of my children."

Simon and his fellow trustees sought to apply Olin's principles to the practical questions of grantmaking, and for the most
part they succeeded. Shortly after Olin's death in 1982, the "Fatter Memo" written by Joyce and Piereson recommended that the
foundation not support endowment drives: "This not only ties
up large amounts of money which, left uncommitted, could be
the source of better leverage, but it also runs the risk that winds
of change will sweep over the endowed institution, and the administration of the endowment fund will consequently pass ultimately to someone who not only does not understand or share
the views and purposes of the founder, but who may have oppo-
site views." The board approved this recommendation.

Yet the board of trustees chose to set aside these guidelines
on a few occasions. In 1984, for instance, the foundation donated
$100,000 to Amherst College to help endow the John J. McCloy
Professorship of American Institutions and International

Diplomacy. A staff evaluation called it a "fitting tribute" to a man who had served as a trustee of the foundation.

The most notable example of the foundation supporting an endowment involved a gift to the business school at Washington University in St. Louis—the largest single grant in the foundation's history. It was also perhaps the foundation's most disappointing use of the Olin fortune. The origins of the grant grew from John M. Olin's personal relationship with the school. As a more or less lifelong resident of the St. Louis area, Olin always took a great interest in Washington University. He joined its board in 1942 and maintained a formal relationship for the rest of his life. He once told Eugene Williams that if the trustees felt their efforts to defend free enterprise were not effective, the foundation's liquidation might take the form of big gifts to Cornell and Washington University. Olin also became an admirer of Murray Weidenbaum, an economist at the school who studied the costs of regulation and enjoyed giving Congress six words of advice: "Don't just stand there, undo something!" In 1974, the foundation helped Weidenbaum establish his Center for the Study of American Business with a grant of $175,000, followed in subsequent years by a series of six-figure donations. Olin was not the only person who appreciated Weidenbaum's work: Ronald Reagan did as well, and he appointed Weidenbaum to serve as his first chairman at the Council of Economic Advisors. The early days of the Reagan administration were busy ones for Weidenbaum, but he still found time for his old patron. At the 1981 dinner held in Olin's honor—the one Richard Nixon attended—Weidenbaum served as master of ceremonies.

Shortly after Olin died, Washington University approached the foundation about a large grant, stressing Olin's personal ties to the school. The Olin steering committee, according to its own notes, "did not feel that this is a school of sufficient influence to warrant an exception to the Foundation's policy not to fund endowments." Consequently, the full board decided against the request. As a consolation prize, however, the trustees approved an endowment gift of $3 million to the Center for the Study of American Business, which was still doing the research into regulation that had made Weidenbaum well known several years earlier. There was some discussion of naming the center after John M. Olin, but Weidenbaum worried that this would limit his ability to solicit donations from other sources, and the idea was dropped.

Through the 1980s and into the 1990s, the Center for the Study of American Business sponsored visiting fellows, held conferences, and conducted research. It continued to focus on regulation and business from a market perspective, sometimes under the direction of Weidenbaum and occasionally under the direction of others when Weidenbaum took leaves of absence. The center never fit neatly into Washington University—Weidenbaum had trouble recruiting faculty associates on his own campus, in large part because prevailing academic trends were not hospitable to his views on the economy.

In the 1990s, the foundation made two more grants to the center worth more than $500,000 in total. When Weidenbaum retired in 2001, the center was renamed in his honor—but the foundation was not consulted on his successor, which had been a condition of the 1984 endowment gift. Its new leader, Steven S. Smith, ended the center's affiliation with several free-market scholars. He also spoke of going in "new directions." Ironically, the Weidenbaum Center's new direction would take it away from the subjects that had most interested Weidenbaum and which had attracted Olin to his work in the first place. "This episode demonstrates the folly of providing endowment funds for university programs," commented Piereson. "It is almost inevitable that such funds will eventually be re-directed for purposes not envisioned by the donor."

Another important factor in the foundation's decision to spend millions on Washington University was its support for the William E. Simon School of Business Administration at the University of Rochester. In the 1980s, business schools hunting for philanthropic dollars often approached executives with proposals to tap fundraising networks in return for naming rights. The dean at Rochester, Paul W. MacAvoy, was an old acquaintance of Simon's. He suggested to Simon that if they raised $30 million together, the school could carry Simon's name. MacAvoy wanted

Simon to come up with half of the money, in part by asking executives and investors to chip in. Simon agreed, and he hoped that in addition to his own large personal contribution the John M. Olin Foundation would provide a donation. From his perspective, this made sense for the foundation because Rochester's business school placed a heavy emphasis on entrepreneurship and markets. Many of its teachers hailed from the University of Chicago, where they learned about economics from Milton Friedman and George Stigler. It was especially strong in finance. Lending it Simon's name would add prestige and possibly encourage it to continue in a healthy direction. When the foundation board considered a grant in 1986, Simon withdrew from the deliberations. There was in fact considerable skepticism about its merits. In the end, however, $2.5 million was pledged. More grants followed in later years, totaling $9.6 million.

Each of these gifts to the Simon School supported specific programs rather than an endowment. Yet they also helped create the conditions for what was to come: If the John M. Olin Foundation was willing to help finance a business school named after Bill Simon, then how could it resist a proposal to name a business school after John M. Olin? Within a few months of the foundation's first grant to the Simon School, trustee Charles Knight suggested finding a business school to name after Olin. Knight was the chief executive of Emerson Electric, a St. Louis company, and he was also deeply involved in supporting Washington University (which is home to the Charles F. Knight Executive Education Center). It did not take long for the John M. Olin Foundation to devote $15 million to endow the John M. Olin School of Business at Washington University. That decision came in the final days of 1987, and it was predicated upon the university matching the gift by raising a similar amount of money on its own—a mission that it would in fact accomplish. Nine years later, the foundation spent an additional $2 million on the John M. Olin Distinguished Professorship in Business, Law, and Economics, another endowment. The first occupant of this position, coincidentally, was recruited from the Simon School.

The school's new name certainly honored the memory of John M. Olin, but did it advance the interests of his foundation?

On one level, spending so much money in this way represented a major departure from the foundation's emphasis on devoting its resources to elite institutions. Washington University's business school was ranked, at best, in the second tier of American business schools. There was simply nothing special about it, apart from the fact of John M. Olin's personal connection. The school did not even have a market-oriented approach to its teaching and research, which was one of the factors that had made support for the Simon School palatable.

Piereson solicited independent judgments on the John M. Olin School of Business in 2003, and the responses were not encouraging. "I find no evidence of concern for free markets and limited government in the curriculum or in the research agenda of the faculty," wrote Paul MacAvoy, who had become a professor at Yale. "I cannot find that the Olin name on this school signifies in any meaningful way principles for which the John M. Olin Foundation is well known." J. Clayburn La Force Jr., the dean emeritus at UCLA's business school—and a longtime advisor to the foundation, going back to the days of Frank O'Connell— reached similar conclusions. "There does not seem to be a group of scholars dedicated to studying the nature of competitive markets, private property, limited government, and so forth," he wrote. "Furthermore, I am certain that such a grouping of academics cannot be created and made to last simply by endowing a school." La Force went on to describe his own experience in raising endowments for chairs at UCLA. He confessed that it would have been better to seek annuities tied to the academic lives of specific individuals. "If [a holder of such a chair] were to die, retire, or go to Harvard, the annuity would end—it would be over and done with and the school would be deprived of the opportunity to fill the endowed chair with a socialist. Henry Ford would have agreed. So would have Bill Simon." Piereson shared many of these views. "I would say our relationship with Washington University was the greatest disappointment during my tenure at the foundation," he said in 2005. "We spent a lot of money there and did little to advance the purposes of the foundation."

As Piereson gained experience at working with the board of trustees, he saw the potential for individual members to advocate for pet causes that did not necessarily reflect the foundation's mission. Some of this arose from social pressures. The board members were constantly assaulted with requests for money, often from groups that had no business expecting to receive support from the John M. Olin Foundation. Simon was especially vulnerable to these appeals. To make sure they did not intrude upon the foundation's main purpose, Piereson came up with the concept of trustee grants: Each trustee was allowed to make grants worth up to $25,000 annually, not subject to board approval. The figure eventually was raised to $100,000. (The grants also were seen as a way of rewarding the trustees for their time; unlike some grantmaking groups, the John M. Olin Foundation did not compensate its trustees.) Most of these special grants wound up supporting charitable organizations with little relationship to the foundation's agenda, such as programs for needy children, summer camps, and medical research.

As a member of the board, Piereson was able to make small grants in this fashion. He typically used his own pool of money to assist conservatives—and one of his trustee grants became controversial when it was made public. In 1993, writer David Brock hit the bestseller lists with *The Real Anita Hill,* an exposé of the woman who collaborated with feminist groups and nearly destroyed the Supreme Court nomination of Clarence Thomas. The book came under withering scrutiny in liberal venues, most notably on the pages of the *New Yorker,* where an article by Jane Mayer and Jill Abramson questioned its objectivity by noting that the John M. Olin Foundation had "helped to bankroll" Brock. Anthony Lewis of the *New York Times* piled on in a column headlined "Sleaze with Footnotes" and specifically fingered Simon as a culprit. What these critics failed to report was the size of the grant: a mere $5,000. (Most of them also seemed unaware of the fact that a few years earlier, the foundation had provided the funds for Brock to have a separate fellowship at the Heritage Foundation.) "I'm darn proud of what we did," wrote Simon in a *Wall Street Journal* op-ed, which went on to reveal that Lewis himself had received a $5,000 honorarium for participating in a John M. Olin lecture series at the Air Force Academy. "If Mr. Lewis feels so strongly about support from the Olin Foundation, why did he accept our $5,000?" asked Simon. It was a compelling rebuttal. Piereson, however, was frustrated to see the foundation's name dragged into a political controversy—especially a controversy to which it had contributed so little.

THE FOUNDATION'S ASSETS DWINDLED between 1988 and 1993, as the trustees remained conscious of their commitment to deplete them entirely—but also aware that they needed to stay in business while John M. Olin's widow, Evelyn, was still alive. The value of the foundation's holdings fell from a high of more than $90 million in the mid-1980s to about $44 million in 1993. Then, on November 7, 1993, Evelyn passed away in St. Louis at the age of eighty-eight. Early in 1994, the foundation inherited the proceeds from a charitable trust that had been established for her. Thus the foundation received its final infusion of cash, worth almost $98 million. "Now," said a report that Piereson prepared for the trustees, "we can begin to . . . make plans to spend the Foundation out of existence."

It was at last possible to start thinking about the foundation's end with some precision. "How long should the Foundation continue to operate?" asked Piereson. He pointed out that Olin had suggested "that the Foundation should not outlive the younger generation of trustees whom he appointed to the board." The memo noted that the oldest trustee at that time was seventy. "Mr. Olin's instruction, when placed in this context, seems practical enough to fix the future life of the Foundation at about 10 years, which would take us out to the year 2003. This might reasonably be extended out to 15 years, if the trustees wish to do so." Piereson expressed special concern that if the foundation were to try to spend its endowment in less than ten years, it would have to increase its rate of annual giving dramatically—and perhaps force the foundation into the practice of giving large endowment gifts, "the value of which (in relation to our objectives) would be open to question."

There were other concerns as well. "Many institutions and programs rely heavily on our support; indeed, in many cases, they may not survive without it," wrote Piereson. "There are only a handful of foundations in the nation with a philosophy and program similar to ours. Funds for the kinds of programs we support are not plentiful. Our funds, once spent, will not be easy to replace."

Conservatives certainly understood this, and it worried them. They were sticklers for donor intent, but at the same time many wished the John M. Olin Foundation could find a way to survive a bit longer. Although nobody at the foundation ever gave serious consideration to anything other than following Olin's instructions, conservatives in the 1990s found themselves wondering, why not extend the life of the John M. Olin Foundation for another generation? It was entirely conceivable, went this line of thinking, that Olin himself would have endorsed such a decision if he had been alive to see the good works his foundation had made possible. Here was the dark side of Olin's sunsetting proviso: Perpetuity may be a long time, but death is forever—its own kind of perpetuity, one might say. Besides, wasn't there something just plain morbid about institutional suicide?

Much of this discussion was self-interested: No recipient organization wants to see a contributor dry up. And few appreciated the fact that if the foundation had tried to stay in business longer, its level of giving would not have been nearly so high. Yet much of the debate was edifying and high-minded—and one of the leading critics of term-limited foundations was Michael Joyce. When Joyce was executive director of the John M. Olin Foundation, he never argued against honoring donor intent. Yet he had come to believe that conservative philanthropists determined to get rid of all their assets were making a grave mistake. From his perch as head of the Bradley Foundation, which had no plans to spend down, he called the mandate of the John M. Olin Foundation unfortunate. He compared it to "the unfounded but powerful belief in the Marxist teleology—embraced, ironically, by many conservatives—that postulates, as a matter of 'scientific' inevitability: History belongs to the left." Despite all the cases of foundations straying from their missions, there were stirring counterexamples to this harmful trend. "It is through a well-established tradition and a body of affirmative authorizing documentation that so perpetual an institution as the Church has been able to survive major deviations from its

Founder's intentions, yet find within itself the capacity for its own regeneration," said Joyce.

Joyce's arguments were by no means the only ones offered. Others pointed out that perpetual foundations had the advantage of acquiring expertise over long stretches of time. Moreover, they were particularly well equipped to focus on enduring problems that have no simple solutions, such as poverty and racial discrimination (or, in the minds of many conservatives, liberal dominance of higher education). Yet there were obvious answers to each of these points: Despite Joyce's optimism, it was difficult to argue with the actual experience of the Ford Foundation and its ilk, and it was far from clear that older and perhaps ossified institutions would do a better job of addressing the troubles that are always with us than newer and more flexible organizations created by a rising generation of philanthropists. The future is fundamentally unknowable and holds many surprises. The Bryan Mullanphy Trust, for example, was created in the middle of the nineteenth century to aid pioneers traveling through St. Louis on their way to settling the West. Its mission was obsolete within half a century of its establishment, but it nonetheless continued to exist (and became the object of several court cases). With the pace of change in an era of technological innovation speeding up rather than slowing down, there was no reason to think that modern philanthropists would have any more success when it came to anticipating the dilemmas of tomorrow. As Heather Richardson Higgins of the Randolph Foundation put it in a debate with Joyce, "It is an astonishing case of moral hubris—born, perhaps, of a generation of progressives—to think that future generations of citizens will be so slack that they will not rise to the challenges of their time."

The John M. Olin Foundation certainly was not alone in resolving to spend itself out of existence. The Lucille B. Markey Charitable Trust underwrote more than $500 million in medical research and went out of business in 1997. The Aaron Diamond Foundation was established in 1986 with a ten-year time limit; it gave away more than $200 million to AIDS research and minority education before closing on schedule. Around the same time, the Vincent Astor Foundation issued its final set of grants—an option it chose in the absence of a mandate to do so from its benefactor. A number of other foundations also planned to exhaust their endowments. One of their most prominent supporters was management guru Peter Drucker. "The idea that foundations should be around forever is a mistake," he said.

In the philanthropic world, however, these views represented only a small minority. Perpetuity was the norm. Most philanthropists did not even consider the possibility of restricting the lives of their foundations. When the media turned its attention to the John M. Olin Foundation's chosen fate, they often treated it as a freakish oddity. The *Boston Globe* referred to its plans as "The right to self-destruct."

The robust stock market of the 1990s made self-destruction a genuine challenge. The foundation's investments produced handsome returns. Even though annual spending from 1994 to 1999 averaged more than $17 million, the foundation's assets declined only slightly, from $115 million to $109 million. The turning point came in 2000, as stocks began to cool off. The foundation also lost its most visible leader when William E. Simon died on June 3 at the age of seventy-two.

For more than two decades, he had served as the foundation's principal leader. Through a combination of his vigorous personality and his impressive résumé—a former Treasury secretary, a bestselling author, and an incredibly successful businessman—Simon exercised a considerable amount of influence over the board of trustees and the foundation staff. At times, he was difficult to work with. But he brought endless amounts of energy to the foundation and he was unwavering in his devotion to the causes that John M. Olin had espoused. When he was gone, almost everybody associated with the foundation missed him right away.

Simon's death, said a comprehensive report to the foundation's board in December 2000, "serves as a reminder that we are all getting older." And so at last the time had come to determine the specifics of how the foundation would shut down. One of the first questions involved its investment portfolio. In its prime, the foundation mostly held stocks because of their long-term performance. Like people planning their retirement, however, the foundation needed more predictability as it approached the end of its life. In 2001, it shifted entirely to bonds at a time when equity markets were at historic highs. This decision allowed it to operate with the confidence that it would be able to meet all of its final obligations.

There were staffing issues as well. The John M. Olin Foundation never took on more than a handful of employees at any one time. To keep them loyal to an organization that was planning its own extinction, the foundation handed out retention bonuses and tried to accommodate transitions into post-foundation life. Janice Riddell, a program officer, departed at the end of 2003, planning to spend more time with her family and consult with other foundations. Her colleague William Voegeli left at the same time and joined the Claremont Institute. By the start of 2004, there were only three employees of the foundation left: Piereson, program officer Caroline Hemphill, and office manager Betty Sturdy.

The most important question, however, focused on the foundation's grant program—and particularly the matter of which groups would continue to receive support and which would not. After Simon's death, the foundation more or less stopped accepting unsolicited applications. These never made up a large portion of the foundation's giving, and so the impact of the decision was negligible. The hardest choices involved determining how to phase out support for traditional recipients. In the fall of 2000, the staff began to prepare a set of recommendations, based upon the quality of each group's work and how much it needed the foundation's funding. There was a strong desire to make several large gifts to recipients that carried John M. Olin's name. Not only did they represent some of the foundation's most important work, but they also relied heavily upon the foundation for their budgets. Moreover, their leaders tended to be academics rather than the quasi-professional fundraisers who headed so many think tanks and other organizations.

These large gifts came to be known as "termination grants," and the biggest beneficiaries were the law and economics centers. The one at Harvard received a promise of $10 million. Yale won a final grant of nearly $3.4 million. Chicago and Stanford took $3 million each, and Virginia $1.2 million. Outside of the law schools, the largest termination grant, worth $2 million, was pledged to the John M. Olin Institute for Strategic Studies at Harvard. The Manhattan Institute earned a going-away present of $1.2 million. The Federalist Society also was promised a donation of $1.2 million, for its general programs as well as administering the John M. Olin legal fellowships. Other noteworthy grantees included the American Enterprise Institute ($750,000 for health policy studies), the Collegiate Network ($450,000), the Law and Economics Center at George Mason University ($600,000), Harvey Mansfield's Program on Constitutional Government at Harvard ($600,000), Paul Peterson's Program on Education Policy and Governance at Harvard ($300,000), and the Intercollegiate Studies Institute ($700,000). Interestingly, neither the William E. Simon School of Business Administration at the University of Rochester nor the John M. Olin School of Business at Washington University received a parting gift.

Although the John M. Olin Foundation planned to close its office and release the remaining members of its staff at the end of 2005, several of these termination grants would require disbursements over the next two or possibly three years. But these would be handled, as Piereson often said, "from a desk drawer." For all intents and purposes, 2005 was the final year of the foundation's life—its final board meeting, its final round of grantmaking decisions, and the final fulfillment of John M. Olin's philanthropic vision.

# THE RIGHT IDEAS

O N THE EVENING OF APRIL 6, 2005, at the Princeton Club in New York City, a group of conservative dignitaries gathered to celebrate the legacy of the John M. Olin Foundation and its longtime executive director James Piereson. The foundation was a few months away from closing for good and the time was fast approaching to say farewell. Master of ceremonies Bill Simon Jr. discussed the foundation's legacy, cracked jokes about his late father, and introduced a small parade of speakers. They included Robert P. George of Princeton, Piereson's old friend Bill Kristol, and foundation trustees Peter Flanigan and Eugene Williams. Paul Brest, president of the William and Flora Hewlett Foundation and previously dean of the Stanford Law School (and not a conservative), spoke about the foundation's support of law and economics. American Enterprise Institute president Christopher DeMuth addressed the group as well. "We all admire Jim Piereson for his sterling character, keen intellect, sound judgment, and self-confident modesty, but the really important reason for us to honor him is that he has shown how nonprofit finance can be purposive and effective," he said.

The handful of listeners who could remember watching Richard Nixon spring into the room at the 1981 dinner honoring John M. Olin must have experienced a sense of déjà vu when Adam Meyerson of the Philanthropy Roundtable stood behind the podium and read a letter from President George W. Bush:

I send greetings to those gathered for The Philanthropy Roundtable's tribute to the John M. Olin Foundation. Congratulations to Jim Piereson and members on being honored for your accomplishments and years of dedicated service.

Today, our Nation is stronger because we have advanced the ideals of private enterprise, freedom, and the rule of law. By supporting policies that strengthen our democracy, the John M. Olin Foundation has helped uphold the vital institutions and values that make America great.

I appreciate all those at the Olin Foundation who give their time, energy, and talents to deepen our understanding of public policy, free government, and the judiciary. Your efforts carry on our proud heritage of freedom and promote our founding principles.

These were the latest tributes among many others that had been pouring in for years, especially from grantees who would feel the full impact of the foundation's pending disappearance. One of the finest had come in 2001, in a letter sent by Nathan Tarcov of the Olin Center at the University of Chicago:

The John M. Olin Foundation will be missed. It has been a wonderful institution with an effect on our times far out of proportion to its size. The foundation's selectively focused grants have had a deep and salutary impact in sustaining independent scholarship and genuine education in the American academy in recent decades. Many foundations in America today can be offered as evidence for how difficult is the practice of intelligent philanthropy. Future generations will look back at the history of our time with profound gratitude that the John M. Olin Foundation was here so long, and knew so well how to get it right.

How did the foundation get it right? As Piereson and company prepared to close shop in 2005, this question increasingly preoccupied conservatives, who pined for a new John M. Olin to fill the vacuum being left by the old one. Liberals also became interested, as they looked at the political landscape and recognized how conservatives had reshaped it over the previous generation. They understood that philanthropy had played an important part, and wondered if studying the experience of the John M. Olin Foundation might teach them some valuable lessons.

There are perhaps eight simple rules that explain why the John M. Olin Foundation was able to do so much and do it so well.

**1. First principles**: John M. Olin gave his foundation a clear mandate to defend America's system of free enterprise. There could be no misunderstanding his intentions. Although the foundation spent the bulk of its assets after he had passed away, Olin made sure that the people to whom he entrusted his philanthropic legacy shared his own devotion to individual liberty and limited government.

**2. Strong leadership**: Not only was William E. Simon fully committed to the foundation's project, he was also a natural leader who knew how to run an organization, inspire excellence and loyalty in others, and invest money wisely. His intimidating personality sometimes presented unnecessary difficulties, but there can be no arguing that the foundation flourished under his direction.

**3. United board**: Every trustee of the foundation had met John M. Olin during his life, and most of them knew him well. All felt obliged to carry out his philanthropic intentions. By staying relatively small—no more than about six or seven members at a time—the board never split into fighting factions. And although there were occasional disagreements, the trustees operated almost totally by consensus. With the semi-exception of Eugene Williams, who was married to Olin's stepdaughter, there were no members of the Olin family on the board during its heyday, and thus there were none of the intergenerational squabbles that have hobbled other foundations with conservative leanings.

**4. Quality staff**: The foundation benefited from three outstanding executive directors and a capable staff. None of them had extensive experience in philanthropy before joining the foundation—they were not professional "philanthropoids." The best of them, such as O'Connell, Joyce, and Piereson, were generalists who could discuss and appraise law and economics theory as well as U.S. foreign policy with intelligence and insight. Although many were of a scholarly bent, they did not function at an academic pace.

**5. Reinvest in success**: Worthy recipients often received support for long periods—they were not cut off so the foundation could move on to something else. The habit of nurturing talent and letting good money follow good allowed the foundation to develop a menu of scholars and organizations with solid track records and promising futures. Over time, this simplified decision making. Rather than investigating new organizations pitching untested products, the foundation devoted a rising portion of its resources to the tried and true.

**6. Patience and serendipity**: The foundation understood that it can take a long time for an idea to have a consequence, and that funding a counterintelligentsia would yield few quick payoffs. Moreover, some of the finest payoffs were completely unexpected, such as the commercial success of *The Closing of the American Mind* or how Francis Fukuyama's end-of-history thesis burst upon America's intellectual scene.

**7. Trickle-down politics**: In a war of ideas, intellectuals fill the boots on the ground. They shape elite opinion, which then spreads into popular culture through books, journals, and other forms of media. The foundation believed that it was far better to support a magazine with a small but influential readership than large-scale campaigns of "public education." From this standpoint, problems are best solved by approaching them on a tectonic level rather than searching for quick fixes.

**8. Sunsetting**: Many conservatives were disappointed that the foundation chose to spend itself out of existence. They wished it could have continued its philanthropy forever. Yet if the foundation had opted for perpetuity, it would not have had nearly the influence it did enjoy—a spending profile of a foundation with assets of $400 million or $500 million, rather than never much more than $100 million. The foundation was important because it had a profound impact on its time, rather than a considerably slighter one that spanned years into a future that probably will be able to take care of itself.

The reason the John M. Olin Foundation mattered, of course, has to do not only with these eight rules but with the awesome power of conservative ideas. At the Philanthropy Roundtable dinner, Pierson drove the point home with a story about Ron Turcotte, the jockey who rode his horse to the Triple Crown in 1973. After he had won the Belmont Stakes by thirty-one lengths, everyone wanted him to answer a single question: What was your secret? "I didn't need a secret," replied Turcotte. "I had Secretariat."

So what was the secret of the John M. Olin Foundation? "Well, we had you—the men and women in this room, and others who are not here: Bill Buckley, Irving Kristol, Norman Podhoretz, Michael Novak, Hilton Kramer, Roger Kimball, Heather Mac Donald, Robby George, and many others," said Piereson. "Milton Friedman and the market economists; the law and economics scholars; Allan Bloom, Harvey Mansfield, and the followers of Leo Strauss; Samuel Huntington, Eliot Cohen, and others in foreign policy; institutions like the Heritage Foundation, the Hoover Institution, the Manhattan Institute, and the American Enterprise Institute; and publications from *Commentary* to *The Public Interest* to *The New Criterion*. The list could go on."

John M. Olin would have appreciated the metaphor. The year after Secretariat raced his way to fame, Olin's own horse, Cannonade, won the Kentucky Derby. His comment on the race, which featured nearly two dozen horses, bears repeating: "There were just too damned many." These are not words that Olin would have uttered in response to Piereson's list. No, the ghost of John M. Olin simply would have smiled.

# APPENDIX
## Financial Summary of the John M. Olin Foundation, 1982–2005

| Year | Assets | Grants |
|------|--------|--------|
| 2005 | 17,000,000 | 12,000,000 |
| 2004 | 30,000,000 | 11,214,000 |
| 2003 | 43,073,000 | 11,310,000 |
| 2002 | 55,258,000 | 17,062,000 |
| 2001 | 71,486,000 | 20,502,000 |
| 2000 | 91,224,000 | 20,819,000 |
| 1999 | 109,498,000 | 19,368,000 |
| 1998 | 110,172,000 | 19,313,000 |
| 1997 | 115,020,000 | 18,370,000 |
| 1996 | 117,971,000 | 18,690,000 |
| 1995 | 117,529,000 | 16,195,000 |
| 1994 | 115,281,000 | 13,852,000 |
| 1993 | 44,700,000 | 14,561,000 |
| 1992 | 58,200,000 | 15,200,000 |
| 1991 | 70,691,000 | 18,726,000 |
| 1990 | 69,646,000 | 19,500,000 |
| 1989 | 90,034,000 | 14,995,000 |
| 1988 | 78,500,000 | 14,383,000 |
| 1987 | 83,846,000 | 14,117,000 |
| 1986 | 90,452,000 | 10,408,000 |
| 1985 | 90,350,000 | 8,591,000 |
| 1984 | 79,784,000 | 7,242,000 |
| 1983 | 72,409,000 | 4,921,000 |
| 1982 | 64,333,000 | 2,364,000 |

Figures are rounded to the nearest $1,000.

Assets are measured as market value on December 31 of each year.

Before John M. Olin's death in 1982, the value of the foundation's grants was never greater than $3.2 million in any year.

Figures for 2005 are estimates.

# ACKNOWLEDGMENTS

"There are three rules for writing the novel," W. Somerset Maugham is reported to have said. "Unfortunately no one knows what they are."

Writing a work of nonfiction can be just as mysterious. The final product does not always look like the book its author envisioned when he first put pen to paper (or set finger to keyboard). But one hard and fast rule, I have learned, is that no good book of any sort is ever written in isolation.

*A Gift of Freedom* owes its existence to the John M. Olin Foundation and its board of trustees, which made the writing of this book possible in every conceivable way. They provided both the subject and the means. The foundation supported me while I worked on the manuscript—something that has inspired me to joke more than once that I was the John M. Olin Fellow at the John M. Olin Foundation. Critics may draw whatever conclusions they wish about this fact. For my part, I will say only that the foundation opened its records to me completely and provided access to virtually every bit of information I requested. At the same time, it made no demands for editorial control. This book is mine, and it is as true a record of the John M. Olin Foundation's history as I am capable of producing.

One of the great pleasures of writing this book has been coming to know the foundation's staff, both professionally and personally. All along, the indispensable man has been James Piereson, who has been more than generous in sharing his time and ideas. His predecessors as executive director, Michael Joyce and Frank O'Connell, always made themselves available. Caroline Hemphill handled intricate questions with grace and speed.

211

Betty Sturdy made every one of my visits to the foundation offices a pleasant experience.

I am grateful to Encounter Books and especially its outstanding editor Peter Collier for agreeing to take on this project. In addition, this book might not have been written—at least not by me—without Adam Meyerson and Scott Walter of the Philanthropy Roundtable. They commissioned me to write a monograph, published in 2003 as *Strategic Investment in Ideas: How Two Foundations Reshaped America*, on the subject of the John M. Olin Foundation and the Lynde and Harry Bradley Foundation. So I tip my hat to them as well.

My employers at *National Review* encouraged me to pursue this project and gave me the freedom to balance the long-term commitment of writing a book with the series of short-term commitments that constitute magazine journalism. I'm especially grateful to my editor Richard Lowry, my publisher Ed Capano, and my Washington bureau chief Kate O'Beirne. In addition, Elizabeth Fisher, Meghan Keane, Stephen Spruiell and John Virtes provided great help chasing down obscure documents on the Internet, at the Library of Congress, and in the *National Review* archives.

At Cornell University, Elaine Engst shared key documents relating to John M. Olin and offered sharp insights. At Lafayette College, Diane Windham Shaw exposed me to the papers of William E. Simon. Tom Fitzgerald of the Olin Corporation helped with some basic questions about the company's business history.

I owe additional thanks to a long list of people. Some consented to long interviews and others helped check a fact or two—but all were willing to help and deserve credit for much of what is good in this book: Stephen Balch, Adam Bellow, William J. Bennett, Walter Berns, David Bernstein, Mark Blitz, Tom Bolan, Karlyn Bowman, Richard Brookhiser, F. H. Buckley, William F. Buckley Jr., Steve Calabresi, Thomas Christensen, Ella Jean Cline, Lloyd Cohen, Dale Corson, Ron Crawford, T. Kenneth Cribb, Glynn Custred, William Danforth, Kim Dennis, Donald Downs, Lee Edwards, Erich Eichman, Fr. Greg Fairbanks, Edwin J. Feulner Jr., Mary Pat Fortier, Francis Fukuyama, Michael Greve, Owen Harries, Steven F. Hayward, Michael Horowitz, Samuel Huntington, Bruce Johnson, Connie Josse, Roger Kaplan, Roger Kimball, Annette Kirk, Hilton Kramer, Irving Kristol, William Kristol, Reed Larson, Walter LeFeber, Leslie Lenkowsky, Tod Lindberg, Frank Luntz, Heather Mac Donald, Henry Manne, Bill Manson, Fred McChesney, David McIntosh, John J. Mearsheimer, Eugene B. Meyer, Charles Murray, Fr. Richard John Neuhaus, Michael Novak, Warren G. Olin, Lee Liberman Otis, A. Mitchell Polinsky, Frances Stonor Saunders, William Schulz, Stephen Shavell, Bill Simon Jr., Nathan Tarcov, Steven Teles, William Voegeli, Evelyn Williams, Bradford P. Wilson, Adam Wolfson, and Thomas Wood.

In the acknowledgments to previous books, I have given my family the last word: My wife, Amy, makes all of my work possible and my children, Brendan, Josie, and Patrick, remind me why nobody should work all the time.

But here I want to say a final word of thanks to Linda Chavez, to whom this book is dedicated. She was my boss for more than five years, first at the Manhattan Institute (where she was a John M. Olin Fellow) and then at its offshoot, the Center for Equal Opportunity. She was the best kind of boss a young man looking to make his way in a world of ideas could hope to have: A mentor who took great personal interest in my own career, and one who helped put me in a position to write books such as this. I am proud to consider myself her protégé, and even prouder to call her my friend.

First, a note on style: There is a strong temptation to refer to the John M. Olin Foundation as simply the "Olin Foundation." I have avoided it throughout, always referring to the organization by its full name. This was how Mr. Olin himself preferred it. After reading a 1981 letter in which his correspondent referred to the "Olin Foundation" rather than the "John M. Olin Foundation," Olin sent a note to executive director Michael Joyce expressing concern over "the confusion which could arise" if people failed to make a distinction between his foundation and his father's. I have chosen to abide by Mr. Olin's wishes on these pages. Call it a case of following donor intent to the letter.

Now, with respect to sources: I did not want footnotes cluttering the narrative of *A Gift of Freedom,* and so I have not used them. When appropriate, I've placed sufficient reference information in the text. Unfortunately, this was not possible everywhere. Some readers may want to check sources or do additional research. The information below is for them.

### Introduction: "Recover the Fundamentals"

Howard S. Goller, "Surprise! Nixon Backs Arms Talks in Visit Here," *St. Louis Post-Dispatch,* April 17, 1981, p. 1.

### Chapter 1: A Man and His Fortune

Following John M. Olin's death in 1982, virtually all of his personal papers were destroyed. "We shredded documents for days," recalled one of his assistants. Despite this loss, important sources about his life and views do exist in scattered places. An excellent history of the Olin Corporation is an undated manuscript, probably written in 1974 or 1975 by Walter Frommer, called "Olin: The Men and the Company." I found a copy in the John M. Olin Foundation's files. A second copy resides in the archives at Cornell, which contain several important documents on Olin, especially with respect to his relationship to his alma mater.

Other sources on Olin's life and work include "Patient Leaps from Hospital to Death," *New York Times,* February 5, 1921, p. 6; Richard Austin Smith, "The Rise of the House of Olin," *Fortune,* December 1953, p. 109; Virginia Kraft, "A Man, a Dog, and a Crusade," *Sports Illustrated,* November 17, 1958; Thomas E. Mullaney, "Olin: Staunch Fighter for Free Enterprise," *New York Times,* April 29, 1977; "Lessons in Mobilization," *National Defense,* February 1981, pp. 41–42; William F. Buckley Jr., "John M. Olin, RIP," *National Review,* October 1, 1982, p. 1197.

Additional information about Amos and Mary Merrill may be found in John M. Olin's letter of April 7, 1982, to his cousin Marjorie S. Davis. The Merrill farm, near Warren, New Hampshire, no longer exists, though its foundations are preserved as a historic site within the White Mountain National Forest. Olin spoke about Emile Chamot in a speech accepting the Charles F. Kettering Award on June 5, 1969. Spencer Olin's golfing is described briefly in Arnold Palmer, with James Dodson, *A Golfer's Life* (New York: Ballantine, 1999), pp. 124–25.

## Chapter 2: The Freedom Persuasion

The *Time* cover story on capitalism appeared in the issue dated July 14, 1975.

For an overview of how the CIA financed academic, cultural, and labor organizations, see Frances Stonor Saunders, *The Cultural Cold War: The CIA and the World of Arts and Letters* (New York: The New Press, 1999); Michael Warner, "Sophisticated Spies: CIA's Links to Liberal Anti-Communists, 1949–1967," *International Journal of Intelligence and Counterintelligence,* vol. 9, no. 4 (Winter 1996–97), pp. 425–33. For a journalistic account of the Vernon Fund, see Gerald Grant, "2 Teacher Units Got CIA Funds," *Washington Post,* February 22, 1967, p. A8.

The best general analysis of what happened at Cornell in 1969 is Donald Alexander Downs, *Cornell '69: Liberalism and the Crisis of the American University* (Ithaca, N.Y.: Cornell University Press, 1999).

A valuable source on philanthropy and classical liberalism is James Piereson, "Investing in Conservative Ideas," *Commentary,* May 2005, pp. 46–53. See also George H. Pearson, "The Business of America: Investment in Ideas," *American Spectator,* June/July 1975, p. 25; F. A. Hayek, "The Intellectuals and Socialism," *University of Chicago Law Review,* Spring 1949, pp. 417–33.

The controversy surrounding David Packard's remarks on philanthropy are covered in Marylin Bender, "Curb Asked on Gifts to Colleges," *New York Times,* October 18, 1973, p. 71; "Not for Sale," *New York Times,* October 29, 1973, p. 34; Leonard Sloane, "Flexible Education Aid Backed," *New York Times,* November 3, 1973, p. 37; McGeorge Bundy, "The Art of Giving: It Requires Practice, Concern, and Trust," *New York Times,* January 16, 1974, p. 66.

## Chapter 3: Simon Says

The best source on the life and ideas of William E. Simon are the man's own books—primarily *A Time for Truth* (New York: Reader's Digest Press, 1978). Also valuable is the posthumous *A Time for Reflection: An Autobiography,* written with John M. Caher (Washington, D.C.: Regnery Publishing, 2004). Less helpful is *A Time for Action* (New York: Reader's Digest/Berkley Books, 1980). See also William E. Simon, "Big Government and Our Economic Woes," *Reader's Digest,* April 1975, p. 57.

There is no shortage of news articles on Simon. Several of the best are: William Schulz, "Bill Simon: Watchdog at the Treasury," *Reader's Digest,* June 1976, p. 61; Herbert Mitgang, "Behind the Best Sellers: William E. Simon," *New York Times,* November 19, 1978, p. 88; Irwin Ross, "Bill Simon's Out of the Limelight and In the Money," *Fortune,* May 3, 1982; Wendy Diller, "Simon Scores on Buy-Outs," *The Record* (Bergen, N.J.), May 9, 1986, p. B11; "Simon Says," *Philanthropy,* January/February 2000, pp. 9–14. *The Economist*'s review of *A Time for Truth* appeared in the issue dated February 10, 1979, on p. 125. Richard A. Riley's comments on free enterprise appear in "Foes Irk New Stock Group Chief," *New York Times,* November 4, 1975, p. 49.

Of all the figures involved in the conservative movement, the one who most desperately needs a biography written about him is Irving Kristol. Despite the lack of one, there is no shortage of material on his life and legacy: Christopher DeMuth and William Kristol, eds., *The Neoconservative Imagination: Essays in Honor of Irving Kristol* (Washington, D.C.: AEI Press, 1995); Geoffrey Norman, "The Godfather of Neoconservatism (And His Family)," *Esquire,* February 13, 1979, p. 37; Walter Goodman, "Irving Kristol: Patron Saint of the New Right," *New York Times Magazine,* December 6, 1981, p. 90; Jacob Weisberg, "The Family Way," *New Yorker,* October 21 & 28, 1996, pp. 180–89. Kristol's letter to Goldwin is quoted in Tevi Troy, *Intellectuals and the American Presidency: Philosophers, Jesters, or Technicians?* (Lanham, Md.: Rowman & Littlefield Publishers, 2002), pp. 117–18. See also Irving Kristol,

"Business and 'The New Class,'" *Wall Street Journal*, May 19, 1975; "Foundations and the Sin of Pride: The Myth of the 'Third Sector,'" Kristol's speech to the Council on Foundations, May 30, 1980, published as a pamphlet by the Institute for Educational Affairs.

### Chapter 4: "Economics to Lawyers?"

There are several good primers on law and economics, beginning with *The Encyclopedia of Law and Economics*, ed. Boudewijn Bouckaert and Gerrit De Geest (Cheltenham, U.K.: Edward Elgar Publishing, 2000—available for free on the Internet at http://encyclo.findlaw.com/). Ejan Mackaay's entry on the history of law and economics is especially helpful. Two good primers on the topic are: Michael McConnell, "The Counter-Revolution in Legal Thought," *Policy Review*, Summer 1987, p. 18; Larissa MacFarquhar, "The Bench Burner," *New Yorker*, December 10, 2001, p. 78. See also Edmund W. Kitch, ed., "The Fire of Truth: A Remembrance of Law and Economics at Chicago, 1932–1970," *Journal of Law and Economics*, vol. 26 (April 1983), pp. 163–234; Ronald H. Coase, "The Problem of Social Cost," *Journal of Law and Economics*, vol. 3 (1960), pp. 1–44. (There is considerable confusion over when Coase's article first appeared in print because it was in an issue that was dated 1960 but was actually published in 1961. Many references say 1962.) The article also may be found in Ronald H. Coase, *The Firm, the Market, and the Law* (Chicago: University of Chicago Press, 1988).

For information on the Law and Economics Center, see Henry G. Manne, "An Intellectual History of the School of Law, George Mason University," published by the LEC, 1993; L. Gordon Crovitz, "George Mason's Entrepreneurial Law Dean Preaches Economics," *Wall Street Journal*, April 4, 1990, p. A25; Paul M. Barrett, "Influential Ideas: A Movement Called 'Law and Economics' Sways Legal Circles," *Wall Street Journal*, August 4, 1986, p. 1; Julie Kay, "Have Gavel, Will Travel," *Miami Daily Business Review*, August 4, 2000. Judge Williams and the *Sweet Home* case is discussed in *Moving a Public Policy Agenda: The Strategic Philanthropy of Conservative Foundations*, published by the National Center for Responsive Philanthropy, July 1997.

The controversy over Critical Legal Studies at Harvard Law School is described in Calvin Trillin, "A Reporter at Large: Harvard Law," *New Yorker*, March 26, 1984, p. 53. See also David Margolick, "Legal Notes: A Professor at Harvard Heads to West and to Right," *New York Times*, September 15, 1985, section 1, p. 58.

Rep. Schumer's letter to the editor concerning John R. Lott Jr. was published in the *Wall Street Journal*, September 4, 1996. Simon's response appeared on September 6. This exchange followed an op-ed by Lott, "More Guns, Less Violent Crime," in the August 28 issue.

For Jerome Culp's comments, see Tony Mauro, "Theory Sees Rehnquist as 'White Supremacist,'" *Legal Times*, March 1, 1993, p. 10. John Brigham's assessment of law and economics may be found in his book *The Constitution of Interests: Beyond the Rights of Politics* (New York: New York University Press, 1996), p. 70.

## Chapter 5: Legal Eagles

The proceedings of the first Federalist Society annual conference were published as a special issue of the *Harvard Journal of Law and Public Policy*, vol. 6, in 1982. The *New York Times* story on the conference appeared April 27, 1982, section A, p. 17. *National Review*'s editorial paragraph appeared in the issue dated April 2, 1982, p. 336. Maurice J. Holland wrote about the Federalist Society's first conference in "America's Federalist Heritage Rediscovered," *American Spectator*, February 1983, pp. 11–14. For a lengthy profile of David McIntosh, see Nina J. Easton, *Gang of Five: Leaders at the Center of the Conservative Ascendancy* (New York: Simon & Schuster, 2000). For a liberal critique of the Federalist Society, see Jerry M. Landay, "The Conservative Cabal That's Transforming American Law," *Washington Monthly*, March 2000. See also Thomas B. Edsall, "Federalist Society Becomes a Force in Washington," *Washington Post*, April 18, 2001, p. A4.

An invaluable source of information on conservative public-interest law firms is Steven Teles, whose forthcoming book *The Evolution of the Conservative Legal Movement* promises to be an excellent work of scholarship. All of my quotes from Horowitz's memo come from Teles. See also Lee Edwards, ed., *Bringing Justice to the People: The Story of the Freedom-Based Public Interest Law Movement* (Washington, D.C.: Regnery Publishing, 2004). A good summary of the Westmoreland case, albeit with a pro-CBS slant, is Connie Bruck, "How Dan Burt Deserted the General," *American Lawyer*, April 1985, p. 117. See also Stephen Klaidman, "CBS Isn't Blameless," *New York Times*, February 24, 1985.

## Chapter 6: A New Beginning

Barry Goldwater's tribute to John M. Olin appears in the *Congressional Record*, September 22, 1982. Simon's obituary, "John M. Olin: In

Memoriam," was published in the *East Hampton Star,* October 21, 1982. News articles about his estate include: Claudia MacLachlan, "Olin Split Estate Between Wife and Foundation He Started," *St. Louis Post-Dispatch,* September 23, 1982, p. 10A; "Wife, Foundation Get Bulk of Olin's Estate," *St. Louis Globe-Democrat,* September 24, 1982.

Helpful background information on this period may be found in Bernard Weinraub, "Foundations Assist Conservative Cause," *New York Times,* January 20, 1981, p. A25; Kathleen Teltsch, "Conservative Unit Gains from Legacy," *New York Times,* October 2, 1983, section 1, p. 41; Roger M. Williams, "An Interview with William E. Simon," *Foundation News,* September/October 1983, pp. 16–21; Richard J. Margolis, "Moving America Right," *Foundation News,* July/August 1983, pp. 44–48.

An excellent history of the Heritage Foundation is Lee Edwards, *The Power of Ideas: The Heritage Foundation at 25 Years* (Ottawa, Ill.: Jameson Books, 1997).

For more on the Bennett-Bradford controversy, see Carla Hill, "Bradford Speaks Out," *Washington Post,* October 28, 1981, p. B1; Paul Gottfried and Thomas Fleming, *The Conservative Movement* (Boston: Twayne Publishers, 1988), pp. 72–73; Patrick J. Buchanan, "The Conservative Crack-Up," *New York Post,* May 1, 1991, p. 27; Jacob Weisberg, "Hunter Gatherers," *New Republic,* September 2, 1991, pp. 14–16. Bradford's most provocative statements about Lincoln may be found in *A Better Guide Than Reason: Studies in the American Revolution* (LaSalle, Ill.: Sherwood Sugden & Co., 1979), pp. 56–57, nn. 36 & 48.

For the early days of *The New Criterion,* see Hilton Kramer, "Reagan Aides Discuss U.S. Role in Helping Arts and Humanities," *New York Times,* November 26, 1980, p. A1; Alfred Kazin, "Saving My Soul at the Plaza," *New York Review of Books,* vol. 30, no. 5 (March 31, 1983). Also "Saving the Free World: An Exchange," *New York Review of Books,* vol. 30, no. 8 (May 12, 1983); Joseph Epstein, "Samuel Lipman at the NEA," *New Criterion,* vol. 13, no. 7 (March 1995).

News stories on the Lay Commission include Marjorie Hyer, "Group Plans to Counter Catholic Bishops' Letter," *Washington Post,* May 19, 1984, p. B8; Ari L. Goldman, "Catholic Bishops Criticized on Poor," *New York Times,* November 5, 1986, p. A20; Kenneth A. Briggs, "Lay Catholic Group Offers Report Praising Capitalism," *New York Times,* November 7, 1984, p. A16; Leonard Silk, "Beyond Parley, Bishops Stir Dispute," *New York Times,* November 14, 1986, p. A15; Michael Novak, "The Bishops and the Poor," *Washington Post,* November 13, 1984, p. A15. For a synopsis of Novak's political journey from Left to Right, see Colman McCarthy, "The Crossing of the Bishops," *Washington Post,* May 11, 1983,

p. B1. Archbishop Weakland discussed the Lay Commission in Paul Wilkes, *The Education of an Archbishop: Travels with Rembert Weakland* (Maryknoll, N.Y.: Orbis Books, 1992). Michael Joyce reflected on the commission's work in "Bad Economics," *Crisis,* November 1996. See also John C. Cort, *Christian Socialism: An Informal History* (Maryknoll, N.Y.: Orbis Books, 1988), p. 332.

The novelist Tom Wolfe discussed Murray and the Manhattan Institute in an essay called "The Manhattan Institute at 25," published in *Turning Intellect into Influence,* ed. Brian C. Anderson (New York: Reed Press, 2004). The early days of the Manhattan Institute are also described briefly in Gerald Frost's biography, *Antony Fisher: Champion of Liberty* (London: Profile Books, 2002). Bill Clinton's quote about Murray appears in a *New York Times Magazine* article by Jason DeParle, "Daring Research or 'Social Science Pornography'?" October 9, 1994.

## Chapter 7: American Minds

For background on the debate over "political correctness," see Richard Bernstein, "The Rising Hegemony of the Politically Correct," *New York Times,* October 28, 1990, section 4, p. 1. For further information on the Collegiate Network, see Dennis A. Williams with Diane Weathers, "God and Man at Dartmouth," *Newsweek,* June 1, 1981, p. 64; Dudley Clendinen, "Conservative Paper Stirs Dartmouth," *New York Times,* October 13, 1981, p. A18; William A. Henry III, "Conservative Rebels on Campus," *Time,* November 8, 1982, p. 80; William E. Simon, "Demagoguery at Dartmouth," *New York Times,* October 20, 1990, p. 23.

An excellent introduction to the thought of Leo Strauss is Steven Lenzner and William Kristol, "What Was Leo Strauss Up To?" *Public Interest,* Fall 2003, pp. 19–39. For details on Bloom at Cornell, see Donald Alexander Downs, *Cornell '69: Liberalism and the Crisis of the American University* (Ithaca, N.Y.: Cornell University Press, 1999), especially p. 146. For responses to *The Closing of the American Mind,* see Christopher Lehmann-Haupt, "Books of the Times," *New York Times,* March 23, 1987, p. C18; Roger Kimball, "The Groves of Ignorance," *New York Times,* April 5, 1987, section 7, p. 7; James Atlas, "Chicago's Grumpy Guru," *New York Times Magazine,* January 3, 1988.

Helpful articles on Dinesh D'Souza include Elizabeth Fox-Genovese, "Education and Its Discontents," *Washington Post,* April 7, 1991, p. X6; Anthony Flint, "Dinesh D'Souza: Conservative Campus Darling," *Boston Globe,* April 14, 1991, p. A35; Charles Trueheart, "Big Man Off Campus," *Washington Post,* April 16, 1991, p. B1.

Robert P. George's program at Princeton is described in Timothy Webster, "A New Birth of Freedom on Campus," *Philanthropy*, November/December 2002.

## Chapter 8: History Clash

Owen Harries discussed his own background and the founding of *The National Interest* in his essay "The Australian Connection," which appears in *The Neoconservative Imagination*, ed. Christopher DeMuth and William Kristol (Washington, D.C.: AEI Press, 1995), pp. 35–45. Fukuyama's review of *The Clash of Civilizations* appeared in the *Wall Street Journal*, November 7, 1996, p. A20. A good introduction to Samuel Huntington is Robert D. Kaplan, "Looking the World in the Eye," *Atlantic Monthly*, December 2001, pp. 68–82. See also James Atlas, "What Is Fukuyama Saying? And to Whom Is He Saying It?" *New York Times Magazine*, October 22, 1989, p. 38; Stanley Kurtz, "The Future of 'History': Francis Fukuyama vs. Samuel Huntington," *Policy Review*, June 1, 2002, p. 43; Peter Berkowitz, "Fukuyama in Tel Aviv," *Weekly Standard* (online edition, a.k.a. the *Daily Standard*), March 19, 2004.

## Chapter 9: "Perpetuity Is a Very Long Time"

Anybody who writes on questions of perpetuity and donor intent is bound to run across the outstanding work of Martin Morse Wooster. His monographs *Should Foundations Live Forever? The Question of Perpetuity* and *The Great Philanthropists and the Problem of "Donor Intent"* (revised edition) were published by the Capital Research Center in 1998. See also Julius Rosenwald, "Principles of Public Giving," *Atlantic Monthly*, May 1929, pp. 599–606; Julius Rosenwald, "The Trend Away from Perpetuities," *Atlantic Monthly*, December 1930, pp. 741–49; Daniel J. Boorstin, *The Decline of Radicalism: Reflections on America Today* (New York: Random House, 1969), pp. 65–66; Thomas C. Palmer Jr., "The Right to Self-Destruct," *Boston Globe*, April 29, 2001; John J. Miller, "Goodbye, Mr. Olin," *National Review*, June 11, 2001, pp. 40–42; Matthew Schuerman, "The Paradox of Perpetuities," *Worth*, January 2004, pp. 120–22.

The perpetuity debate between Joyce and Higgins was published by the Philanthropy Roundtable in 1996 as *Should Foundations Exist in Perpetuity?*

A helpful discussion of what happened to the Center for the Study of American Business is Geoffrey S. Underwood, "CSAB R.I.P.," UPI, June 19, 2001.

For the David Brock controversy, see Jane Mayer and Jill Abramson, "The Surreal Anita Hill," *New Yorker,* May 24, 1993, pp. 90–96; Anthony Lewis, "Sleaze with Footnotes," *New York Times,* May 28, 1993; William E. Simon, "Tony Lewis's $5,000," *Wall Street Journal,* June 1, 1993.

## Conclusion: The Right Ideas

The letter from President Bush was dated March 30, 2005. See also Gary Shapiro, "Saluting James Piereson," *New York Sun,* April 8, 2005. For Piereson's views on the future of conservative philanthropy, see his op-ed "You Get What You Pay For," *Wall Street Journal,* July 21, 2004.

# INDEX

Aaron Diamond Foundation, 198

*ABA Watch,* 96

Abraham, Spencer, 89

Abrams, Elliott, 141

Abramson, Jill, 195

*Academic Questions,* 161

Accuracy in Media, 41

Ackerman, Bruce, 70

Adams, John, 28

African-American Institute, 26

Agnew, Spiro, 33

Allen-Bradley Company, 133

*Alternative, The,* 40, 140–41

Alternative Educational Foundation, 40

American Academy for Liberal Education, 161–62

American Bar Association, 92, 95–96

American Catholic Committee, 119

American Civil Liberties Union, 101

American Constitution Society, 97

American Council of Trustees and Alumni, 162

American Enterprise Institute, 6, 37–38, 53, 113, 172, 203, 207; Bork at, 64; as Brookings rival, 40; D'Souza at, 158; and Harries, 173–74; vs. Heritage,

105; Lott at, 73; Novak at, 117; termination grant, 201

American Historical Association, 160, 162

American Jewish Committee, 113

American Law and Economics Association, 79

*American Law and Economics Review,* 79

*American Mercury, The,* 29

American Museum of Natural History, 41

*American Spectator, The,* 40, 41, 90, 114, 136; origins, 140–41

Amherst College, 190

Applebaum, Anne, 169

Areeda, Phil, 75–76

Arrow, Kenneth J., 33

arts & culture, 110–12, 114–15

Ashcroft, John, 96

Association of Literary Scholars and Critics, 162

*Atlantic Monthly,* 158, 178, 186

Baker International, 103

Balch, Stephen, 160

Baroody, William J., 38

Baruch College, 161

Bator, Paul, 74–75

Baxter, William, 65

Beacon Fund, 26

Becker, Gary, 65, 66, 71